Lecture Notes in Artificial Intelli

Edited by J. G. Carbonell and J. Siekmann

Subseries of Lecture Notes in Computer Science

Sven A. Brueckner   Salima Hassas
Márk Jelasity   Daniel Yamins (Eds.)

Engineering
Self-Organising Systems

4th International Workshop, ESOA 2006
Hakodate, Japan, May 9, 2006
Revised and Invited Papers

 Springer

Series Editors

Jaime G. Carbonell, Carnegie Mellon University, Pittsburgh, PA, USA
Jörg Siekmann, University of Saarland, Saarbrücken, Germany

Volume Editors

Sven A. Brueckner
NewVectors, LLC, Emerging Markets Group (EMG), Ann Arbor, USA
E-mail: Sven.Brueckner@newvectors.net

Salima Hassas
CExAS Team - LIRIS, Université Claude Bernard Lyon 1, Villeurbanne, France
E-mail: hassas@liris.cnrs.fr

Márk Jelasity
University of Szeged, Institute of Informatics, Hungary
E-mail: jelasity@inf.u-szeged.hu

Daniel Yamins
Harvard University, Div. of Engineering and Applied Sciences, Cambridge, USA
E-mail: yamins@fas.harvard.edu

Library of Congress Control Number: 2006940399

CR Subject Classification (1998): I.2.11, C.2.4, C.2, D.2.12, D.1.3, H.3, H.4

LNCS Sublibrary: SL 7 – Artificial Intelligence

ISSN	0302-9743
ISBN-10	3-540-69867-1 Springer Berlin Heidelberg New York
ISBN-13	978-3-540-69867-8 Springer Berlin Heidelberg New York

Springer is a part of Springer Science+Business Media

springer.com

© Springer-Verlag Berlin Heidelberg 2007
Printed in Germany

Typesetting: Camera-ready by author, data conversion by Scientific Publishing Services, Chennai, India
Printed on acid-free paper   SPIN: 11976783   06/3142   5 4 3 2 1 0

Preface

The Fourth International Workshop on Engineering Self-Organizing Applications (ESOA) was held on May 9, 2006 in conjunction with the 2006 Conference on Autonomous Agents and Multi-Agent Systems (AAMAS 2006), in Hakodate, Japan. The present post-proceedings volume contains revised versions of the seven papers presented at the workshop, and six additional invited papers. Continuing the tradition of previous editions, this book discusses a broad variety of topics in an effort to allow room for new ideas and discussion, and eventually a better understanding of the important directions and techniques of our field.

In "Hybrid Multi-Agent Systems: Integrating Swarming and BDI Agents"—an article based on an invited talk at the workshop by Van Parunak—Parunak et al. address an important question facing the ESOA community: how should self-organizing swarm-like agent approaches relate to the techniques of the multi-agent community at large? ESOA techniques primarily rely on simple *reactive* agents, whose intelligence emerges at the group level via carefully designed interaction rules. These simple agents might have some *internal state* that allows them to remember the history of their interactions at some (low) level of detail, but generally the complexity in such systems arises from the dynamics. In contrast, the mainstream multi-agent systems community uses intelligent agents, which apply sophisticated algorithms to build up internal models of their environments and complex protocols to communicate about their models. This general approach, of which the BDI frameworks are an example, warrant a more cognitive analogy than the typical ESOA ideas. Parunak et al.'s work shows how the two approaches could profitably interact.

Two of the articles advance novel "design concepts"—that is, architectures that are optimized for achieving decentralized behavior from the algorithm design perspective. In "An Analysis and Design Concept for Self-Organization in Holonic Multi-Agent Systems," Rodriguez et al. describe the concept of a *holon* as a particular kind of multi-agent hierarchy, and apply it to design adaptive systems. Tom De Wolf and Tom Holvoet fold the standard motifs of emergent multi-agent systems into the programming techniques of standard computer science. By making gradients, a technique of spatial distributed systems, and market-mechanisms, a technique of non-spatial distributed systems, into standardized design patterns, they provide the beginnings of a framework for systematic design of self-organizing systems.

In "Measuring Stigmergy: The Case of Foraging Ants," Gulyas et al. begin to explore well-defined system-level observables that can quantitatively capture the qualitative sense of *emergence* in multi-agent systems. In the specific case of ant agents foraging in a 2D spatial environment for a conserved food resource, they define an entropy-like measure of disorder on the ant positions and food positions, and observe the dynamics off these measures. Although preliminary, this paper raises the important question of whether there are underlying statistical mechanics-like principles that apply to emergent multi-agent systems. Answering this question will in the long run provide an important part of the underlying theory of emergent distributed systems.

In "Dynamic Decentralized Any-Time Hierarchical Clustering," Parunak et al. introduce a technique for maintaining the hierarchical clustering of dynamically changing, streaming data using strictly local computations. The algorithm is inspired by ant nest-building.

Mamei and Zambonelli's work on "Programming Modular Robots with the TOTA Middleware" and Shabtay et al.'s paper on "Behaviosites: A Novel Paradigm for Affecting Distributed Behavior" shared the common theme of developing frameworks for the simple manipulation and control of distributed systems. The TOTA middleware, as developed in the past few years by Mamei and Zambonelli, is an efficient and elegant language through which general distributed behaviors can be designed and propagated through multi-agent systems. A *Tuple on the Air* is a data structure that contains a behavioral program, together with rules for its propagation and maintenance. If a single robot in a system is infected with the appropriate TOTA, its behavior can effectively propagate and emergently control the functioning of the system as a whole. Here, Mamei and Zambonelli apply the TOTA approach to programming a variety of motion routines (walk, crawl, roll, etc.) in snake-like robots.

While the Mamei and Zambonelli work is inherently spatial, referring as it does to the geometric motions of physical robots, the Shabtay et al. work is about behavioral programming in non-spatial systems. Their behaviosites are pieces of code that infect and multiply within a community of functioning agents, manipulating the responses of the agents so as to change and potentially improve their behavior. They apply their idea to the El Farol bar problem. Although the two papers are applied to quite different problems, their common idea of standardized code fragments that affect global behavior as they infect local agents is striking.

In "An Adaptive Self-Organizing Protocol for Surveillance and Routing in Sensor Networks," Jorge Simao exploits the diffusion of information around a sensor network to design a decentralized routing protocol that is efficient both in identifying an emergency situation as well as in using energy at each sensor. By using the correlations between sources of information and event types, the algorithm propagates information along a gradient in much the way the De Wolf and Holvoet design patterns describe.

In "Towards the Control of Emergence by the Coordination of Decentralized Agent Activity for the Resource Sharing Problem," Armetta et al. propose an agent communication model, called a negotiation network, in which (situated) agents and contracts are assigned to each other, and stigmergic coordination procedures, where agents can dynamically evaluate and select contracts. The performance of the resulting system, CESNA, is comparable to centralized optimization techniques.

A number of contributions apply or target evolutionary techniques, a main source of inspiration for achieving self-organization. Eiben et al. optimize evolutionary algorithms on the fly in "Reinforcement Learning for Online Control of Evolutionary Algorithms." They use a control loop that involves a reinforcement learning component to capture the abstract structure of the ongoing optimization, that is, the way performance depends on parameters.

In "Greedy Cheating Liars and the Fools Who Believe Them", Arteconi et al. apply an important idea originating from evolutionary computing: tags. In the protocol they present, the tag-based evolutionary system can successfully resist certain types of malicious attacks. All network nodes make local decisions to implement selection, replication and fitness evaluation, and still, through the application of tags, it becomes possible to implicitly reward *groups* that work together in a cooperative way.

In Nowostawski and Purvis' work on "Evolution and Hypercomputing in Global Distributed Evolvable Virtual Machines Environment," the authors exhibit a blend between evolving genetic algorithms and distributed spatial structures. They develop agents on a discrete grid that can cooperate with (or parasitize) each other to evolve solutions to linear polynomial computations. In doing so, they are able to observe the diffusion of knowledge and know-how through the multi-agent system, providing a clear and effective demonstration of the abstract principles of collective intelligence and learning.

In "A Decentralized Car Traffic Control System Simulation Using Local Message Propagation Optimized with a Genetic Algorithm," Kelly and Di Marzo Serugendo describe a decentralized approach to control traffic in an urban environment. The control system is based on emergent phenomena that can be tuned using a few simple parameters. In the article these parameters are set using a genetic algorithm that utilizes a simulation of the control system to evaluate candidate settings.

Finally, we need to mention that this edition is the last in the ESOA series as the workshop will merge into the *International Conference on Self-Adaptation and Self-Organization (SASO)*: a federated conference series covering our field starting in 2007. This signals the growth of interest in engineering self-organization. We believe that this last volume represents interesting contributions in this direction that the readers will find inspiring and useful in their research.

November 2006   Sven Brueckner
                                                                Salima Hassas
                                                                Márk Jelasity
                                                                Daniel Yamins

Organization

Organizing Committee

Sven Brueckner   NewVectors LLC, USA
Salima Hassas   University of Lyon, France
Márk Jelasity   University of Szeged and MTA, Hungary
Daniel Yamins   Harvard University, USA

Program Committee

Sergio Camorlinga   University of Manitoba, Canada
Vincent Cicirello   Drexel University, USA
Giovanna Di Marzo Serugendo Birkbeck College, London, UK
Maria Gini   University of Minnesota, USA
Marie-Pierre Gleizes   IRIT Toulouse, France
Manfred Hauswirth   Swiss Federal Institute of Technology,
                               Switzerland
Christophe S. Jelger   University of Basel, Switzerland
Anthony Karageorgos   University of Thessaly, Greece
Manolis Koubarakis   Technical University of Crete, Greece
Marco Mamei   University of Modena and Reggio Emilia, Italy
Paul Marrow   BT, UK
Philippe Massonet   CETIC, Belgium
Alberto Montresor   University of Bologna, Italy
Andrea Omicini   University of Bologna, Italy
H. Van Dyke Parunak   NewVectors LLC, USA
Martin Purvis   University of Otago, New Zealand
Mikhail Smirnov   Fraunhofer Fokus, Berlin, Germany

Table of Contents

Self-organization and Evolutionary Computing

Hybrid Multi-agent Systems: Integrating Swarming and BDI Agents

H. Van Dyke Parunak[1], Paul Nielsen[2], Sven Brueckner[1], and Rafael Alonso[3]

[1] NewVectors LLC, 3520 Green Court Suite 250, Ann Arbor, MI 48105
{van.parunak, sven.brueckner}@newvectors.net
[2] 28095 Hawberry Rd, Farmington Hills, MI, 48331
paul_eric_nielsen@yahoo.com
[3] SET Corporation, 1005 North Glebe Road, 4th Floor, Arlington, VA 22201
ralonso@setcorp.com

Abstract. The individual agents that interact in a multi-agent system typically exist along a continuum ranging from heavyweight cognitive agents (often of the "BDI" type) to lightweight agents with limited individual processing (digital ants). Most systems use agents from a single position along this spectrum. We have successfully implemented several systems in which agents of very different degrees of internal sophistication interact with one another. Based on this experience, we identify several different ways in which agents of different kinds can be integrated in a single system, and offer observations and lessons from our experiences.

1 Introduction

It has been said that to a small boy with a hammer, every problem looks like a nail. Technologists often seek to press every problem into the mold of their favorite mechanism. In the domain of multi-agent systems, a wide range of agent models have been developed. Some are highly sophisticated cognitive agents that aspire to individual human level intelligence, while other emulate insect-level cognition and exhibit intelligence only at the level of collective behavior.

For several years, we have been exploring different ways of combining heterogeneous models of cognition in a single system. Our experiences show that this approach is not only possible, but that it yields benefits that would be difficult to obtain within a homogeneous framework.

Just as there is no single best agent model, there is no single best way to combine different models. We exhibit a number of different architectures and discuss the situations in which they can be most profitably applied.

Section 2 describes the range of agent models that we hybridize in our work. Section 3 surveys and illustrates the different modes of integration that we have explored. Section 4 offers discussion and conclusion.

2 Alternative Agent Models

Software agents exist across a range of complexities. At some risk of oversimplification, we describe two extremes, and then illustrate some points in the middle. For expository

S. Brueckner et al. (Eds.): ESOA 2006, LNAI 4335, pp. 1–14, 2007.

purposes, we call the two extremes "heavyweight" and "lightweight" agents, but these titles are more mnemonic than definitive. Table 1 summarizes the differences between these two extremes.

2.1 Heavyweight Agents

Heavyweight agents are based on the cognitively-inspired AI programs developed in the heyday of artificial intelligence. Each such program then, and each individual agent now, aspires to human-level intelligence. In this domain, an intelligent agent system consists of a system composed of individually intelligent agents. Well-known researchers in the heavyweight tradition include Durfee [7], Jennings [16], Laird [19], Lesser [21], Sycara [34], and Wooldridge [37].

Heavyweight agents have inherited classical AI's emphasis on symbolic representations manipulated with some form of formal logic. The symbols are intended to represent cognitive constructs that are meaningful to people, such as beliefs, desires, and intentions (thus the common rubric "BDI agent" [13, 30]). These constructs, and the logical entailments among them, are elicited by a process of knowledge engineering. This process seeks to capture human intuitions about the appropriate partitioning of a problem domain and self-reflective models of how people reason about the domain.

Because heavyweight agents are built around human-inspired cognitive constructs, they facilitate communication with their users. If an agent has a concept of "danger" that corresponds to a human's concept, there is a good chance that when the agent tells the human that a situation is dangerous, the human will understand.

This benefit comes at a cost. The process of knowledge engineering is intensive and time-consuming. In addition, logical computation is subject to a number of limitations. For example, logical computations are often

Table 1. Two Extreme Types of Software Agents

Class of Agent	Heavyweight	Lightweight
Origins	Artificial Intelligence/Cognitive Science	Artificial Life
Locus of intelligence	Within a single agent	In the interactions among agents
Internal representations and processing	Symbolic	Numeric: polynomials, neural networks, matrix manipulations
Concepts represented	Explicit beliefs, desires, intentions/goals, plans	Sensor states, actuator levels
Development approach	Knowledge engineering	Optimization
Strengths	Intelligible to humans	Computationally efficient Degrades gracefully
Weaknesses	Computationally intractable for large problems Brittle	Difficult to understand

- Intractable, their computational complexity increasing exponentially or worse in the size of the problem, so that problems of realistic size cannot be executed fast enough for the answer to be useful [10],
- Undecidable, so that some questions expressible in the logic simply cannot be answered [11], or
- Brittle, with performance that degrades rapidly (either in accuracy or speed) as one nears the limits of the domain.

2.2 Lightweight Agents

At the other extreme, lightweight agents draw their inspiration from computerized work in ethology, the study of animal behavior. Biologists often construct computer models of animals in order to study their interactions with one another. In many cases (such as ants), no one imagines that the individual agent has anything like human-level intelligence, but the society as a whole can exhibit impressive behavior that might be described as intelligent. In this context, an intelligent agent system is a system of agents that is collectively intelligent. Well-known researchers in this tradition include Bonabeau [3], Brueckner [4], Ferber [8], Ilachinski [15] and Parunak [22].

Lightweight agents do not rely on cognitively meaningful internal representations, for two reasons. First, biologists tend to resist anthropomorphizing the mental behavior of ants and termites. Second, even if it were appropriate to describe their mental operations in the same terms that emerge from human introspection, we would have no way to interrogate the organism about these constructs. What is accessible to the biologist is the entity's environment and its observed actions, so the representation tends to focus on sensory inputs and signals sent to actuators. These are customarily described in analog terms, leading to widespread use of numerical reasoning, usually as some form of matrix algebra (a framework that includes weighted polynomials and neural networks).

Programming such an agent is a matter of identifying the appropriate numerical parameters and setting their values. Knowledge engineering is of little use with a digital insect. Instead, one uses optimization methods such as evolutionary computation to explore the parameter space. We can compare the observed behavior of the agent either with the observed behavior of the domain entity (in a modeling application) or with the desired behavior (in a control application), and use the difference between the two as an objective function [32].

Because their internal processes are essentially numerical, lightweight agents are usually more computationally efficient than heavyweight agents, avoiding issues of tractability and decidability. Their representations extrapolate naturally, avoiding the challenge of brittleness. But they can be difficult for users to understand, for two reasons.

1. The mapping from internal numerical parameters to cognitively meaningful constructs may not be direct. An agent's behavior may be dominated by the fact that the weight between two nodes in a neural network is 0.375, but that knowledge is of little use to a human seeking to validate the agent.

2. Lightweight agents often yield useful behavior, not as individuals, but as a collective. The dynamic of emergence, by which global behavior arises from individual behaviors, is often counter-intuitive [31].

2.3 Intermediate Agents

The two categories of "heavyweight" and "lightweight" agents as described above are extreme cases, and a number of intermediate architectures have been used.

Scripted agents use a state machine to shift from one cognitively meaningful state to another, based on external stimuli. Thus they avoid some of the computational complexity issues associated with richer computational models such as theorem proving.

One mechanism for scripted agents is the Task Frame [5]. Task Frames are used in military simulations such as OneSAF, JSAF, and ModSAF to decompose tasks, organize information, and sequence through the steps of a process. Finite state machines are used to sequence through the task states, however the code within these states is unrestricted.

Sometimes scripted transitions are combined with lighter-weight mechanisms. MANA [20] is a combat model whose agents make decisions based on matrix multiplications, along the line of EINSTein [15]. However, the personality vector that weights the effect of environmental stimuli can be changed discontinuously by certain distinguished events, allowing the agent to change among different behavior patterns depending on environmental stimuli.

Bayes networks [29] combine symbolic and numeric processing, in a manner similar to iconic neural networks. Each node corresponds to a concept or proposition that is meaningful to a human, in a manner consistent with symbolic representations, but the links among the nodes represent conditional probabilities, and processing consists of numeric computations of the propagation of evidence through the network.

Bayes networks have proven most useful at interpretation of activity from observations. For example, seeing a person with wet hair enter the office could either imply that it is raining or they have just taken a shower. However, if we observe several people with wet hair the belief that it is raining would increase.

These intermediate agent architectures combine in a single agent mechanisms from different points in the spectrum *in a single agent*.

3   Integration Modes

In this section, we discuss why it is difficult to integrate agents with different cognitive levels in a single system, and then exhibit a number of different approaches that we have explored. Our list of examples is open-ended, and we invite other researchers to expand it on the basis of their experience.

3.1 Why Is Integration Difficult?

The hybrid systems that we discuss here differ from the "intermediate agents" discussed in Section 2.3. Those examples combined mechanisms from different points in the spectrum *in a single agent*. Here, we explore patterns for combining *distinct agents* that differ in their cognitive mechanisms.

There are three challenges in developing a hybrid system: issues internal to individual agents, issues relating an individual agent to its external environment, and issues dealing with the overall structure of the system.

Internal Issues: Any agent, however simple or complex, is responsible to perceive its environment and take some action based on that perception. Each agent in the system must have the capacity to solve the problem with which it is tasked.

External Issues: The widespread use of heavyweight agents leads naturally to agent interactions that draw on the cognitive constructs that the individual agents are presumed to support. This assumption is the basis of messaging standards such as KQML/KIF and FIPA ACL. Lightweight agents interact through their sensors and actuators rather than through messages with explicit cognitive content. Thus communication between the two types of agents requires special attention.

System Issues: When we provide our small boy with a screwdriver and a wrench in addition to his hammer, we have made his life much more complicated. Now he has to decide which tool to use in which situation. When we permit the use of multiple levels of agent cognition in a single system, we need to think about which kind of agent to use where, and why.

3.2 Swarm as Subroutine

Sometimes a community of lightweight agents can perform a specialized task in support of a heavyweight agent. We used this approach in an experimental extension of TacAir-Soar [17]. The basic TacAir-Soar system is a classic heavyweight architecture based on the Soar architecture for general AI. Geospatial reasoning such as path planning is cumbersome in such an architecture [9], but straightforward for a swarm of lightweight agents. Biological ants use a simple pheromone mechanisms to generate minimal spanning trees that connect their nests with food sources [12], and these mechanisms have been applied successfully in robotic path planning to approach targets while avoiding threats [33].

We merged these two classes of agents by having the Soar agent invoke a swarm of lightweight agents to plan paths. Fig. 1 shows the structure of the implemented system. Communication between the agents is at the cognitive level required by the pilot agent. A wrapper around the path planning swarm handles the translation. In a typical dialog, the pilot reports its current location and its destination, and requests a route. The wrapper instantiates a nest of agents at the current location, a food source at the destination, and turns the swarming agents

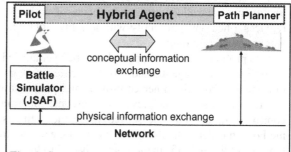

Fig. 1. Swarming path planner as subroutine to Soar AI pilot

loose. They generate a field of digital pheromones whose crest indicates the desired path. The wrapper then translates the turning points in this path into a series of waypoints, which it reports to the pilot.

3.3 Polyagent

Closely related to the previous example is the use of multiple lightweight agents to explore alternatives being considered by the heavyweight agent. We have formalized this construct as the polyagent [23], and other researchers have developed similar mechanisms under the rubric of "delegate Multi-Agent Systems" (because the heavyweight agent delegates its task to the lightweight agents) [14, 18].

The justification for using lightweight agents to explore alternatives is computational efficiency. If there were no constraint on computational resources, the heavyweight agent could just explore the alternatives itself (perhaps through parallel invocations of its environment). By using lightweight agents, it can explore more alternatives in shorter time.

The difference between the polyagent and the swarm as subroutine is that the heavyweight agent in the polyagent (the "avatar") considers each of its lightweight agents ("ghosts") individually in making use of their results, rather than simply consuming their aggregate output as in the swarming subroutine. As a result, instead of wrapping a translator around the lightweight agents to enable them to speak the language of the heavyweight agent, we require the heavyweight agent to examine the environmental changes (e.g., digital pheromones) produced by the actions of the lightweight agents.

3.4 Transitional Agents

Transitional agents morph between heavy and light weight agents depending on the needs of the application.

For example, in a large scale simulation it is infeasible to simulate every entity at a very high level of fidelity, yet humans who participate in the simulation will not be challenged by the actions of an insect level intelligence. To provide both the desired breath of scale and richness of interaction, the majority of the entities can be controlled by lightweight agents, while those few agents who come into contact with humans can be controlled by heavyweight agents.

The simplest interface simply notes that an interaction is imminent, destroys the lightweight controlled entity and replaces it with a heavyweight controlled entity, or replaces a heavyweight entity with a lightweight when the entity is no longer within human interaction range.

One problem with this approach can be exemplified as "waking up in the middle of a dogfight." The agent needs to acclimate itself to the situation, obtain historical information from the other controller, and plan a strategy for the encounter. During this time the agent is helpless. To overcome this transition interval, an entity's new control method should be started while the entity is under control of the previous method. In order to facilitate the transition, each controller must incur an overhead of logging additional information that is useful to the other controller.

3.5 Swarming Integration of Cognitive Reasoners

Sometimes it is desirable to integrate the results of multiple reasoning engines operating on a single domain. Within the paradigm of symbolic AI, the standard approach is to construct yet another reasoner that does meta-level reasoning over the knowledge produced by each of the component reasoners. This process is liable to the same challenges of tractability, decidability, and brittleness as any symbolic process. It is often exacerbated by the increased size of the problem (involving the union of the results of multiple reasoners) and the difficulty of ensuring semantic compatibility across the reasoners.

Instead of *reasoning* about the intermediate results, an alternative approach is to treat them as *constraints* that are imposed on an

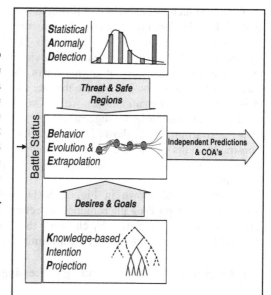

Fig. 2. Three Synergistic Reasoners.—Statistical reasoner estimates threat regions; Bayes network projects intentions; swarming emulation integrates these results by using the to constrain dynamics of emulated entities

emulation of the domain. This approach uses the semantics of the emulation as the interface standard across the different reasoners. Whether the emulation is tractable or not depends on its underlying technology. An equation-based model of the domain is completely tractable and decidable, but has a number of shortcomings compared with an agent-based model [28]. If the agents in an agent-based model are heavyweight agents, the emulation itself may be no more efficient than metalevel reasoning. The highly efficient execution of lightweight agents enables us to run an emulation fast enough to support real-time fusion of results from multiple reasoners. This approach is in some sense a mirror image of the "Swarm as Subroutine" model of Section 3.2. There, a swarm of lightweight agents solved a specific problems for a heavyweight agent. Here, the heavyweight agents are the focused problem-solvers, and it is the swarm that integrates their results.

An important challenge to this approach is the question of fidelity. Whether a model can accurately fuse constraints imposed by component reasoners depends on how faithfully it represents the domain, and *a priori* one might expect lightweight agents, with their simplified internal modeling, to yield less accurate models of behavior than heavyweight agents. In many domains, the constraints imposed by the environment are more important to determining the system-level outcome of a model than the internal reasoning of the agents, a phenomenon that we have termed "universality" [25]. In such domains, lightweight agents are equal to the task.

We have taken this approach in fusing multiple reasoners in a system for predicting battlefield behavior. Fig. 2 shows the structure of this system. The central element, Behavioral Evolution and Extrapolation (BEE), is a swarming model of the battlespace that itself predicts entity behavior using polyagents (Section 3.3). It also fuses the results of two other reasoners. Statistical Anomaly Detection (SAD) identifies regions of the battlespace that are likely to be perceived as threatening, and thus repulsive, to domain entities, while Knowledge-based Intention Projection (KIP) uses Bayesian networks to suggest entity goals, which are attractors. Fig. 3 shows how the swarming BEE ghosts form predictions of entity movement that satisfy these constraints. This prediction technology outperforms human experts, and also other technical approaches (such as game-theoretic predictors) with which it has been compared [24].

In the example shown in Fig. 2, SAD and KIP interface with the swarming simulation by depositing pheromones reflecting their results. In principle, they could also modulate the simulation by changing the structure of its underlying topology, or by modifying the personalities of the swarming agents.

3.6 Cognitive Interface, Swarming Processing

The cognitive transparency of heavyweight agents makes them a natural candidate for a user interface to an underlying swarming system. In this approach, the heavyweight agent maintains a model of the user's interests. It focuses the behavior of the swarm in accordance with those interests, and then translates the swarm's results into terms understandable to the user. Metaphorically, the heavyweight agent constructs the DNA that guides the behavior of the lightweight agents.

An example of this architecture is the Ant CAFÉ, a system that supports Indications and Warnings analysts as they try to connect clues gleaned from massive quantities of complex data [35]. The system is an iterative loop: analysts ask the system to find evidence that supports a hypothesis, the system returns assemblies that organize relevant evidence, and the analyst reviews the evidence and in the process improves her understanding of the problem. The analyst-system interaction leads to a revised representation of the hypothesis, and the loop iterates repeatedly in this manner as the investigation advances. Fig. 4 provides a high level overview.

Hypotheses are repre-sented as concept maps [6]. The concept maps are utilized in every stage of processing; they essentially act as templates for the

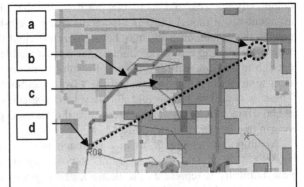

Fig. 3. Results of Fused Reasoners.—For red unit at d (red tail shows recent past), BEE integrates predicted goal (a) from KIP and threat regions (c) from SAD with dynamics of interactions with environment to yield predicted path (b) in the face of future threats, engagements, and force activity

construction of evidence assemblies. Concept maps are graphs with labeled nodes and edges. The nodes are nouns and the edges are verbs or verb-prepositions. We call the nouns and verbs *concepts*. We call two nodes and their connecting edge, together, a *relation*. We consider concept maps to be a low-commitment form of ontology-like symbolic knowledge representation. They are becoming quite ubiquitous for modeling

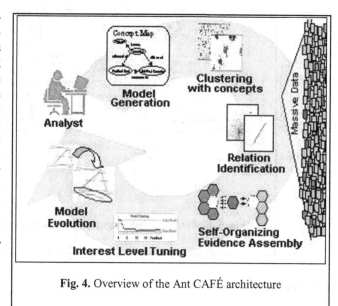

Fig. 4. Overview of the Ant CAFÉ architecture

domain knowledge, and are now widely taught in middle schools and elsewhere.

The left side of Fig. 4 (the Analyst Modeling Environment, or AME) involves modeling the analyst's interests as represented in the concept maps, using a heavyweight agent that explicitly manipulates high-level concepts. Issues include initial acquisition of concept maps, tuning weights associated with concepts and relations to reflect analyst interests by observing their behavior, and evolving concept maps in semi-automatic ways to capture increasing understanding as investigations progress [1]. The use of a heavyweight agent to model the analyst and interpret the results returned by the Ant Hill is necessary to enable humans to use the system effectively.

The right side of Fig. 4 is the Ant Hill, which uses lightweight agents in swarming processes to cluster data, identify relations, and assemble evidence. Each of these stages employs a distinct swarming mechanism. They are sequential in terms of logical data flow, but execute concurrently. All of the processes use *anytime* algorithms: where some answer is available at any time, and the quality of the answer improves as time passes. Lightweight swarming agents are appropriate for the Ant Hill because they can efficiently process the massive dynamic data that the system must handle.

The concept maps form the interface between the Analyst Modeling Environment and the Ant Hill. The AME can interpret them as symbolic structures to capture the analyst's interests and explain the structure of results, while the Ant Hill can use the concepts and their associated weights to define a feature vector that supports low-level self-organizing processes such as dynamic distributed hierarchical clustering [27].

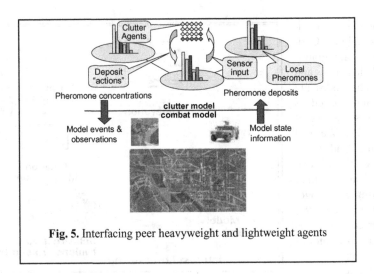

Fig. 5. Interfacing peer heavyweight and lightweight agents

3.7 Peer Interactions

Because lightweight agents do not require the degree of knowledge engineering that heavyweight agents do, and because of their relative efficiency of execution, they can often be attractive as a way to increase the population of a multi-agent model without unduly increasing its cost or its computational expense. In this approach, lightweight and heavyweight agents function as peers in an agent-based model.

Military operations unfold within the constraints of a particular physical environment. Operational effectiveness is a product of the joint "system" of the military operations and the environment. These emergent dynamics often vary widely as the state of the environment varies, to the point where the dynamics and thus the outcome of particular military operations may be completely dominated by the environment in which they are embedded. Recognizing this relationship between the operations and their environment is important at different levels. At the level of sensors and communication networks, local variations in environmental factors such as weather, soil conductivity, and foliage can lead to wide variation in system performance. At the level of fighting units such as urban combat with small distributed teams, FCS system of systems, or highly distributed mixed-initiative systems, the outcome depends on the availability of information and the interaction of numerous entities and the complex environment in which they are embedded.

The interaction of various noncombatants with different states within the environment of a military operation may also strongly determine the outcome of the operations. Noncombatants interact with the operations in two ways. On the one hand, they are simply affected by the ongoing operations (e.g., seeking refuge, being injured, etc.), but on the other hand, they may also influence the progress of the operation directly or indirectly. A direct impact occurs when some of the objectives of the operation are contingent on the state of the noncombatants (e.g., minimize casualties, control refugee flows). Noncombatants indirectly influence the progress of the operations as they may provide cover for combatants or obstruct the line-of-sight to targets.

We have implemented this approach to add swarming non-combatants to the scripted combatants in an urban combat modeled in COMBAT XXI [2]. Fig. 5 shows how we interface them. The swarming clutter agents live on a graph model whose nodes maintain digital pheromone concentrations. The scripted combatants live on a map. We add a process to the computational environment that translates between pheromone concentrations on the swarming side and events and state information on the heavyweight side. Such a process is an instance of the kind of services that make it important to consider the environment a first-class object in multi-agent systems [36].

4 Discussion and Prospectus

We can now return to the challenges to integration that we raised in Section 3.1, and also outline some directions for further research.

4.1 Internal and System Issues

Fig. 6 summarizes the relative strengths and complementarity of heavyweight (e.g., BDI) and lightweight (typically swarming) agents. In one way or another, each of our examples seeks to combine the strengths of the two models.

This prototypical summary of the capabilities and weaknesses of the different models is moderated by the principle of agent universality [25]. As the level of constraint imposed by the environment increases, differences in the cognitive capability of agents become less important. In effect, there is a trade-off between the information that agents can gain from the environment and the information they must generate by their own reasoning. Highly-constrained environments may provide so much exogenous information that even very simple agents are all that is needed, while in environments with no constraints, swarming lightweight agents may not be able to function effectively.

4.2 External Issues: Agent Interfacing

Our examples show a number of different approaches to agent interfacing. Lightweight agents are by their nature representationally impoverished relative to heavyweight agents, so it is natural that heavyweight agents will need to learn to "speak their language" rather than the other way around. This may take the form of depositing and reading pheromones that are visible by stigmergic agents (as KIP and SAD do in the swarming integration example).

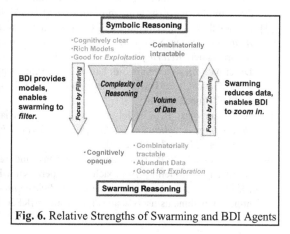

Fig. 6. Relative Strengths of Swarming and BDI Agents

Because lightweight agents are so simple, it is possible to have heavyweight agents custom-craft them for specific tasks (as in the Polyagent, or along the lines of the cognitive interface example).

4.3 Future Research

Once we begin to think in terms of using lightweight and heavyweight agents together in the same system, a number of research questions become evident.

To what extent can we construct a unified development methodology that supports both extremes (and thus intermediate agent types as well)? It is clumsy to have to use one methodology [38] for BDI agents, and a completely separate one [26] for swarming agents. Hybrid systems will only become commonplace when both kinds of agents can be developed within an integrated framework.

Sometimes the cognitive complexity of an agent may need to differ during its lifetime. For example, imaging a crowd of lightweight agents representing non-combatants. At some point, an intelligence operative might want to engage one of them in conversation about what she has seen recently, a process that requires the cognitive capabilities of a heavyweight agent. One approach is the transitional agent approach described in Section 3.4. Another would be to add an interpreter to the lightweight agent along the lines of Section 3.6. Such a dynamic change in agent complexity has not been explored to any great degree, and poses a number of interesting research challenges.

The schemes summarized in this paper are the result of surveying projects that we have executed. A further stage of analysis might yield a more systematic theory of how one can integrate different agent models, which in turn might suggest further approaches to this important problem.

References

[1] R. Alonso and H. Li. Model-driven Information Discovery for Intelligence Analysis. In *Proceedings of In preparation*.

[2] Army MSRR. Combined Arms Analysis Tool for the XXIst Century (COMBAT XXI). 2006. http://www.msrr.army.mil/index.cfm?RID=MNS_A_1000185.

[3] E. Bonabeau, M. Dorigo, and G. Theraulaz. *Swarm Intelligence: From Natural to Artificial Systems*. New York, Oxford University Press, 1999.

[4] S. Brueckner. *Return from the Ant: Synthetic Ecosystems for Manufacturing Control.* Dr.rer.nat. Thesis at Humboldt University Berlin, Department of Computer Science, 2000. http://dochost.rz.hu-berlin.de/dissertationen/brueckner-sven-2000-06-21/PDF/Brueckner.pdf.

[5] A. Ceranowicz, P. E. Nielsen, and F. Koss. Behavioral Representation in JSAF. In *Proceedings of Ninth Annual Computer Generated Forces and Behavior Representation Conference*, Orlando, FL, 2000.

[6] J. W. Coffey, R. R. Hoffman, A. J. Cañas, and K. M. Ford. A Concept Map-Based Knowledge Modeling Approach to Expert Knowledge Sharing. In *Proceedings of IASTED International Conference on Information and Knowledge Sharing*, 2002. http://www.ihmc.us/users/acanas/Publications/IKS2002/IKS.htm.

[7]   E. H. Durfee. *Coordination of Distributed Problem Solvers*. Boston, MA, Kluwer Academic Press, 1988.

[8]   J. Ferber and E. Jacopin. The framework of eco-problem solving. In, *Decentralized Artificial Intelligence 2*, pages 181-193. Elsevier/North-Holland, Amsterdam, 1991.

[9]   K. D. Forbus, P. Nielsen, and B. Faltings. Qualitative Spatial Reasoning: The Clock Project. *Artificial Intelligence*, 51(1-3):417-471, 1991.

[10] M. R. Garey and D. S. Johnson. *Computers and Intractability*. San Francisco, CA, W.H. Freeman, 1979.

[11] K. Gödel. Über formal unentscheidbare Sätze der Principia Mathematica und verwandter Systeme, I. *Monatshefte für Mathematik und Physik* 38:173-198, 1931.

[12] S. Goss, S. Aron, J. L. Deneubourg, and J. M. Pasteels. Self-organized Shortcuts in the Argentine Ant. *Naturwissenschaften*, 76:579-581, 1989.

[13] A. Haddadi and K. Sundermeyer. Belief-Desire-Intention Agent Architectures. In G. M. P. O'Hare and N. R. Jennings, Editors, *Foundations of Distributed Artificial Intelligence*, pages 169-185. John Wiley, New York, NY, 1996.

[14] T. Holvoet and P. Valckenaers. Exploiting the Environment for Coordinating Agent Intentions. In *Proceedings of Third International Workshop on Environments for Multi-Agent Systems (E4MAS06)*, Hakodate, Japan, Springer, 2006.

[15] A. Ilachinski. *Artificial War: Multiagent-Based Simulation of Combat*. Singapore, World Scientific, 2004.

[16] N. R. Jennings and J. R. Campos. Towards a Social Level Characterisation of Socially Responsible Agents. *IEE Proceedings Software Engineering*, 144(no 1):11-25, 1997.

[17] R. M. Jones, J. E. Laird, P. E. Nielsen, K. J. Coulter, P. Kenny, and F. V. Koss. Automated intelligent pilots for combat flight simulation. *AI Magazine*, 20(1 (Winter)):27-41, 1999.

[18] J. Kant and S. Thiriot. Modeling one Human Decision Maker with a MultiAgent System: the CODAGE Approach. In *Proceedings of Fifth International Conference on Autonomous Agents and Multi-Agent Systems (AAMAS06)*, Hakodate, Japan, ACM, 2006.

[19] J. E. Laird, A. Newell, and P. S. Rosenbloom. Soar: An Architecture for General Intelligence. *Artificial Intelligence*, 33(1): 1-64, 1987.

[20] M. K. Lauren and R. T. Stephen. Map-Aware Non-uniform Automata (MANA)—A New Zealand Approach to Scenario Modelling. *Journal of Battlefield Technology*, 5(1 (March)):27ff, 2002. http://www.argospress.com/jbt/Volume5/5-1-4.htm.

[21] V. Lesser and D. D. Corkill. Functionally accurate, cooperative distributed systems. *IEEE Transactions on Systems, Man, and Cybernetics*, SMC-11:81-96, 1981.

[22] H. V. D. Parunak. 'Go to the Ant': Engineering Principles from Natural Agent Systems. *Annals of Operations Research*, 75:69-101, 1997. http://www.newvectors.net/staff/parunakv/gotoant.pdf.

[23] H. V. D. Parunak and S. Brueckner. Modeling Uncertain Domains with Polyagents. In *Proceedings of International Joint Conference on Autonomous Agents and Multi-Agent Systems (AAMAS'06)*, Hakodate, Japan, ACM, 2006. http://www.newvectors.net/staff/parunakv/AAMAS06Polyagents.pdf.

[24] H. V. D. Parunak, S. Brueckner, R. Matthews, J. Sauter, and S. Brophy. Real-Time Evolutionary Agent Characterization and Prediction. In *Proceedings of Social Agents: Results and Prospects (Agent 2006)*, Chicago, IL, Argonne National Laboratory, 2006.

[25] H. V. D. Parunak, S. Brueckner, and R. Savit. Universality in Multi-Agent Systems. In *Proceedings of Third International Joint Conference on Autonomous Agents and Multi-Agent Systems (AAMAS 2004)*, New York, NY, pages 930-937, ACM, 2004. http://www.newvectors.net/staff/parunakv/AAMAS04Universality.pdf.

[26] H. V. D. Parunak and S. A. Brueckner. Engineering Swarming Systems. In F. Bergenti, M.-P. Gleizes, and F. Zambonelli, Editors, *Methodologies and Software Engineering for Agent Systems*, pages 341-376. Kluwer, 2004. http://www.newvectors.net/staff/ parunakv/ MSEAS04.pdf.

[27] H. V. D. Parunak, R. Rohwer, T. C. Belding, and S. Brueckner. Dynamic Decentralized Any-Time Hierarchical Clustering. In *Proceedings of Proceedings of the Fourth International Workshop on Engineering Self-Organizing Systems (ESOA'06)*, Hakodate, Japan, Springer, 2006. http://www.newvectors.net/staff/parunakv/SODAS06.pdf.

[28] H. V. D. Parunak, R. Savit, and R. L. Riolo. Agent-Based Modeling vs. Equation-Based Modeling: A Case Study and Users' Guide. In *Proceedings of Multi-agent systems and Agent-based Simulation (MABS'98)*, Paris, FR, pages 10-25, Springer, 1998. http://www.newvectors.net/staff/parunakv/mabs98.pdf.

[29] J. Pearl. *Probabilistic Reasoning in Intelligent Systems, Morgan-Kaufmann, 1988.* San Francisco, CA, Morgan-Kaufmann, 1988.

[30] A. S. Rao and M. P. Georgeff. Modeling Rational Agents within a BDI Architecture. In *Proceedings of International Conference on Principles of Knowledge Representation and Reasoning (KR-91)*, pages 473-484, Morgan Kaufman, 1991.

[31] M. Resnick. *Turtles, Termites, and Traffic Jams: Explorations in Massively Parallel Microworlds*. Cambridge, MA, MIT Press, 1994.

[32] J. A. Sauter, R. Matthews, H. V. D. Parunak, and S. Brueckner. Evolving Adaptive Pheromone Path Planning Mechanisms. In *Proceedings of Autonomous Agents and Multi-Agent Systems (AAMAS02)*, Bologna, Italy, pages 434-440, ACM, 2002. www.newvectors.net/staff/parunakv/AAMAS02Evolution.pdf.

[33] J. A. Sauter, R. Matthews, H. V. D. Parunak, and S. A. Brueckner. Performance of Digital Pheromones for Swarming Vehicle Control. In *Proceedings of Fourth International Joint Conference on Autonomous Agents and Multi-Agent Systems*, Utrecht, Netherlands, pages 903-910, ACM, 2005. http://www.newvectors.net/staff/parunakv/ AAMAS05SwarmingDemo.pdf.

[34] K. Sycara. Intelligent Software Agents. 2001. Web Page, http://www-2.cs.cmu. edu/~softagents/retsina.html.

[35] P. Weinstein, H. V. D. Parunak, P. Chiusano, and S. Brueckner. Agents Swarming in Semantic Spaces to Corroborate Hypotheses. In *Proceedings of AAMAS 2004*, New York, NY, pages 1488-1489, ACM, 2004. http://www.newvectors.net/staff/parunakv/ AAMAS04AntCAFE.pdf.

[36] D. Weyns, A. Omicini, and J. Odell. Environment as a first-class abstraction in multiagent systems. *Journal of Autonomous Agents and Multi-Agent Systems*, 17, 2007.

[37] M. Wooldridge. *Reasoning about Rational Agents*. Cambridge, MA, MIT Press, 2000.

[38] M. Wooldridge, N. R. Jennings, and D. Kinny. The Gaia Methodology for Agent-Oriented Analysis and Design. *International Journal of Autonomous Agents and Multi-Agent Systems*, 3(Forthcoming), 2000.

An Analysis and Design Concept for Self-organization in Holonic Multi-agent Systems

Sebastian Rodriguez, Nicolas Gaud, Vincent Hilaire, Stéphane Galland,
and Abderrafiâa Koukam

Multiagent Systems and Applications Group,
Systems and Transportation Laboratory (SeT),
University of Technology of Belfort-Montbéliard (UTBM),
F-90 000 Belfort, France
sebastian.rodriguez@utbm.fr
http://set.utbm.fr/info/

Abstract. Holonic Multi-Agent Systems (HMAS) are a convenient way to engineer complex and open systems. HMAS are based upon self-similar entities, called holons, which define an organizational structure called holarchy. An open issue of HMAS is to give holons means of self-organization to satisfy their goals. Our works focus on modeling and engineering of complex systems using a holonic organizational approach. This paper introduces the concept of *capacity* as the description of agents know-how. This concept allows the representation and reasoning about agents know-hows. Even more, it encourages a reusable modeling and provides agents with means to self-organize.

1 Introduction

Software agents and multi-agents systems (MAS in the sequel) are recognized as both abstractions and effective technologies for modelling and building complex distributed applications. However, they are still difficult to engineer. The current practice of MAS design tends to be limited to individual agents and small face-to-face groups of agents that operate in closed systems [13]. However, MAS aim large scale systems operating in open environments. Moreover, agents are expected to organize and cooperate in order to fullfill system's goals. It seems improbable that a rigid unscalabe organization could handle real world problems in this context. The holonic paradigm [7] has proven to be an effective solution to several problems with such complex underlying organizations [10,21,22]. Holons are defined as self-similar structure composed of holons as substructure. They are neither parts nor wholes in an absolute sense. The organizational structure defined by holons, called holarchy, allows the modelling at several granularity levels. Each level corresponds to a group of interacting holons. One issue is that holons need a representation of their know-hows in order to efficiently group, cooperate and achieve their respective goals.

In this paper, we introduce the notion of capacity as a description of a know-how or a service. We define this notion and integrate it into a holonic framework to enable holons to find the right holon to cooperate with.

S. Brueckner et al. (Eds.): ESOA 2006, LNAI 4335, pp. 15–27, 2007.

This paper is organized as follows : secion 2 introduces the holonic framework we use and defines the concept of capacity. Section 3 shows how to use capacities and finally section 4 concludes and future research directions are presented.

2   Concepts

2.1   An Organizational Approach for Holonic Systems

A holon is a self-similar structure composed of holons as sub-structures. This hierarchical structure composed of holons is called a *holarchy*. A holon can be seen, depending on the level of observation, either as an autonomous "atomic" entity or as an organization of holons. This duality is sometimes called the *Janus Effect*[1], in reference to the two *faces of a holon*. A holon is a whole-part construct that is composed of other holons, but it is, at the same time, a component of a higher level holon. Examples of holarchies can be found in every-day life. Probably the most widely used example is the human body. The body cannot be considered as a whole in an absolute sense. It is, in fact, composed of organs, that in turn are composed of cells, molecules, etc.

Holonic Systems have been applied to a wide range of applications. Thus it is not surprising that a number of models and framework have been proposed for these systems[11,22,23]. However, most of them are strongly attached to their domain of application and use specific agent architectures. In order to allow modular and reusable modelling that minimizes the impact on the underlying architecture we propose a framework based on an organizational approach. We have selected the Role-Interaction-Organization (RIO) model [5] to represent organizations. We have leaned for this model since it enables formal specification, animations and proofs based on the OZS formalism [4].

In order to maintain this framework generic, we need to distinguish between two aspects that overlap in a holon. The first is directly related to the holonic character of the entity, i.e. a holon (super-holon) is composed of other holons (sub-holons or members). This aspect is common to every holons, thus called *holonic* aspect. And the second is related to the problem the members are trying to solve, and thus specific to the application or domain of application.

A super-holon is an entity in its own right, but it is composed by its members. Then, we need to consider how members organize and manage the super-holon. This constitutes the first aspect of the holonic framework. To describe this aspect, we define a particular organization called *Holonic Organization*. We have adopted the *moderated group*[3] as management structure of the super-holon, due to the wide range of configurations it allows. In a moderated group, a subset of the members, namely *heads*, will represent all the sub-holons with the outside world.

The *Holonic Organization* represents a *moderated group* in terms of roles and their interactions. To describe the status of a member inside a super-holon, it

---

[1] Roman god with two faces. Janus was the god of gates and doorways, custodian of the universe and god of beginnings.

defines three main roles: The *Head* role players are the *representatives* or *moderators* of the group, and a part of the visible interface. For the represented members we define two different roles. The *Part* role represents members belonging to only one super-holon. The *Multi-Part* role is played by sub-holons shared by more than one super-holon.

In our approach, every super-holon must contain at least one instance of the *Holonic Organization*. Every sub-holon must play at least one role of this organization to define its status in the composition of the super-holon.

Super-holons are created with an objective and to perform certain tasks. To achieve these goals/tasks, the members must interact and coordinate their actions. Our framework also offers means to model this second aspect of the super-holons. This goal-dependent interactions are modeled using organizations. We give them the name of *Internal Organizations*, since they are specific to each holon and its goals/tasks. The behaviors and interactions of the members can thus be described independently of their roles as a component of the super-holon. The set of *internal organizations* can be dynamically updated to describe additional behaviors. The only strictly required organization is the Holonic organization that describes member's status in the super-holon.

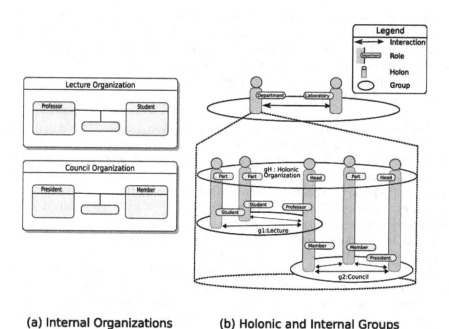

(a) Internal Organizations   **(b) Holonic and Internal Groups**

Fig. 1. Computer Science Department Holon

This approach guarantees a clear separation between the management of the super-holon and the goal-specific behaviors and favors modularity and re-usability.

For example, lets consider a department in a university. The holonic aspect makes reference to the fact that the students and teachers compose and manage the department. This is modeled using the *Holonic Organization*. On the other hand, the department is created with a specific purpose and, thus, to fulfill precise goals/tasks in the system. How members coordinate and interact to achieve these goals is modeled using the *internal organizations*. In the department example, we use two organizations: *Lecture* and *Council*. The RIO diagrams of these organizations are shown in figure 1(a).

At the holon level, an organization is instanciated into *groups*. In our example, the Department Holon is decomposed into three groups. The first represents an instance of the *Holonic Organization*. The other two groups instanciate the goals-dependent organizations : *Lecture* and *Council*. The notation *g1:Lecture* denotes that the *g1* group is an instance of the organization *Lecture*. A holon may contain several instances of the same organization.

Further details on the framework can be found in [14,16]. A formal specification of the roles described above can be found in [15].

2.2   Capacity

Large scale systems are expected to organize and cooperate in open environments. To satisfy their needs and goals, agents often have to collaborate. Thus an agent has to be able to estimate the competences of its future partners to identify the most appropriate collaborator. We have introduced the notion of capacity to deal with this issue. The capacity allows to represent the competences of an agent or a set of agents.

Definition. A capacity is a description of a know-how/service. This description contains at least a name identifying the capacity and the set of its *input* and *output* variables which may have default values. The *requires* field defines the constraints that should be verified to guarantee the expected behavior of the capacity. Then the *ensures* field describe what properties the capacity guarantees if *requires* is satisfied. Finally we add a textual description to informally describe the behavior of the capacity.

In our model the capacity can thus be represented using the structure presented in figure 2 (inspired by [19] and [12]) :

By logical constraints we refer to pre/post conditions on operations and invariants on states. For example, lets consider a capacity called *FindShortestPath*. This capacity finds the shortest path in a weighted directed graph G from a source node s to a destination d. The description of this capacity can be stated as depicted in the figure 3. This capacity takes as input : a directed graph G consisting of nodes N and edges E valued by a weight function w, a source and a destination node. The output produced by this capacity, P, consists in a sequence of nodes. The *requires* clause states that the node and edge sets must not be empty. It also impose that the source and destination nodes belong to the graph nodes and that the weight function gives only positive values. The *ensures* clause says that there cannot be a shorter path than P from s to d.

Name : the name of the capacity
Input : the declaration of input variables, their type and possibly a default value.
Output : the declaration of output variables, their type and possibly an expected value for input default value.
Requires : Logical constraints defined on input variables
Ensures : Logical constraints defined on output variables
Textual Description : A textual description of the capacity

Fig. 2. The general structure of a capacity

Name : FindShortestPath
Input :

- $\mathcal{G} = (N, E)$, directed graph. $E = N \times N$
- $w : E \to \mathbb{R}$, weight function.
- $s \in N$, source node.
- $d \in N$, destination node.

Output : $P = \langle s = i_0, i_1, \cdots, i_{n-1}, d = i_n \rangle$, with $\forall k \in \{0..n\}, i_k \in N$ the shortest path P between s and d.
Requires : $N \neq \emptyset$ and $E \neq \emptyset$ and $\forall (u, v) \in E / w(u, v) \geq 0$
Ensures : $\forall j_t \in N, t \in \{0..m\}$

$$\forall Q = \langle s = j_0, j_1 \cdots, j_m = d \rangle : \quad P = Q \vee \sum_{t=0}^{m-1} w(j_t, j_{t+1}) \geq \sum_{k=0}^{n-1} w(i_k, i_{k+1})$$

There exists no path Q in the graph linking s to d shorter than P.
Textual Description : provides a solution to the single-source shortest path problem for a directed graph with non-negative edge weights.

Fig. 3. The *FindShortestPath* capacity

The definition of the capacity doesn't include any references to entities exhibiting this know-how/service. Indeed, we want to clearly separate the capacity of how it is realized.

However, from the super-holon point of view, we can categorize its capacities in three subcategories:

Atomic. The capacity is already present in one of the members of the super-holon. In this case, the head has to simply request the member possessing the required capacity to perform it.
Liaised. The capacity is obtained from a subset of the member's capacities following a known protocol.

Emergent. The capacity is not present as an atomic capacity nor it can be obtained as composition of them. The capacity *emerges* from the interactions of the members.

The capacity is *atomic* for the super-holon if one of the members provides the capacity, but it does not have any implications on how this member obtains this capacity. This taxonomy of capacity is only relative to the super-holon point of view. The distinction between the capacity and the means to obtain it, and how we have integrated this concept into our holonic organizational model, will be detailed in the next section.

2.3   Integrating Capacities into a Holonic Organizational Perspective

As we already mentioned, we use an organizational approach to model holonic MAS. We propose an extension of the RIO model[5] to integrate the concepts of *Holon* and *Capacity*. An overview of this meta-model is presented in figure 4 using an UML-like diagram.

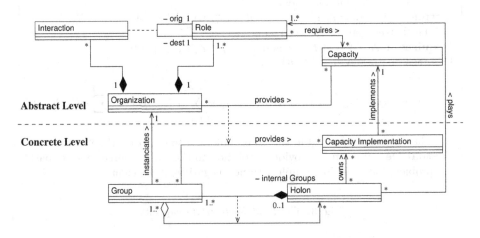

Fig. 4. Overview of the Organizational Meta-Model

As in RIO, the behaviors of the members are specified in terms of roles and their interactions. A role is defined as the abstraction of a behavior or/and a status in an organization. An interaction is a link between two roles such that an action in the first role produces a reaction on the second one. An organization is defined by a set of roles, their interactions and a common context. Finally a capacity is defined as presented in the previous section.

To obtain a generic model of organization, we need then to define a role without making any assumptions on the architecture of the holon which will play this role. Basing the description of these behaviors (Roles) on capacities enables a modular and reusable modeling of holonic MAS. Indeed, capacities describe what the holon is capable of doing (Abstract Level), independently of how it does it (Concrete Level). So to catch these two different levels of abstraction in our organizational model, we introduce the notion of capacity implementation. The capacity is the description of a given competence/service, while its implementations are the way to obtain that competence or service. For the example of the capacity *FindShortestPath*, the *Dijkstra's* and the *Bellman-Ford* algorithms constitute two available implementations. From a programming point of view, the notion of capacity implementation promotes re-usability and modularity and in this sense can be considered as a basic software component. Multiple implementations can be associated to a single capacity.

A role defines a behavior based on what the holon is capable of doing (i.e. the holon's capacities). Thus, a role requires that the role player has specific capacities. A holon has to possess all capacities required by a role to play that role.

On the other hand, a role confers to its player a certain status in the organization and the right to perform its capacities. A role thus confers holon the authorization to wield some of its capacities in the context defined by the organization. This context is materialized at the Concrete Level by the Group. A group represents then an instance of an organization. A holon belonging to a group must play at least one role in this group. A holon can belong to several groups.

In addition a holon may be composed of groups. A super-holon contains at least the holonic group and possibly a set of internal groups, instances of internal organizations. Of course a super-holon cannot be a member of one of its internal groups.

We suppose that every holon has a set of basic capacities. It may also have a set of specific capacities (e.g. *FindShortestPath*) that, as we will see in section 3.2, can dynamically evolve.

3 Using Capacities to Enable HMAS Self-organization

3.1 Organization Capacities

As described by John H Holland : "The behavior of a whole complex adaptive system[*cas*] is more than a simple sum of the behaviors of its parts; *cas* abound non linearity" [6].

The notion of capacity provides means to control and exploit these additionnal behaviors, emerging from members interactions, by considering an organization as a capacity implementation. Organizations used to model members interactions offer a simple way to represent how these capacities are obtained from the members. This becomes specially useful to represent *Liaised* and *Emergent* Capacities.

For example, we have already mentioned that the *Dijkstra's* and *Bellman-Ford* algorithms can be two possible implementations of the capacity *FindShortestPath*. If we consider that organizations can also be seen as possible implementations, the *Ant Colony* organization may then be also considered as an implementation of the capacity *FindShortestPath*. The *Ant Colony* is a well known organization able to determine a solution to the shortest path problem in a directed graph. The solution (the shortest path) results from Ants interaction in their environment. According to the description stated at the figure 3, the environment is represented by the graph $\mathcal{G}$, the source node s is assimilited to the Ant-hill, and the destination node d to a source of food.

The figure 5 shows an example of three holons in interactions. Holon 1, playing the *Route Requester* role, is looking for the shortest route to a given destination, and thus asks the *Route Providers*. The behavior, described by the *Route Provider* role, is based on the assumption that the role player has the *FindShortestPath* capacity. As long as the implementation honors the constraints established by the capacity, the holon is authorized to play the role. In our example, two implementations are present. The holon 2 owns an implementation based on the *Dijkstra*'s algorithm while holon 3 obtains its capacity through an *Ant Colony*. Holon 3 contains an instance of the *Ant Colony* organization (depicted in figure 6) noted $g1 : Ant\ Colony$. This denomination indicates that group $g1$ is an instance of the *Ant Colony* organization. As such, members involved in the group play one of the roles defined on the RIO diagram given at figure 6.

The fact that an organization can provide a capacity takes all its sense when we associate it to the holonic vision. Because the super-holon can exploit the additional behavior emerging from its members interactions and so play roles inaccessible to its members. It remains one more issue in order to integrate it into the holonic modelling : how to map the external stimuli of the super-holon to the actions and capacities of the members. The *head* represents the solution to this problem. The members playing this role are part of the interface of the super-holon. Thus, in charge of redistributing or translating the external incoming information to the other members of the holon (playing *Part* and *MultiPart* roles). Certain organizations may require to be adapted to this mode of representation. For the *Ant Colony* organization (cf. figure 6), a special role : the *Supervisor*, played by the *Head*, have been added. First of all, the *Supervisor* is in charge of initializing the environment of the colony with the specified input graph $\mathcal{G}$ and emitting the signal to launch the Ants. Then it observes the *Ant Colony* to determine when the result is available and forward it to its super-holon. This result being emergent, the presence of an observer to determine the availablity of the result is imperative. The holon 3 in figure 5 contains a group $g1$ which is an instance of the *Ant Colony* Organization.

In this sense, an organisation can, under certain conditions, provide one or more capacities. Thus, it represents a way to implement or obtain a capacity. This feature can be exploited in the Analysis and Design phase. To that end, the capacities provided by an organization have to be added to its description (especially in Organizational Design Pattern).

The self-organization mechanisms enabled by the notion of capacity will be detailed in the following section.

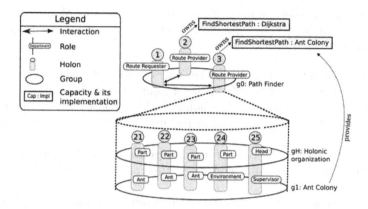

Fig. 5. Atomic or Emergent Capacity

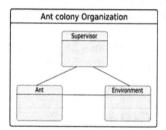

Fig. 6. RIO Diagram of the *Ant Colony* Organization

3.2   Capacity Dynamics

As we have already precised, each holon originally possess a set of capacities that can dynamically evolve. In order to acquire a new capacity a holon may instanciate a new internal organization providing the required capacity. This process can be summarized by the following steps and is depicted in figure 7 :

1. First, the holon tries to match the capacities provided in organizations' descriptions with the required capacity. To assure this matchmaking process in an open system a common description language is required to match holon capacites, [19,20] propose a model to deal with dynamic service matchmaking that can be easily adapted to our case.
2. If matches are found the holon has to choose among the different organizations the one which seems the fittest. This choice is essentially based on the capacities required by the chosen organization and the already present member's capacities.
3. When an organization has been chosen the holon has yet to instantiate the defined roles and interactions. Either the chosen organization's roles are played by sub-holons member, or it has to recruit new members capable of playing those roles.

4. When each role defined in the chosen organization has a player in the freshly instanciated group. The super-holon is able to obtain the capacity implementation and can thus play new roles.

To illustrate these steps, lets now consider our *FindShortestPath* capacity example. We suppose that the group g_0 of figure 5 contains a *Route Requester* and only one *Route Provider*. The holon 3 wish integrate this group as *Route Provider* but it doesn't possess the required capacity *FindShortestPath* (cf. fig. 7, step 1).

It has thus two possibilities. First, the recruitment of a member, already owning the *FindShortestPath* capacity. In this case it would also obtain it as an atomic capacity.

Second, instanciate an organization able to provide it, like the *Ant Colony* organization. This organization is found using a matchmaking process (cf. fig. 7, step 2). Lets condiser the situation where holon 3 choses this alternative and integrates an additional internal group, instanciating the *Ant Colony* organization (cf. fig. 7, step 3). It recruits new members able to play the various role of this organization (cf. fig 6).

Owning henceforth the required capacity, it's able to play the *Route Provider* role and thus joins the group g_0 (cf. fig. 7, step 4).

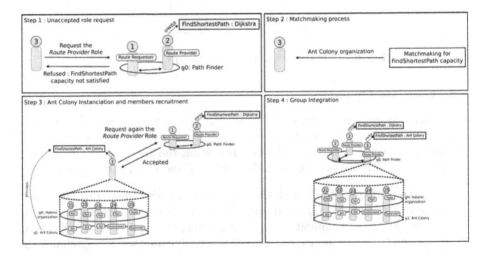

Fig. 7. Acquiring a new capacity by integrating a new internal organization

4   Related Works

Several approaches related to agent capabilities have been already proposed in various domains of MAS.

In the domain of Semantic Web and Web Agents, [19,20] propose an Agent Capability Description Language (LARKS) and discuss the Service Matchmaking process using it. Thus a first description of Agent Capability using LARKS is given. However this decription is only used in the Service Matchmaking process and not used during the analysis nor the modelling phases. These aspects are tackled in our approach with the notion of capacity as a basic decription of an agent know-how.

To distinguish the agent from its competences, [17] and [18] have introduced the notion of *skill* to describe basic agent abilities and allowing the definition of an atomic agent, that can dynamically evolve by learning/acquiring new *skills*. Then [1,2] have extended this approach to integrate this notion of *skill* as a basic building block for role specification. [8,9] also consider agent capability as a basic building block for role specification in their meta-model for MAS modeling. But these capabilities are inherent to particular agents, and thus to specific architectures. In these models the role is considered as a link between agents and a collection of behaviors embodied by the skills. This really differs from our view of the notion of role. For us a role is a first class entity, the abstraction of a behavior or/and a status in an organization (extension of [5]), that should be specified without making any assumptions on its susceptible players. In other words, in these approaches, the skill is directly related to the way to obtain a service, and thus represents a basic software component. However, the description of the general class of related services and the fact that a given agent ability can be obtained by various implementations is not developed. We can thus consider that these aspects are captured in our model with the notion of capacity implementation.

In a more general way, we can consider that our approach is situated in the confluence of these various models, linking the description of an agent capability and its various possible implementations. We thus provide agents with means to reason about their needs/goals and to identify the way to satisfy/achieve them. We thus benefit of the advantages of both approaches, increasing reuasibility and modularity by separating the agent from its capacities, and the capacity from its various implementations.

Considering an organization as a possible capacity implementation constitutes our main contribution. We can thus consider that a group of interacting agent can provide a capacity to an upper level. This takes all its interest in the case of holonic MAS, where the super-holon can exploit additionnal behaviors emerging from members interactions to obtain a new capacity. In a same way, we also provide a modeling tool to deal with intrinsic emergent properties of a system and catch them directly from the analysis phase.

5   Conclusion

In this paper, we have presented the concept of capacity to enable a modular and reusable model of organizations. To achieve that, the role specification is based on the description of required know-hows, described using capacities. To play a role, a holon has to possess an implementation (that could be specific according to its architecture) for each required capacity.

By considering, an organization as a possible capacity implementation, we provide means to exploit additional behaviors emerging from a group of agents in interaction. Combining this representation with the holonic approach, the super-holon, by instanciating specific organizations, can obtain new capacities from the collaboration of its members and therefore play roles, inaccessible to its members as individuals.

Finally we introduce self-organization mechanisms allowing a holon to dynamically change its set of capacities and so achieve its new goals.

This work is part of larger effort to define a well founded framework for Holonic MAS applications. Future research will deepen the formal specification of capacities and define a matchmaking process to find capacities implementations.

References

1. Emmanuel Adam and René Mandiau. A hierarchical and by role multi-agent organization: Application to the information retrieval. In *ISSADS*, pages 291–300, 2005.
2. Emmanuel Adam and René Mandiau. Roles and hierarchy in multi-agent organizations. In M. Pechoucek, P. Petta, and L.z. Varga, editors, *4th International Central and Eastern European Conference on Multi-Agent Systems, CEEMAS 2005*, number 3690 in LNAI, pages 539–542, Budapest, Hungary, September 2005. Springer-Verlag.
3. Christian Gerber, Jörg H. Siekmann, and Gero Vierke. Holonic multi-agent systems. Technical Report DFKI-RR-99-03, Deutsches Forschungszentrum für Künztliche Inteligenz - GmbH, Postfach 20 80, 67608 Kaiserslautern, FRG, May 1999.
4. Pablo Gruer, Vincent Hilaire, Abder Koukam, and P. Rovarini. Heterogeneous formal specification based on object-z and statecharts: semantics and verification. *Journal of Systems and Software*, 70(1-2):95–105, 2004.
5. Vincent Hilaire, Abder Koukam, Pablo Gruer, and Jean-Pierre Müller. Formal specification and prototyping of multi-agent systems. In Andrea Omicini, Robert Tolksdorf, and Franco Zambonelli, editors, *Engineering Societies in the Agents' World*, number 1972 in Lecture Notes in Artificial Intelligence. Springer Verlag, 2000.
6. John H. Holland. *Hidden order: how adaptation builds complexity*. Addison Wesley Longman Publishing Co., Inc., Redwood City, CA, USA, 1995.
7. Arthur Koestler. *The Ghost in the Machine*. Hutchinson, 1967.
8. Eric Matson and Scott A. DeLoach. Autonomous organization-based adaptive information systems. In *IEEE International Conference on Knowledge Intensive Multiagent Systems (KIMAS '05)*, Waltham, MA, April 2005.
9. Eric Matson and Scott A. DeLoach. Formal transition in agent organizations. In *IEEE International Conference on Knowledge Intensive Multiagent Systems (KIMAS '05)*, Waltham, MA, April 2005.
10. F. Maturana, W. Shen, and D. Norrie. Metamorph: An adaptive agent-based architecture for intelligent manufacturing, 1999.

11. Francisco Maturana, Weiming Shen, and Douglas Norrie. Metamorph: An adaptive agent-based architecture for intelligent manufacturing. *International Journal of Production Research*, 37(10), 1999. 2159-2174.
12. B. Meyer. Applying 'design by contract'. *IEEE Computer*, 25(10):40–51, October 1992.
13. James Odell, Marian Nodine, and Renato Levy. A metamodel for agents, roles, and groups. In James Odell, P. Giorgini, and Jg Mller, editors, *Agent-Oriented Software Engineering (AOSE) IV*, Lecture Notes on Computer Science. Springer, 2005.
14. Sebastian Rodriguez, Vincent Hilaire, and Abder Koukam. Towards a methodological framework for holonic multi-agent systems. In *Fourth International Workshop of Engineering Societies in the Agents World*, pages 29–31, Imperial College London, UK (EU), October 2003.
15. Sebastian Rodriguez, Vincent Hilaire, and Abder Koukam. Fomal specification of holonic multi-agent system framework. In *Intelligent Agents in Computing Systems, International Conference on Computational Science (3)*, number 3516 in LNCS, pages 719–726, Atlanta, USA, 2005.
16. Sebastian A. Rodriguez. *From analysis to design of Holonic Multi-Agent Systems: a Framework, methodological guidelines and applications*. PhD thesis, Université de Technologie de Belfort-Montbéliard, 2005.
17. JC. Routier, P. Mathieu, and Y. Secq. Dynamic skill learning: A support to agent evolution. In *AISB'01 Symposium on Adaptive Agents and Multi-Agent Systems*, pages 25–32, 2001.
18. M. Savall, M. Itmi, and J-P. Pecuchet. Yamam : a new organization model for multi-agent systems and its platform named phoenix. In *Conference SCSC 2000*, Orlando, USA, 2001.
19. K. Sycara, M. Klusch, S. Widoff, and J. Lu. Dynamic service matchmaking among agents in open information environments. *SIGMOD Record (ACM Special Interests Group on Management of Data)*, 28(1):47–53, March 1999.
20. K. Sycara, J. Lu, M. Klusch, and S. Widoff. Matchmaking among heterogeneous agents on the internet. In *Proceedings of the 1999 AAAI Spring Symposium on Intelligent Agents in Cyberspace*, March 1999.
21. F. Tecchia, C. Loscos, R. Conroy, and Y. Chrysanthou. Agent behaviour simulator (abs): A platform for urban behaviour development. In *GTEC'2001*, 2001.
22. M. Ulieru and A. Geras. Emergent holarchies for e-health applications: a case in glaucoma diagnosis. In *IECON 02 [Industrial Electronics Society, IEEE 2002 28th Annual Conference of the]*, volume 4, pages 2957– 2961, 2002.
23. J. Wyns. *Reference architecture for Holonic Manufacturing Systems - the key to support evolution and reconfiguration*. PhD thesis, Katholieke Universiteit Leuven, 1999.

Design Patterns for Decentralised Coordination in Self-organising Emergent Systems

Tom De Wolf and Tom Holvoet

AgentWise@DistriNet Research Group
Department of Computer Science, KULeuven
Celestijnenlaan 200A, 3001 Leuven, Belgium
{Tom.DeWolf,Tom.Holvoet}@cs.kuleuven.be
http://www.cs.kuleuven.be/~tomdw

Abstract. There is little or no guidance to systematically design a self-organising emergent solution that achieves the desired macroscopic behaviour. This paper describes decentralised coordination mechanisms such as gradient fields as design patterns, similar to patterns used in mainstream software engineering. As a consequence, a structured consolidation of best practice in using each coordination mechanism becomes available to guide engineers in applying them, and to directly decide which mechanisms are promising to solve a certain problem. As such, self-organising emergent solutions can be engineered more systematically, which is illustrated in a packet delivery service application.

1 Introduction

Modern distributed systems exhibit an increasingly interwoven and completely decentralised structure [13] (e.g. ad-hoc networks, transportation systems, etc.). Different subsystems interact with each other in many, often very complex, dynamic, and unpredictable ways. More systems need to achieve their requirements autonomously [15]. A promising approach is to use a group of agents that cooperate to autonomously achieve the required system-wide or macroscopic behaviour using only local interactions, local activities of the agents, and locally obtained information. Such decentralised multi-agent systems (MASs) exhibit *self-organising emergent behaviour* [5].

When engineering a self-organising emergent solution, the problem-solving power mainly resides in the interactions and coordination between the agents instead of in the intelligent reasoning of single agents. Therefore, a major architectural design decision is the choice of suitable decentralised coordination mechanisms such as digital pheromones [3], gradient fields [22], market-based control [26], tags [12], or tokens [31]. Many of such mechanisms are already applied to a number of case studies in literature [3,21,22,18,20,19,25,12,31,26,32,4,10,11,17,24]. However, a fundamental problem is the lack of guidance on how to systematically choose and use the most suitable coordination mechanism. The main reason is that, currently, all existing knowledge and best practice on coordination mechanisms is spread over hundreds of papers without a clearly structured and directly usable description of the mechanisms.

S. Brueckner et al. (Eds.): ESOA 2006, LNAI 4335, pp. 28–49, 2007.

The main contribution of this paper, and the extended report in [7], is twofold. First, the paper shows how decentralised coordination mechanisms can be structurally described as design patterns. Secondly, the paper illustrates how an engineer can use these patterns to systematically choose how to coordinate agents and achieve the desired global behaviour. Section 2 motivates design patterns as a description to support engineers in their choice of decentralised coordination mechanisms. The section also outlines in detail the structure of the pattern description. After that, sections 3, 4 and 5 give an usable pattern summary of a number of coordination mechanisms and apply the design pattern description in detail to two example mechanisms, i.e. gradient fields and market-based control. In section 6, a case study on a packet delivery service illustrates how design patterns allow to engineer more systematically a self-organising emergent solution. Finally, section 7 concludes and discusses future work.

2   Decentralised Coordination Mechanisms as Design Patterns

Typically, engineering MASs means having 99% of the effort go to conventional computer science and only 1% involves the actual agent paradigm [8]. Therefore, to engineer self-organising emergent MASs, developers should exploit conventional software technologies and techniques wherever possible [29]. Such exploitation speeds up development, avoids reinventing the wheel, and enables sufficient time to be devoted to the value added by the multi-agent paradigm [30]. From this point of view, [6] proposes a step plan based on an existing industry-ready software engineering process, i.e. the Unified Process [14]. The UP process is customised to explicitly focus on how to address the desired macroscopic behaviour of self-organising emergent MASs. Figure 1 shows that almost every discipline in the UP process is customised.

This paper focusses on the Design which emphasises a solution that fulfills the requirements, rather than its implementation or the requirements themselves. More specifically the focus is on the coarse-grained architectural design. The author of [16] states that architectural design is partially a science and partially an art. The *science* of architecture is the collection and organisation of information about architectural significant requirements (e.g. non-functional and macroscopic functionality). The *art* or architecture is making skillful choices and constructing a solution that meets the requirements, taking into account trade-offs, interdependencies, and priorities. The 'art' of architectural design is the creative step where designers exploit knowledge and best practice from a number of areas (e.g. architectural styles and patterns, technologies, pitfalls, and trends) to reach a suitable solution. For self-organising emergent systems the main source of knowledge to exploit in this creative step are the different mechanisms to coordinate the desired macroscopic functionality such as digital pheromones [3], gradient fields [22], and market-based coordination [26]. This paper captures this knowledge on decentralised coordination mechanisms as architectural design patterns.

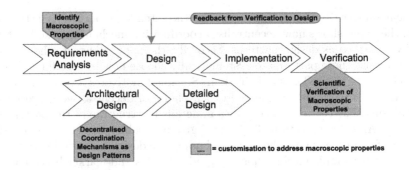

Fig. 1. A Unified Process engineering iteration annotated with customisations for issues specific for self-organising emergent MASs

2.1 Motivation for Design Patterns

As stated earlier, the main problem-solving power resides in the coordination between agents and a major architectural design decision concerns the choice of one or more decentralised coordination mechanisms to achieve the desired macroscopic behaviour. The mechanism used to coordinate has a strong impact on what is and can be communicated [21]. A lot of such mechanisms are used in literature but experience and knowledge about how to use them is currently spread out over hundreds of articles. A more structured and useful description is needed to consolidate this best practice.

In mainstream software engineering, current best practice and knowledge about known solutions is captured in what is called 'design patterns'. The most famous reference is the Gang of Four design patterns book [9]. This paper supports applying decentralised coordination mechanisms by describing them as design patterns, similar to patterns used in mainstream software engineering. An important issue in engineering self-organising emergent solutions is to understand for which kind of macroscopic behaviour each coordination mechanisms is useful, which is more appropriate in which situation, etc. Design patterns describe each decentralised coordination mechanism in a structured way, inherently including this kind information. Using such a set of structured patterns, self-organising emergent system can be designed more systematically.

2.2 The Pattern Description Format

Patterns can be described at several levels of abstraction. The patterns in the Gang of Four book [9] are described at the class or implementation level. Another level of abstraction to describe design patterns is the architectural or even conceptual level in which the focus is more on the coarse-grained and conceptual structure. The decentralised coordination mechanisms in this paper are described at the architectural and conceptual level. The class level is not described because such mechanisms can be implemented in multiple ways and little is known about the best way to do this.

This paper uses the guidelines and patterns for describing patterns from [23]. As such, the decentralised coordination mechanisms are described in a format known in mainstream software engineering which promotes their usage. For example, also the Gang of Four patterns book [9] uses a similar format. The general structure is extended in subsections to better describe issues specific for decentralised coordination in self-organising emergent solutions. The format used involves the following sections:

- **Pattern Name/Also Known As:** A clear name and aliases referring to the solution used or a useful metaphor. The name is given in the title of the pattern's section.
- **Context/Applicability:** The circumstances in which the problem being solves requires a solution. Often described via a 'situation'. In this paper this context typically indicates when a self-organising emergent solution is promising.
- **Problem/Intent:** What is solved by this pattern? Engineers compare this section with their problem in order to select coordination mechanisms.
- **Forces:** Often contradictory considerations that must be taken into account when choosing a solution to a problem.
- **Solution:** A description of how the problem is solved and described in close relation to the forces it resolves. This section has a more detailed structure:
  - *Inspiration:* Most coordination mechanism are inspired by some natural, biological, physical, or social phenomena.
  - *Conceptual Description:* A conceptual description of how the inspirational mechanism works and is used in computer systems. This section allows to map the concepts used in the coordination mechanism to domain-specific entities in the system under construction, i.e. the concepts and their relationships indicate what is needed in order to use this coordination mechanism.
  - *Parameter Tuning:* Typically, such coordination mechanisms have a lot of parameters that need to be tuned. This section enumerates them and gives some guidelines to tune them.
  - *Infrastructure:* Some mechanisms need a supporting infrastructure. More specifically, what is needed to support the design at the class level.
  - *Characteristics:* Using the mechanism imposes some characteristics on the solution including advantages, disadvantages, and other useful properties.
- **Related Mechanisms/Patterns:** An enumeration of patterns that are related in which the differences and similarities are emphasised.
  - *Variations:* Variations of the same pattern which can be more general or (domain) specific variations.
  - *Other Coordination Mechanisms:* Alternative coordination mechanisms that solve the same (or related) problem.
- **Examples/Known Uses:** Examples of known uses of the pattern in case studies.

In addition to a separate description for each pattern, a 'Problem/Solution Summary' is provided to help the reader find the pattern(s) which solve(s) their specific problems. Such a summary is typically a table with a brief description of the problem each pattern solves and how. In what follows, section 3 gives such a summary for a limited set of widely used coordination mechanisms and sections 4 and 5 describe two patterns in more detail following the structure given in this section.

3   Problem/Solution Summary

This section summarises the patterns by giving a so called 'Problem/Solution Summary'. An engineer uses this to find the pattern(s) or coordination mechanism(s) which solve(s) their specific problem(s). The Problem/Solution Summary can be found in Table 1 where a brief description of the problem and the corresponding solution is linked to the pattern to use. Due to space limitation only two pattern descriptions are given in (limited) detail in the following sections. However, a full detailed pattern catalogue can be found in [7].

4   Pattern 1: Gradient Fields

Also Known As: Computational Fields, Co-Fields, Morphogen gradients [18], Field-based coordination, Force Fields [21].

4.1   Context/Applicability

A solution is needed to coordinate multiple autonomous entities, situated in an environment, in a decentralised way to achieve a globally coherent spatial movement of the agents. The coordination mechanism has to be robust and flexible in the face of frequent changes. Also, local estimates of global information are the only possible way to coordinate. As such, decentralised coordination is the only possible alternative.

4.2   Problem/Intent

- *Spatial Movement:* How to adaptively orchestrate in a decentralised way the spatial movement of a large set of agents in large-scale distributed systems [21,20,18]? As such global *Pattern Formation* can be achieved.
- *Structure Formation:* How to adaptively self-configure a modular structure achieving the desired shape/structure (e.g. modular robots) [18]?
- *Routing:* How to achieve routing for messages, agents, etc. [18]?
- *Integration of Contextual Information:* How to provide agents with abstract, simple yet effective contextual information from various sources supporting and facilitating the required motion coordination activities [21,20,18] (i.e. spatial information such as distance/direction to source)?

Table 1. Problem/Solution Summary

Problem(s)	Solution	Pattern
Spatial Source to Destination Routing, Task Recruitment, Relation Identification, Integration of various information sources	*Agents explicitly search* for goals, tasks, or related items and drop pheromones to gradually form historical paths for other agents to follow. Reinforcement of an existing path by other agents can be seen as a reinforcement of the relation between source and destination. Evaporation, Aggregation, and Propagation keep the pheromones up-to-date and support integration of information.	Digital Pheromone Paths [3]
Spatial Movement, Pattern Formation, Structure Formation, Routing, Integration of Contextual Information	Spatial, contextual, and coordination information is automatically and instantaneously propagated by the environment as computational fields. *Agents simply follow the "waveform"* of these fields to achieve the coordination task, i.e. *no explicit exploration.*	Gradient Fields [22]
Resource Allocation in general (resource=task, power, bandwidth, space, time, etc.) , Integration of resource Usage/Need Information	A virtual market where resource users sell and buy resource usage with virtual currency. The price evolves according to the market dynamics and indicates a high (high price) or low (low price) demand. This information is used by agents to decide on using the resource or not. Economic market theory states that the prices converge to a stable equilibrium.	Market-based Coordination [26]
Trust and reputation, Team-formation, Discourage selfish behaviour in Teams, Specialisation of skills within Teams	Agents put and modify tags on other agents and a team is formed by only collaborating with agents with the same tag or some other condition. If tags indicate how well agents behaved in collaborations with others then trust and reputation information can be available.	Tags [12]
Resource Access Control/Allocation, Role Allocation, Enforce Organisation Structure, Information Sharing	Information, resources, or roles are represented by a token. Only the holder has exclusive access to the information and resource. Holding a role token commits to executing that role. Tokens are passed among agents to get adaptive coordination.	Tokens [31]
etc.	etc.	etc.

4.3 Forces

– *Explore vs. Exploit*: In order to be adaptive the solution has to explore sufficiently compared to only exploiting already known information. Otherwise the approach can get trapped in local optima or never find new targets at all. However, to much exploration may result in an approach that is very inefficient.

- *Centralised vs. Decentralised*: A decentralised solution often requires a huge amount of communication and coordination overhead which a centralised solution has not. A centralised solution often optimally controls the system. However, a centralised solution is often a bottleneck and single point of failure in a very dynamic context.
- *Optimality vs. Robustness/Flexibility*: An adaptive approach that has no central means to optimise its efficiency may result in suboptimal solutions. However, an optimal solution only exists with respect to a static situation, which is never reached in the face of frequent changes. As such, a robust and flexible approach may be preferred to an approach that is optimal but inflexible.
- *Responsibility of Environment vs. Agents*: Coordination needs complex processing and communication. There is a trade-off to make the agents themselves or the environment responsible. Making the agents responsible allows agents to explicitly reason about and control how information is distributed but sometimes requires complex algorithms. On the other hand, making the environment responsible allows agents to simply be guided by the results in the environment, i.e. a "red carpet' that avoids complex processing within agents, but the agents are no longer in control of the information distribution. Such coordination can be more dynamic and adaptive because the source of changes, i.e. environment, also supplies the coordination information.
- *Greedy vs. Focussed*: A "greedy" approach to coordination disregards that a small sacrifice now, i.e. not exploiting a piece of coordination information, could possibly lead to greater advantages in the future. However, it is a general drawback of distributed solutions, where the possibility of globally informed decisions by distributed agents is often ruled out due to the need for efficient and adaptive coordination [19].

4.4   Solution

Inspiration. The Gradient Field coordination mechanism takes its *inspiration from physics and biology*. In physics [20,19,21], the same mechanism can be found in the way masses and particles in our universe adaptively move and globally self-organise their movements accordingly to the locally perceived magnitude of gravitational/electro-magnetic/potential fields. The particles follows the "waveform" of the fields (see figure 2). In biological organisms, a coherent, reliable and complex behaviour is achieved from the local cooperation of large numbers of identically "programmed" cells [18]. In particular, chemicals are diffused among cells and cells are driven in their behaviour by the locally sensed gradients of diffused proteins ("morphogen gradients"). Morphogen gradients is a mechanism used to determine positional information and polarity. For example, cells use the concentration of different morphogens to determine whether they lie in the head, thorax, or abdominal regions to achieve wing and limb development.

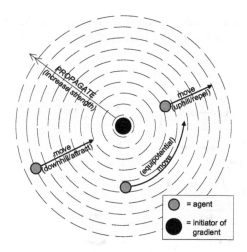

Fig. 2. A gradient field with propagation direction and agent movements shown

Conceptual Description. To use this as a decentralised coordination mechanism in software systems such a gravitational/electro-magnetic/chemical field has to be translated into an artificial data structure representing the Gradient Field, i.e. a computational field or Co-Field [22,21,19]. Figure 3 illustrates the conceptual structure of such a solution in UML class diagram notation. A Gradient Field is data structure which is spatially distributed, as Gradient Parts, over Locations in the Environment. Each field is characterised by a unique identifier, the necessary contextual information such as a location-dependent numeric value (representing the field strength in that location), and a Propagation Rule determining how the numeric value should change in space.

A gradient field is started, initiated, or injected into the environment from a certain "source" location by a Gradient Initiator (i.e. a Location itself, an Agent, or some other entity in the system) conveying some application-specific information about the local environment and/or about the initiator itself [21]. The Environment makes sure that the Gradient Field is propagated, according to its Propagation Rule, from the starting location to the neighbours of that location (typically increasing the strength of the gradient, initially set to zero; decreasing gradients are also possible). In turn, the neighbouring locations modify the strength and re-broadcast the gradient to their neighbours which is repeated until the gradient has propagated far enough. Each intermediate location stores and forwards only the gradient part with the minimum strength value it has received for that particular gradient field. As such a "waveform" gradient map is formed in the environment which conveys useful context information for the coordination task.

Agents observe multiple Gradient Parts on the neighbouring locations of the location on which the agent is situated. Then agents follow the waveform (deterministically or with some probability) by moving to a neighbouring location. This allows agents to coordinate their movement with respect the the gradient initiator. For example, in figure 2 agents move downhill (attracted by the initiator), uphill (repelled by the initiator), or on an equipotential line (equal strength around initiator).

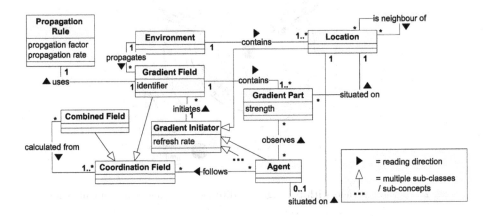

Fig. 3. A conceptual model of the gradient coordination mechanism

The gradient field mechanism can be schematised as follows [22,21,20,19]:

- The *environment is represented and abstracted by "computational fields"* which provide agents with a location-dependent and local perspective on the global situation of the system to facilitate the required motion coordination.
- The coordination policy is realised by letting the agents move locally *following the "waveform" of these fields.* Agents can autonomously decide whether to follow the gradient fields or not.
- Environmental *dynamics* and movement of entities *induce changes in the fields' surface.* For example, when the initiator of a gradient field moves, the field -with some propagation delay- has to be updated in the environment to reflect that move. As such, a feedback cycle is formed that consequently influences agent movement.
- This *feedback cycle* lets the system *self-organise.* A globally coordinated and self-organised behaviour in the agent's movements emerges in a fully decentralised way due to the interrelated effects of agents following the fields' shape and of dynamic field re-shaping [21,20].

However, the achievement of an application-specific coordination task is rarely relying on the evaluation, as it is, of an existing computational field. Rather, in most cases, an application-specific task relies on the evaluation of an application-specific Coordination Field [21,20,19]. This coordination field can be an existing gradient field but typically it is a Combined Field, calculated as a combination (e.g. linear) of some of the locally perceived fields or other coordination fields. The coordination field is a new field in itself, and it is built with the goal of encoding in its shape the agent's coordination task. Once a proper coordination field is computed, agents can achieve their coordination task by simply following the shape of their coordination field.

Parameter Tuning. Every gradient field has a number or parameters, or "settings": a *Propagation Factor* determining how much is added to or removed from the gradient strength each propagation step and a *Propagation Rate* indicating how fast propagation occurs; a dynamic gradient has to be updated regularly which is determined by a certain *Refresh Rate*; the *Initial Strength of a Gradient* is the strength at the source location; each propagation rule can have its own *rule-specific parameters*, e.g. using another propagation factor at a distance of X from the initiator.

Infrastructure. A proper infrastructure or middleware is required (e.g. TOTA [20]) that supports data storage (to store field values), communication (propagate field values), event notification and subscription mechanisms (notify interested agents about field changes, as well as update fields to support changes), mobile-code services (dynamically configure field-propagation algorithms and coordination fields composition rules), and localisation mechanisms (to discover where agents are).

Characteristics

- Typically, following the gradient field downhill is the *shortest path* towards the initiator of the field [18].
- The structure of the environment in which the agents are working should reflect the current "problem" the agents are working on and the gradient structure and distribution should guide the agents to the current "solution" to that problem.
- *Spatial Context Information is distributed:* Gradients support *information spreading/distribution*. Gradient-Fields mainly deliver spatial information such as the direction or distance to a gradient initiator [20]. However, gradients can also embed any other necessary information.
- *Feedback Cycle [22]:* Feedback is given by the fact that gradients can change when changes occur in the environment or when the agent that emits the gradient decides to move or change the gradient. Other agents or gradient-emitting entities can then take that change in the gradient into account and react on it by for example changing its own gradient info. As such a feedback cycle is established to self-organise.
- *Simple Agents - Complex Environment:* Field-based approaches delegate to a middleware infrastructure in the environment the task of constructing and automatically updating the gradient field [20]. As such, the environment makes sure that not too much computational and communication burden is imposed on the agents themselves [19]. The context is represented as gradient fields, i.e. a kind of "red carpet", which represents how to achieve a coordination task by simply following the field.

- *Greedy Approach [20,19]:* A weakness of field-based approaches is that they are "greedy" because of the strictly local perspective in which agents act. Agents disregard whether as small sacrifice now, climbing a field hill instead of descending it - could possibly lead to greater advantages in the future.
- etc. (see [7] for more characteristics)

4.5 Related Mechanisms/Patterns

Variations

- *Propagation Inhibition or Selective Propagation [20,18]:* The propagation of a field can be bounded to a portion of space by having the propagation procedure to check conditions such as the local spatial coordinates, the gradient type or its strength to decide on further propagation or not.
- *Multiple Types of Fields [20,21,19]:* As mentioned earlier, multiple gradient instances can be combined in a coordination field to follow as a whole. All used gradients are typically of the same type. A logical extension is using different types of fields depending on the specific motion pattern to enforce. As such, they can be propagated and combined in coordination fields according to field-specific rules.
- etc. (see [7] for more variations)

Other Coordination Mechanisms. *Digital Pheromone Paths* is a specific instance of *Gradient Fields* where a number of small fields or pheromones aggregate into a gradient path and evaporate over time [20]. Also pheromone paths are constructed explicitly and, as such, agents also explicitly have to discover targets. Gradients make targets immediately and automatically (by the environment) visible through the presence of a gradient field for that target. Agents do not have to explore pro-actively. In addition, pheromones constitute a memory of the recent past, while gradient fields are instantaneous.

4.6 Examples/Known Uses

Some known uses or possible applications are: spatial shape formation [18], urban traffic management [21], reconfiguring modular robots' shape [21,25], control of autonomous characters in video games [21,19], tourist movement in museum [19,20], forklifts activity in a warehouse [19], software agents exploring the web [19], etc.

5   Pattern 2: Market-Based Control

Also Known As: Market Control, Market-Oriented Programming [32].

5.1 Context/Applicability

You need to coordinate multiple autonomous entities in a decentralised way to achieve a common and globally coherent goal while sharing a set of scarce

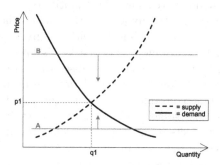

Fig. 4. The theory of Supply and Demand

resources. The coordination mechanism has to be robust and flexible in the face of frequent changes. Also, local estimates of global information are the only possible way to coordinate. As such, decentralised coordination is the only possible alternative. Some locally available information is needed indicating the global usage of resources.

5.2 Problem/Intent

- *Resource Allocation:* How to do efficient resource allocation [26,4,10,32] in a distributed and decentralised manner? Resources can be interpreted as tasks, bandwidth, manufacturing devices, etc.
- *Integration of Resource Usage/Need Information:* How to have locally available information about the global usage of and need for resources?

5.3 Forces

- *Centralised vs. Decentralised* (see section 4.3 in Gradient Field pattern).
- *Optimality vs. Robustness/Flexibility* (see section 4.3).
- *Responsibility of Environment vs. Agents* (see section 4.3).

5.4 Solution

Inspiration. The inspiration and metaphor came from human economies and market mechanisms, i.e. the free-market economies. In such an economy, goods or resources are allocated to the participants in a decentralised, robust, and self-organising manner. Participants act as buyers and/or sellers of goods by offering to buy or sell a good to other participants for a certain price. As long as the participants act completely self-interested then the market achieves a globally optimal allocation of goods. Transaction prices converge to a global equilibrium price, i.e. the market price. Note, that the degree of convergence depends on the market characteristics (e.g. elasticity, shape of demand and supply curves, etc.).

This price mechanism depends on the evolution of the demand and available supply of goods. Figure 4 illustrates this by plotting the evolution of supply and demand. The demand curve shows the quantity of good that consumers are willing and have the capacity to buy at the given price. The supply curve shows the quantity that suppliers are willing to sell at a given price. If the quantity of a good demanded by consumers in a market is greater than the quantity supplied, competition between consumers causes the price of the good to rise. As such, according to situation A in figure 4 this can both reduce the quantity demanded (because some consumers can no longer afford it) and increase the quantity supplied (because some suppliers may be more interested in selling at higher prices). Similar effects occur when the quantity supplied is greater than the quantity demanded (situation B in figure 4). According to classical economic theories the market equilibrates (see arrows in figure 4): transaction prices approach an equilibrium value $(p1, q1)$ where the quantity demanded matches the quantity supplied. As such, an efficient means of societal resource/goods allocation exists.

Conceptual Description. The aim of market-based coordination in computer science is fundamentally different from the aim of economic theory [32]. In market-based coordination, microeconomic theory is taken as given. Whether or not the microeconomic theory actually reflects human behaviour is not the critical issue. The important question is instead how microeconomic theory can be utilised for the implementation of successful resource allocation mechanisms in computer systems. Although decision-making is only local, economic theory, which has an immense body of formal study [28], provides means to generate and predict macroscopic properties such as the equilibrium price and others that can be deduced from that price information. The aim is that computer systems exhibit the same decentralisation, robustness, and capacity for self-organisation as do real economies [4]. In designing a market of computational agents, a key issue is to identify the consumers and producers [11]. Various preferences and constraints are introduced through the definition of the agents' trading behaviour. This ability to explicitly program the trading behaviour is an important difference from human markets. Finally, the mechanism for matching buyers and sellers must be specified.

Figure 5 illustrates market-based coordination conceptually in UML class diagram notation. A group of `agents` negotiate and trade with each other on an virtual market of scarce resources. The agents `communicate` with messages encapsulating `offers`, `bids`, `commitments`, and `payments` for resources [10]. The agents' goal is to acquire the `resources` of a certain `Resource Type` that they need. All agents start with an initial amount of `Currency` [11]. `Resources` are at each moment in time owned/used by one `agent`. Some agents act as 'consumers' or 'buyers' and have a `Demand` for a certain *quantity* of a resource and are willing to pay a certain *price* for it, based on the `Currency` they have and possibly other conditions. Other agents act as 'producers' or 'suppliers' and have a `Supply` of a certain *quantity* of a resource and are willing to sell at a certain *price*. The goal is to maximise their profit. Each `Agent` is self-interested and decides to participate as a *buyer/consumer* in an `Transaction` with a *supplier/producer* to transfer a certain *quantity* of resources. The behaviour of each agent depends on its local

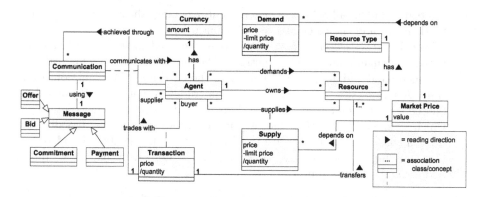

Fig. 5. Conceptual model of Market-based Coordination

information as well as market prices that communicate global information. For each unit to trade, each agent has a `limit price` that is unknown to others [4]. A buyer couldn't pay more than its limit price, and a seller couldn't sell for less than its limit price. The distribution of limit prices determines the evolution of the supply and demand curves.

Similar to a real free-market economy the process of **demand** and **supply** determines the **Market Price** to which the transaction prices evolve. When supply is greater than demand (resources are plentiful), the price of the resource will fall; and when demand exceeds supply (resources are scarce), the price rises. The aim then is that prices rise and fall, dynamically matching the quantity demanded to the quantity supplied, while these quantities also vary dynamically [4]. Agents set their prices solely on the basis of their implicit perception of supply and demand [10] through their success of bidding at particular prices. A special case occurs when an agent is at the same time a seller and a buyer [10] which implies a strategy to maintain an inventory level (i.e. number of owned resource units) that maximises its profit, i.e. that suits the market demand. The amount of available resources can be limited [11]. This is taken into account in the demand and supply. For instance, if the amount of available resources increases suddenly then the supply curve on figure 4 shifts to the right because suppliers are willing to supply more for each price. This results in an equilibrium increase in the supply and decrease in price (similarly demand curve shifts when agents suddenly need more resources). A globally limited amount of resources makes the market mechanism a resource allocation mechanism that generates an equilibrium distribution of resources that maximises global welfare [10].

There are two approaches to establish a market in a computer system [10,4,32,11,1]:

- *Auctioneer-mediated Markets (Centralised):* The market is mediated by an auctioneer agent. Agents send demand/supply functions or bids telling how much they like to consume/produce at different prices. The auctioneer then immediately establishes an equilibrium market price vector such that supply meets demand for all resources. Then agents exchange the resources as stated by their bid and the calculated equilibrium price.

- *Direct Markets (Decentralised):* Real bids are used instead of calculating based on demand and supply functions. The market is executed for real and the agents bid and adapt their bidding to the outcomes of the auctions over time. A transaction occurs whenever one trader accepts an offer or a bid quoted by another trader. Transactions depend on pairwise encounters in which agents exchange their bid or price for a resource (e.g. traders distributed in space only transact with nearby traders). The agents bid and adapt their bidding to their success over time which iteratively balances supply and demand at the equilibrium [10].

Note, that the speed or stability of equilibration in a market can be affected by the type of market. An auction-mediated market typically equilibrates immediately in each auction cycle while a decentralised market needs multiple transactions cycles before the market equilibrates. However, the system should not rely on the operation of any single critical component, i.e. a centralised auctioneer [4]. The failure of any one trading agent in a market-based system should result in only a minor impairment to the overall behaviour of the system, rather than a total breakdown. A truly decentralised and robust system in which agents bargain directly with each other is preferred to a failure-prone and inflexible central one. However, firm guarantees that the (optimal) equilibrium price is reached are not always available because less theory is available for decentralised markets compared to centralised markets.

Parameter Tuning. Depending on the specific use of the market mechanism, a number of parameters have to be tuned: *limit prices* determine the demand and supply curve behaviour and the profit of agents, the *initial amount of currency* influences the limit prices, the *number of agents* participating influences the convergence to equilibrium, and the *price-adaptation behaviour* (speed and size of increase/decrease of prices) influences the demand/supply curves and thus the speed and efficiency of the market. For the decentralised market, the specification of who trades with who is also an important parameter (e.g. a distance-limit between agents in a 2D world can determine if they can trade or not).

Infrastructure. Because most of the coordination happens directly between agents no real infrastructure support is needed, except for communication infrastructure.

Characteristics

- *Information Distribution.* Markets deliver to agents information on the resource-usage through the price mechanism. A high price reflects a high demand and/or low remaining supply, i.e. high usage. A low price reflects a low demand and/or high remaining supply, i.e. low usage.
- *Feedback Cycle.* The price mechanism serves as a feedback cycle. A high price implies that agents buy less which diminishes the demand and as

such the price reflects this by decreasing. In turn, a lower price changes the behaviour of agents to start buying again which increases the demand. As such feedback about the global market is given through the price evolution.

- *Agents have all responsibility.* The responsibility of coordination is completely situated with the agents themselves, i.e. no environment-mediated coordination. However, for auction-based markets the auctioneer can be considered as the environment.
- *Decentralisation - Robustness - Self-Organisation [32,10,4]:* Market-based control without an auctioneer allows for truly distributed systems with the same decentralisation, robustness to participant failures, and self-organising properties as real free-market economies. A central auctioneer would be a single point of failure.
- *Price Information indicates Global and Local Performance:* For example for network routing in [10], the cost of each network call can be computed from the available price information which allows more efficient call charging. Trading resources for some sort of money enables evaluation of local performance and valuation of resources [32] based on the price, so that it becomes apparent which resources are the most valuable and which agents are using the most of these.
- *Stabilisation at Equilibrium - Pareto Optimality [4,17,32]:* For markets to be of genuine use in applications, they should exhibit smooth and fast convergence to the equilibrium. Transaction prices stabilise rapidly at an equilibrium that is predictable from economic theory and which is stable and robust with respect to sudden changes in the market. Actions of groups of individuals, engaging in simple trading interactions driven by self-interest can result in optimal resource allocation. Market-based systems are termed Pareto optimal. Pareto optimality means that no agent can do better without diminishing the performance of another. However, there are indications in theoretical economic studies that the dynamics of some decentralised markets may converge to stable but highly sub-optimal equilibria.
- etc. (see [7] for more characteristics)

5.5   Related Mechanisms/Patterns

Variations

- *Multiple Markets [10]:* Multiple related markets are used. An example on how such markets can be related is when resources on one market are a composite of resources on another market (e.g. 'network path' contains 'network links' [10]).
- etc. (see [7] for more variations)

Other Coordination Mechanisms. Another coordination mechanism that can solve resource allocation is the *Tokens* mechanism. A token then represents the capability and authority to use a certain resource exclusively and the number of tokens in the system is limited to the available amount of resources.

5.6 Examples/Known Uses

Some known uses and possible applications are: manufacturing control [24] (re-source = machine), power distribution [32] (resource = power), routing in net-works [10] (resource = bandwidth), stabilisation of unstable (civil) structures [11,17] (resource = power to push somewhere), climate control in buildings [32] (resource = cold air), and other cases on distributed resource allocation [32,4].

6 Case Study: A Packet Delivery Service

This section considers the design of a packet delivery service application to illustrate the use of decentralised coordination patterns. First the requirements are described and then a design is proposed using the patterns.

Problem Statement and Requirements. A packet delivery service [27] al-lows customers to submit an order to come and pick up a packet and transport it to a given destination or delivery location (see figure 6). At each moment in time, new pickup and delivery locations can be added to the system by customers. A fleet of trucks is available which has to self-organise efficiently to accommodate the current request for transport. As such, the orders of customers form a dy-namic overlay network of pickup and delivery locations between which trucks have to move routing themselves through a street map. So basically there are two main requirements for this problem:

- Dispatching: every new order has to be assigned to a truck that will be responsible for handling the requested transport.
- Routing: trucks have to be adaptively routed through a street map in order to reach new pickup locations for orders to which they were assigned and to reach delivery locations for orders already inside the truck.

These requirements have to be achieved in the face of frequent changes: new orders arriving at any moment, changes to the delivery location of existing or-ders, congestion and obstacles on streets, trucks failing, etc. On the other hand there are a number of timing constraints that have to be reached: pickup time-window in which the pickup should occur, delivery time-window, regular breaks for drivers to rest, etc. This is a highly dynamic problem in which the informa-tion needed to decide how to route or dispatch is inherently decentralised over a number of trucks, customers, streets, etc. As such a self-organising emergent solution is promising.

Design with Decentralised Coordination Patterns. As mentioned earlier, the problem-solving power resides in the interaction between agents. Therefore for each of the requirements that have to be coordinated one has to discover which information is needed to take the appropriate decisions and actions. And especially, which decentralised coordination mechanism allows to exchange that kind of information and to coordinate the agents to achieve the requirements.

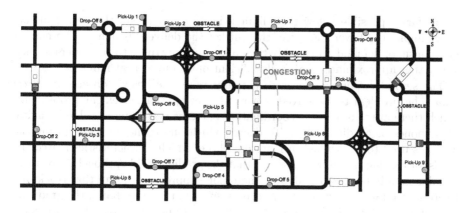

Fig. 6. The Packet-Delivery Problem

Consider the *dispatching requirement* for which new orders have to be assigned as a task to available trucks. Information is needed to decide which truck is chosen, such as the distance of the truck to the pickup location or its estimated arrival time, the trucks available with enough room to carry the packet, and the estimated delivery times of trucks. The best truck at that moment should be allocated. To solve this problem systematically, the 'Problem/Solution Summary' described in Table 1 is used. The engineer has to find a problem description matching the dispatching problem. Some kind of allocation of resources is required. The resource is the room available in trucks that has to be allocated to an order. Table 1 states that a Market-based Coordination mechanism may be suitable. Therefore, the consumers and suppliers of the resource market have to be determined. For example, consider the trucks as the suppliers of available transportation room, and order agents, representing orders, are the consumers of that room. Another important aspect of markets is the instantiation of the price mechanism. According to the pattern, a number of price values are involved such as limit prices under which the room is not bought or sold, prices offered in individual bids, and the market price. These prices should depend on information important for making the allocation decisions because in a market limit prices, offered prices, and market price determine what is allocated to whom. As such, for the order dispatching a truck could have a limit price that increases with the distance or estimated travel time to reach the pickup, increases with the estimated delivery time, decreases with the amount of available room in the truck, etc. The order's limit price can depend on the wanted delivery and pickup time constraints so that an order willing to pay a high price is willing to wait longer before pickup and/or doesn't require a short delivery time. A market is started when an order is submitted by a customer and stops only when it has been assigned to a truck. During the market execution trucks will offer to supply room at a certain price as far as possible above their limit price to maximise their profit (i.e. for example, the higher the price payed, the more time the truck has to deliver the order). Orders will bid to buy the room at certain prices that are as far as possible below their limit price in order to get the best deal (i.e. for example, the lower the price, the quicker the delivery is done). The market mechanism of demand and supply then allocates the trucks to the orders in such a way that approximates a globally efficient optimum at that moment.

The second requirement was to actually *route the trucks through the street map*. The problem to be solved is a routing or spatial movement problem for which there are two possible coordination patterns according to table 1: digital pheromones or gradient fields. To decide which one is the most promising the patterns need to be studied in more detail, i.e. which characteristics match the needs for routing trucks, etc. Assume that the gradient field approach is the most suitable mainly because the digital pheromone approach requires that trucks actively search for delivery locations, orders, etc. On the other hand, the gradients are automatically propagated by the environment and trucks only have to follow their coordination gradient to be routed through the street map efficiently. As such new orders are immediately found by trucks which is an important requirement. Without giving a more detailed solution the main idea is using different types of gradients:

- *Delivery Location Gradients:* each delivery location emits a gradient as soon as the order is assigned to a truck. The truck then simply follows that gradient.
- *Pickup Location Gradients:* each pickup location emits a gradient to signal the presence of a new order. The truck assigned to the order simply follows the gradient to reach the pickup.
- *Market Communication Gradients:* to facilitate direct interaction and negotiation needed for markets between trucks and orders at pickup locations each can emit a market gradient. That gradient is used to actively send bids to buy room, offers to sell room, payments, etc. These messages can route themselves by simply following the right gradient. Each truck and order have their own gradient.

Note that a requirements was to cope with dynamics such as congestion and obstacles. The gradients used above all take into account these changes in their propagation rules. For example, the propagation occurs slower, not at all, or with a higher increase in strength through congested streets. Similar for other dynamics.

Once the coordination mechanisms are chosen, the pattern description offers a guide to actually apply them: different variants can be considered, the parameters to tune are known, guidelines are available, etc. In particular, a gradient solution requires an environment capable of storing and propagating gradients, i.e. an infrastructure. Such an environment is not available or too expensive on a real street network. Alternatively, a decentralised solution which is not distributed on the street network can be used. As such a server emulates the street network as a graph environment in which gradients propagate and on which truck agents move in sync with and actively coordinate the movement of the real trucks. Changes such as information on congestion and obstacles is updated in that emulated environment in a decentralised manner by directly linking the real world trucks with the agents. Customers submit their orders to this server. The advantages of a self-organising solution are preserved because the solution is constantly adapting to changes without a central controlling entity and is still robust to truck failure. Of course, a failure of the server emulating the environment would break the system. However, making the server failure-safe remains cheaper than embedding a gradient infrastructure in a real street network.

7 Conclusion and Future Work

To systematically design a self-organising emergent solution, guidance on which decentralised coordination mechanisms to use is essential because the problem-solving power resides in the coordination process. Decentralised coordination mechanisms can be described as design patterns, similar to patterns used in mainstream software engineering. Such a clear and structured description format helps in making the engineering process more systematic for two reasons:

- Firstly, pattern descriptions allow to *directly find a solution based on the problem.*
- Secondly, each *pattern is a consolidation of best practice* to use it, which *systematically guides engineers* in applying the coordination mechanisms.

However, the patterns in this paper and in [7] have a conceptual focus. More work is needed on patterns for designing coordination mechanisms at the class or implementation level. Even for the conceptual patterns given, more structure is possible. For example, identifying the participants and interactions and representing this structurally in UML interaction diagrams; or identifying new sections in the pattern format that address issues specific for self-organising emergent systems. Also, many other coordination mechanisms should be captured as design patterns to easily compare and choose between them when engineering a self-organising emergent solution. Exemplary work can be found in [2].

Acknowledgements. This work is supported by the K.U.Leuven research council as part of the concerted research action on Autonomic Computing for Decentralised Production Systems (project 3E040752).

References

1. R. Axtell and J. Epstein. *Distributed Computation of Economic Equilibria via Bilateral Exchange*. Brookings Institution, Washington DC, 1997.
2. O. Babaoglu, G. Canright, A. Deutsch, G.A. Di Caro, F. Ducatelle, L.M. Gambardella, N. Ganguly, M. Jelasity, R. Montemanni, A. Montresor, and T. Urnes. Design patterns from biology for distributed computing. *ACM Transactions on Autonomous and Adaptive Systems*, 1(1):26–66, September 2006.
3. S. Brueckner. *Return From The Ant - Synthetic Ecosystems For Manufacturing Control*. PhD thesis, Humboldt-Universitt, Berlin, 2000.

4. D. Cliff and J. Bruten. Simple bargaining agents for decentralized market-based control. Technical Report HPL-98-17, HP Labs, Bristol, UK, 1998.
5. T. De Wolf and T. Holvoet. Emergence and Self-Organisation: a statement of similarities and differences. In *Proc. of the 2nd Int. Workshop on Engineering Self-Organising App.*, 2004.
6. T. De Wolf and T. Holvoet. Towards a methodolgy for engineering self-organising emergent systems. In H. Czap, R. Unland, C. Branki, and H. Tianfield, editors, *Self-Organization and Autonomic Informatics (I)*, volume 135 of *Front. in Artif. Intell. and App.* IOS Press, 2005.
7. T. De Wolf and T. Holvoet. A catalogue of decentralised coordination mechanisms for designing self-organising emergent applications. CW 458, Department of Computer Science, K.U.Leuven, August 2006.
8. O. Etzioni. Moving Up the Information Food Chain: Deploying Softbots on the World Wide Web. In *Proc. of the 13th Int. Conf. on Artificial Intelligence*, 1996.
9. E. Gamma, R. Helm, R. Johnson, and J. Vlissides. *Design Patterns: Elements of Reusable Object-Oriented Software*. Professional Computing Series. Addison-Wesley, 1995.
10. M. A. Gibney, Nicholas R. Jennings, N. J. Vriend, and José-Marie Griffiths. Market-based call routing in telecommunications networks using adaptive pricing and real bidding. In *IATA '99: Proceedings of the Third International Workshop on Intelligent Agents for Telecommunication Applications*, pages 46–61, London, UK, 1999. Springer-Verlag.
11. O. Guenther, T. Hogg, and B. Huberman. Power markets for controlling smart matter. Computing in Economics and Finance 1997 62, Society for Computational Economics, 1997.
12. D. Hales. Choose your tribe! - evolution at the next level in a peer-to-peer network. In *Proc. of the 3rd Workshop on Engineering Self-Organising Applications (EOSA 2005)*, 2005.
13. K. Herrmann, G. Mhl, and K. Geihs. Self-Management: The Solution to Complexity or Just Another Problem? *IEEE Distributed Systems Online*, 6(1), 2005.
14. I. Jacobson, G. Booch, and J. Rumbaugh. *The unified software development process*. Addison Wesley, 1999.
15. J. O. Kephart and D. M. Chess. The vision of autonomic computing. *IEEE Computer Magazine*, 36(1):41–50, Jan 2003.
16. C. Larman. *Applying UML and Patterns: An Introduction to Object-Oriented Analysis and Design and Iterative Development*. Prentice Hall, 3rd edition, 2005.
17. J.P. Lynch and K.H. Law. Decentralized control techniques for large-scale civil structural systems. In *Proc. of the 20th Int. Modal Analysis Conference (IMAC XX)*, 2002.
18. M. Mamei, M. Vasirani, and F. Zambonelli. Experiments of morphogenesis in swarms of simple mobile robots. *Applied Artificial Intelligence*, 18(9-10):903–919, 2004.
19. M. Mamei and F. Zambonelli. Motion coordination in the quake 3 area environment: A field-based approach. In Danny Weyns, H. Van Dyke Parunak, and Fabien Michel, editors, *Environments for Multi-agent Systems - First E4MAS workshop, New York, NY, July 19, 2004, Revised Selected Papers*, volume 3374 of *Lecture Notes in Computer Science*, page 264. Springer Verlag, 2005.
20. M. Mamei and F. Zambonelli. Theory and practice of field-based motion coordination in multiagent systems. *J. Appl. Artif. Intell.*, 19, 2005. to be published.

21. M. Mamei, F. Zambonelli, and L. Leonardi. Distributed motion coordination with co-fields: A case study in urban traffic management. In *Proc. of the The 6th Int. Symp. on Autonomous Decentralized Systems (ISADS'03)*, page page 63, Washington, DC, USA, 2003. IEEE CS.
22. M. Mamei, F. Zambonelli, and L. Leonardi. Co-fields: A physically inspired approach to motion coordination. *IEEE Pervasive Computing*, 3(2), 2004.
23. G. Meszaros and J. Doble. Metapatterns: A pattern language for pattern writing. In *The 3rd Pattern Languages of Programming conference*, Monticello, Illinois, USA, September 1996.
24. H. V. D. Parunak, A. D. Baker, and S. J. Clark. The aaria agent architecture: From manufacturing requirements to agent-based system design. *Integrated Computer-Aided Engineering*, 8(1):45–58, 2001.
25. E. Rimon and D. E. Kodischek. Exact robot navigation using artificial potential functions. *IEEE Transactions on Robotics and Automation*, 8(5):501–518, 1992.
26. Editor S. H. Clearwater. *Market-Based Control: A Paradigm for Distributed Resource Allocation*. World Scientific, Signapore, 1996.
27. M. W. P. Savelsbergh and M. Sol. The general pickup and delivery problem. *Transportation Science*, 29:1729, 1995.
28. H. Varian. *Intermediate Microeconomics*. W.W.Norton, New York, USA, 1999.
29. D. Weyns, A. Helleboogh, E. Steegmans, T. De Wolf, K. Mertens, N. Bouck, and T. Holvoet. Agents are not part of the problem, agents can solve the problem. In *Proc. of the OOPSLA Workshop on Agent-Oriented Methodologies*, 2004.
30. M. Wooldridge and N.R. Jennings. Software engineering with agents: Pitfalls and pratfalls. *IEEE Internet Computing*, 3(3):20–27, 1999.
31. Y. Xu, P. Scerri, B. Yu, S. Okamoto, M. Lewis, and K. Sycara. An integrated token-based algorithm for scalable coordination. In *Proceedings of the fourth international joint conference on Autonomous agents and multiagent systems (AAMAS)*, pages 407–414, Utrecht, NL, 2005.
32. F. Ygge and H. Akkermans. Decentralized markets versus central control: A comparative study. *Journal of Artificial Intelligence Research*, 11:301–333, 1999.

Measuring Stigmergy: The Case of Foraging Ants

Laszlo Gulyas[1], Laszlo Laufer[2], and Richard Szabo[3]

[1] AITIA International Inc.
1039 Czetz J. utca 48-50, Budapest, Hungary
lgulyas@aitia.ai
[2] Dept. of Ergonomics and Psychology,
Budapest University of Technology and Economics
1111 Egry J.u.1.E, Budapest, Hungary
[3] Dept. of Software Technology and Methodology &
Dept. of History and Philosophy of Science,
Lorand Eotvos University
1117 Pazmany Peter setany 1/c, Budapest, Hungary

Abstract. Software today is no longer monolithic, but typically part of a system consisting of many components. As engineers are no longer in control of the entire system, novel methods are sought to design complex software systems that are built from the bottom up and are robust in a dynamically changing environment. The coordination method called stigmergy that is inspired by the collective behavior of social insects is one of the candidates to help solving this problem. In this paper we make a first step in formally understanding the essence of stigmergetic behavior by studying the famous ant foraging model of Deneubourg et al. We explore the relationship between the initial (dis)order in the environment and the performance of the ant foraging behavior. We further study how this configuration of the task to solve governs the behavior of the ant colony, with special focus on the level of coordination that is achieved.

1 Introduction

Software today is not as it used to be. [26] Systems are no longer monolithic, but they are typically part of a larger system consisting of many components, which are partly interconnected and partly co-existing or competing. Software engineers are no longer in control of the entire system; rather, they design solutions that are intended to co-exist with other components, so that the emerging behavior at the system level conforms to the stated goals. As a consequence, novel methods to design 'complex software systems' are sought.

Stigmergy is one of the promising concepts to attack the problems of complex software systems. The concept is that of a spatial self-regulatory community of active components, where the product of the ongoing work motivates the workers and regulates the process. This is underlined by the term itself, which was coined by Pierre-Paul Grassé, a French biologist, in 1959 and originates from the Greek words of

S. Brueckner et al. (Eds.): ESOA 2006, LNAI 4335, pp. 50–65, 2007.

stigma (sign) and *ergon* (work). [9] Stigmergy is common in insect societies. One of the most known examples is the foraging behavior of any colonies.

In this paper we explore the relationship between the initial (dis)order in the environment and the performance of the ants' foraging behavior. We further study how this configuration of the task to solve governs the behavior of the ant colony, with special focus on the level of coordination that is achieved. Our motivation is best summarized by Parunak and Brueckner, who state that *"The natural tendency of a group of autonomous processes is to disorder, not to organization. (...) We will be successful in engineering agent-based systems just to the degree that we understand the interplay between disorder and order."* [18] In a sense, we explore formally the phenomena of Herbert Simon's famous ant. [23] According to Simon, an ant crawling on the beach may appear to exhibit complex behavior, even though it is only following simple rules that make it mirror the complexity of the terrain. Applying this metaphor, we seek to understand the relationship between the complexity of the food collecting task at hand, and the complex behavior of the ant colony that solves it. Here we present the preliminary results of a larger project aiming at the understanding of the role of order/disorder in self-organization methods that use the environment of the agents as the primary medium for coordination.

1.1 Foraging Ants

When ants swarm out of their nest they appear to wander randomly at first, but soon they form a well-pronounced trail between the nest and the food source. Surprisingly, the trail found is typically fairly close to the shortest possible path. When there are multiple food sources, the ant colony usually exploits them in the order of their distance.

Individual ants wander out of the nest in random directions, leaving a trail of 'homing pheromone' (a volatile chemical substance) behind. When an ant finds food, it sets out for the nest, this time dropping 'food pheromone' as it goes. Food-seeking ants follow the gradient of 'food pheromone' in their local neighborhood, while homing ants seek places with high amounts of 'homing pheromone'. Below a certain threshold pheromone level and also with a constant probability, the ants move randomly. This latter component controls the balance between 'exploitation' and 'exploration', the essence of optimizing behavior.

Foraging in ant societies is a complex, organized behavior at the colony level, while individual ants apply a simple, probabilistic rule set. It is exactly this agent-level simplicity what makes ant behavior appealing when seeking to tackle complex distributed problems. The key in organizing the colony level behavior is *communication via the environment*, i.e. via pheromones. The communication is always local on the part of the ants (they always leave the pheromone on their actual location), but it is channeled by the physical environment (diffusion and evaporation). Thus, the individual ant has a local communication method using the chemical pheromone, but the colony itself has no global communication methods. The colony must therefore achieve its macro-goals by coordinating or tuning the individual micro-level ant behavior.

2 A Formal Model of Foraging Ants

In the rest of the paper we will work with the following *model* of the above described behavior, after Deneubourg et. al. [6] Let's consider N ants (indexed by integers from 1 to N) living on a discrete, two-dimensional lattice L of size S with periodic boundary conditions (i.e., a torus). Let $l_i^t \in L$ denote the location of ant i at time t, and $f(p) \geq 0$ the amount of food (in discrete units) at position $p \in L$. Initially, all ants are located in the nest, i.e., $l_i^0 \in K$, for all $i \in [1..N]$. The nest is defined as a disc of radius R located at an arbitrary position in L. (Due to the periodic boundary conditions of the lattice, the location of K may always be interpreted as being in the 'middle'.) The task of the ants is to collect all food units to the nest. For future reference, let F be the amount of food to be collected: $F = \sum_{p \in L} f(p)$.

The ants leave a trail by depositing pheromone at their current location. The type of the substance depends on whether the ant is homing or seeking food, while the amount A depends on the time T the ant has spent on its current activity: $A = max(m - (T-1) \cdot d, 0)$, where m and d are model parameters. The emitted pheromone diffuses to neighboring cells and also slowly evaporates. Thus, $\phi_z^t(p)$ gives the amount of pheromone type z at time t at location p.

$$\phi_z^t(p) = \left[\rho \cdot \phi_z^{t-1}(p) + (1-\rho) \cdot \frac{\sum_{q \in L, |p-q|=1} \phi_z^{t-1}(q)}{8} \right] \cdot (1-\delta) + \sum_{i \in [1,N], l_i^t = p} A_i^t$$

where δ is the evaporation rate and ρ is the rate of diffusion, both model parameters. A_i^t stands for the amount of pheromone emitted by ant i at time t.

During their walk, ants follow a simple probabilistic rule: they move to the neighboring cell with the highest pheromone level (depending on their destination, they either seek 'homing pheromone' or 'food pheromone' locations). Below a certain threshold, and with a given probability w, they move randomly. However, the ants prefer not to turn, i.e., their selection of new location is biased by their direction. Let h_i^t be the direction of ant i's head at time t, given as one of the cells neighboring l_i^t. Moreover, let *left(h)* and *right(h)* denote the directions immediately to the left and right from direction h, respectively. The ants' moving rule is then defined as

$$l_i^{t+1} = \begin{cases} random(h_i^t) \text{ with probability } w, \\ pheromone\_seeking(h_i^t) \text{ with probability } 1-w \end{cases}$$

where functions *random(·)* and *pheromone_seeking(·)* are defined as follows.

$$random(h_i^t) = \begin{cases} h_i^t \text{ with probability } \dfrac{2}{3} \\ left(h_i^t) \text{ with probability } \dfrac{1}{6} \\ right(h_i^t) \text{ with probability } \dfrac{1}{6} \end{cases}$$

$$pheromone\_seeking(h_i^t) = \begin{cases} random(h_i^t) & \text{if } \max\{\phi_z^t(D)\} < \alpha \\ \arg\max\{\phi_z^t(D)\} & \text{otherwise} \end{cases}$$

where $D = \{h_i^t, left(h_i^t), right(h_i^t)\}$ and α is a model parameter.

3   Order In and Out of the Ant Colony

The efficiency and flexibility of the above 'algorithm' is very appealing, because it is exactly in line with the anticipated needs of modern software systems. However, as Simon observes, an ant crawling on a beach, simply following the erratic surface of sand, will leave an intricately complex pattern of movement. [23] Therefore, it is possible that the efficiency, seen here as a demonstration of complexity, of the foraging ant colony originates from the order present in the initial environment. (Here we use the term 'order' to describe the non-randomness of food-placement.)

3.1   Ant Efficiency Depends on Order in the Environment

To test our hypothesis, we have performed computer simulations. During these we have explored various initial configurations of the F units of food. We distributed food equally among G *food sources*, placed randomly on L. Units of food were placed in the sources with a deviation of σ. We varied G between 1 and 10, and σ between 1 and 50. The other parameters of the model were set according to Table 1. Notice that we kept all parameters directly governing the 'ant algorithm' constant. We only varied the *task* to be solved.

   In order to quantify the order in a configuration of food, we calculated the *average distance between pairs of food units*. This measure, which clearly depends on S and F, *increases* with decreasing order. Therefore, in the following we will loosely call it the *disorder* of the food configuration. (The dependence on system size can be neglected in case of the experiments reported here, since the two parameters were held constant.)

   On the other hand, as a measure of ant colony performance, we used the simulated time that it took to collect $0.9 \cdot F$ units of food in the nest. The reason for the 90% threshold is that the location of the last few remaining food units is essentially random (within the source), and thus they are almost always collected by random walk, since no pheromone trail can prevail that connects them. Accounting for this last random period would add an amount of 'random noise' to our measurements. Nonetheless, our findings hold even if the limit is raised to 100%, albeit in a little less strict form.

Table 1. The parameter settings of our experiments

Parameter	Value	Parameter	Value
N	100	W	0.1
S	100	α	1
R	5	δ	0.01
F	800	ρ	0.86
m	100	D	2

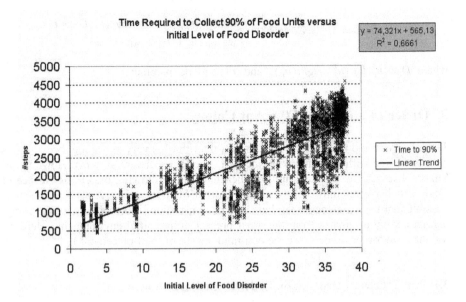

Fig. 1. The dependence of the ant colony's performance on the initial order in food placement. The horizontal axis shows the measure of disorder in the initial food configuration, while the vertical axis represents the number of time steps that it took for the ant colony to collect 90% of the food in the nest. Each mark represents the result of a simulation run with the default parameter set. Food placement parameters were varied: G took the values of 1, 2, 5 and 10, while σ varied between 1, 2, 5, 10, 15 and 20. For G=1 we also explored 8, 20, 25, 30, 40 and 50 for σ. Each combination was run with 10 different pseudo random number generator (RNG) seeds for food placement, and each initial configuration was tested with 10 different RNG seeds. That is, the figure shows 10x10 marks for each combination of G and σ.

Fig. 1 summarizes the dependence of ant colony performance on the initial order in food placement. The horizontal axis shows the measure of order in the initial food configuration, while the vertical axis represents the number of time steps that it took for the ant colony to collect 90% of the food in the nest. It is evident that the performance decays (the number of time steps required to collect the food increases) about linearly as the disorder of the initial configuration increases. However, the variance in performance also increases dramatically, which blurs the picture. Therefore, on Fig. 2 we separate the two 'sources of disorder', i.e., the cases when we increased the number of food sources and those when the original order was disrupted by increased deviation from the source. The figure shows the results for $G>1$, and those with $\sigma>1$ separately. (The cases when both placement parameters were varied are omitted.)

It is clear that the foraging ants favor more 'pointed' food sources, even to the extent of being quicker in collecting *several* 'compact' food sources than a single, but 'disordered' source. The reason for this tendency is that information about a pronounced food source can be 'communicated' (even if indirectly) within the ant

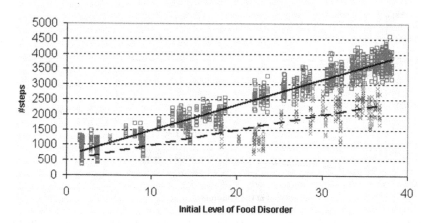

Fig. 2. The dependence of the ant colony's performance on the initial order in food placement, separating single food source cases from ones with multiple sources. The horizontal axis shows the measure of disorder in the initial food configuration, while the vertical axis represents the number of time steps that it took for the ant colony to collect 90% of the food in the nest. Each mark represents the result of a simulation run with the default parameter set. Food placement parameters were varied. Hollow squares represent runs with G=1 and σ taking values of 1, 2, 5, 8, 10, 15, 20, 25, 30, 40 and 50. Crosses stand for runs where σ=1 and G varies over 2, 5 and 10. Each combination was run with 10 different pseudo random number generator (RNG) seeds for food placement, and each initial configuration was tested with 10 different RNG seeds. That is, the figure shows 10x10 marks for each combination of G and σ.

community, while this is less efficient for dispersed sources. The thus identified food sources can even be exploited in parallel, explaining the better performance for multiple sources.

It may appear that these results so far are not much more than saying that the algorithm's performance depends on the difficulty of the task at hand. While this is evidently true, it is important to see that it is not much known about *what* kind of tasks can be solved efficiently by ant-like systems. Albeit analyzing worst-, best-, and average-case performance is common in studies of algorithms, the efforts dedicated to analyze the capabilities of ant algorithms have been limited. [16] Moreover, the point here is that performance depends on the *level of (dis)order* in the initial food placement and that this dependence is vaguely linear. Fig. 3 demonstrates that this kind of dependence is not trivial, by comparing our findings to the performance of a colony of uncoordinated ants performing random walks. The main message of this figure is not that stigmergetic ants outperform the uncoordinated colony, but the clearly different nature of the dependence between the two societies' performance and the initial level of order in the environment.

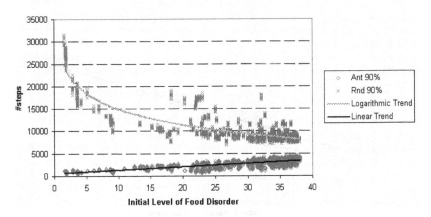

Fig. 3. Comparison of the ant colony's performance to the performance of 'ants' performing random walks. The horizontal axis shows the measure of disorder in the initial food configuration, while the vertical axis represents the number of time steps that it took for the colony to collect 90% of the food in the nest. Hollow squares represent the same runs as on Fig. 1, while crosses stand for the performance of the 'random ant' colony for the same initial configurations. To implement the 'random ant' colony we used the above ant algorithm with w=1.0.

3.2 Order in the Ant Colony Corresponds to Order in the Environment

Computer programs solve problems by processing information. That is, they *convert* data from one format to another, changing its information content. In case of the foraging ant society, food units are carried from the source to the nest. That is, the colony changes the configuration of food in the environment. It would be nice to say that the ant colony's task is to reduce the disorder of the food, but this is not always true. Especially, it is often not true in the simplest case, when there is only a single food source. In this case, whether the overall disorder of food decreases or not depends on the size of the food source, compared to that of the nest.

Therefore, we are interested in how the disorder (cf. information content) of the environment changes during the foraging process, and how this change is reflected in the order of the ant colony itself. In the following, we will focus our study on the single food source case.

We measure the (dis)order in food configuration as in the previous section. Similarly, we quantify the ant colony's (dis)order by the *average distance between pairs of ants in the colony*.

Fig. 4 and Fig. 5 show the development of food and ant colony disorder in case of a single food source. Each panel on the figures shows the change of both food (solid lines) and ant colony disorder (dashed lines) for 10 runs (with different random seeds for ant behavior). Each row contains results for a specific value of food variation (σ) around the randomly selected single food source. The value increases from the top to the bottom. The two figures show two examples of food source placement (values resulting from two different seeds).

The initial value of the ant colony's disorder is the same (low value) on each graph, because the ants start by hiving out from the nest. When the ants start exploring the environment, their disorder rises radically. It reaches its peak when the colony discovers the food source. Then, the ants start forming a trail between the source and the nest, which decreases their disorder. The timing and height of the peak depends on the actual location of the food source. When it is closer to the nest, the random exploration period is shorter and thus the disorder of the ant colony is lower. The peak is also affected by the variation parameter (σ). If the food source is spread out more, this brings its edge closer to the nest.

At the end of the foraging, when most of the food is already in the source, the disorder of the ant colony raises again. This is because there is no more enough food to occupy all the ants, so they start exploring again. However, the persistence of the pheromone trail may delay this phenomenon, as observable on the panels of the first two rows of Fig. 4 and Fig. 5. In some cases, the disorder of the colony in this last period is even higher than its former peak. This depends on two factors. First, on the time it took for the colony to discover the food source. If they were quick, the peak is likely to be at a lower value. The other factor is a measuring effect: namely, when the recording of the process was stopped. When all food units are in the nest, in the long run, the ant colony's disorder should approach the theoretical maximum value of disorder defined by the parameters of the closed system. This is because the ants move randomly in the absence of food.

On the other hand, the initial disorder of food is the same in each row, as it is governed by the variation around the center of the single food source, but increases with the growth of σ. After the initial random exploration phase of the foraging, a few ants find the food source, and the disorder of the food changes gradually. As the ants' disorder starts to drop, that of the food raises. This is because some of the food units are now taken away from the relatively ordered configuration of the food source, and are now on their way to the nest. Later during the process, the food units are divided in three classes. Some still reside in the source; others are already collected in the nest, while the remaining is in transit. This results in an initial increase in the disorder of food. However, after half of the food units are collected in the nest, each additional unit that leaves the source will bring the disorder down. Even those in transit will, since they are almost certainly traveling *towards* the nest, thus decreasing their distance to more than half of the other food units. (For larger food sources, i.e., when σ is high, the initial disorder of food is so high that the first part of the above described 'hill' in the trajectory partially disappears.)

A significant observation is that the ant colony reaches its minimum disorder about the same time when the food disorder peaks. This is when the ants found the 'optimized' trail between the source and the nest, and most of them are walking this path back and forth, carrying food to the nest. Clearly, this is the most ordered (or coordinated) behavior that the ant colony displays during the whole process. On the other hand, this is when they are most effective in transferring food. Therefore, this is when the highest number of food units are 'in transit', i.e., scattered along the ant trail. This explains the peak in food disorder.

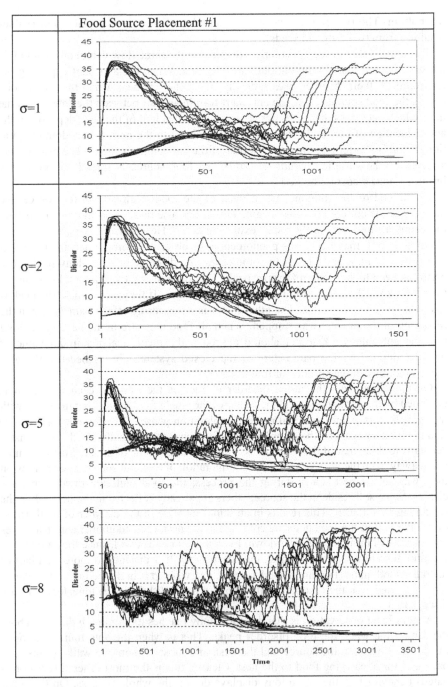

Fig. 4. The in-run development of food and ant colony disorder in case of a single food source. Each figure shows the time-trajectories of both food (solid lines) and ant colony disorder (dashed lines) for 10 runs (with different random seeds for ant behavior). The rows represent increasing values of food variation (σ) around the randomly selected food source.

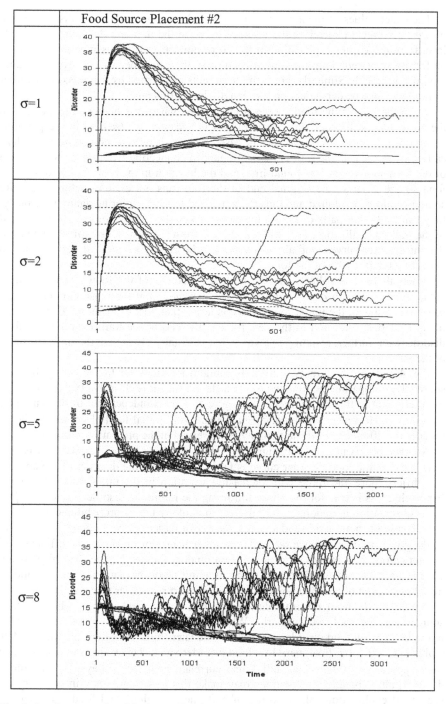

Fig. 5. Another example of the in-run development of food and ant colony disorder in case of a single food source (using a different seed for food source placement)

The exact values of the ants' minimum disorder and the maximum disorder value of food placement depend on the distance between the nest and the source. This follows from our earlier explanation of the correspondence. If we assume the ants to be uniformly scattered along the trail at each time, their disorder will clearly be a function of trail length. Similarly, since the food units are carried by the ants, the disorder of food will also be dependent on trail length during this phase.

When the size of the food source is larger (i.e., when σ is higher), the increase in the ant colony's disorder starts earlier. This is because, as observed in the previous section, the colony is less efficient in case of more dispersed food sources. Technically, this is because the trail is most efficient in connecting two points, i.e., the area of the food source that was found first, and the location in the nest closest to it. If the food source is large, the original end of the trail runs out of food before the entire source would be exploited and thus the ants need to start exploring again. Obviously, they can find other parts of the source easily, since they start exploring from the end of the trail, but still, some ants will wander off from the nest. This explains the tail of the ant disorder curves, and also accounts for the colony's degraded performance in collecting the last 10% of the food.

When all food is collected in the nest, the disorder of the food reaches its final value. In case of high σ, this value is lower than the initial food disorder. This is because the radius of the initial food source is larger than that of the nest. Also, ants are likely to deposit the food in the nest right at the end of the trail, lowering the food disorder even further, resulting in a value that is slightly lower than the initial disorder of the ant colony.

Fig. 4 and Fig. 5 show two different random locations for the center of the food source. By comparing the timeline of the different runs it is clear that the ant colony is more efficient in the environments on Figure 5. This is independent of the particular values of σ. However, *within each figure*, increasing initial food placement variation reduces the efficiency of the ant colony, as observed in the previous section.

Another observation is that higher σ values result in higher variance across the runs. That is, the food disorder curve is fairly similar, but the disorder of the ant colony differs more and more with increasing variation in the initial food placement. Especially, this is true for the phase following the minimum disorder value. The previous observation is important, because the ant colony uses a probabilistic algorithm. Yet, in case of 'point like' food sources, *the performance appears almost independent of the given random number seed*. On the other hand, for higher σ, the efficiency of the ant colony becomes more dependent on random factors. Notice that this dependence is on probabilistic elements in the foraging algorithm, and not in the random initial placement of the food units, even though the σ parameter controls the latter.

Above we focused on environments with a single food source. Multiple food sources may be analyzed similarly. When food sources are exploited sequentially, multiple 'hills' in food disorder are visible. The later 'hills' are often superimposed on a plunge towards the final, very low food disorder value. This is due to the amount of food approaching $0.5 \cdot F$. The 'hills' also correlate with the 'valleys' of ant colony disorder, albeit parallel explorations may make this less clear. Also, in between two sequential exploitations, the disorder of both the ant colony and food may increase simultaneously. This is caused by the explorative behavior of the ants switching from one source to the other.

4   Discussion and Related Work

The behavior of social insects has inspired a growing body of work in computer science. [19] A fair amount of this work was based on different models of the ant foraging behavior. Dorigo et al. give an extensive overview on various theoretical and practical applications of this approach, which amounts to the traveling salesman and quadratic assignment problems, graph coloring, routing in telecommunications networks, task scheduling, etc. [8] They also describe the original phenomena, as observed in [6], by Deneubourg et al. on the ant species *Linepithema humile*.

The algorithms inspired by ant foraging behavior has been grouped and generalized under the Ant Colony Optimization (ACO) metaheuristic. [5] Although this approach supersedes the ant foraging model of Deneubourg et al. in detail and in practical applicability, we constrained our analysis to the latter in this paper. This is due to our different motivation: we were seeking the underlying reasons why ant foraging works, for which a simpler model seems more appropriate.

The theoretical analysis of the above range of algorithms so far amounted to showing various convergence properties of ACO, to establishing that a colony of ants can approximate the shortest path between the nest and the food source, and to discovering second order phase transitions separating random and ordered behavior. [8][4] However, less effort has been dedicated to analyze *why*, in essence, ant algorithms work; a step of reasonable necessity in order to devise ant-like algorithms not directly mimicking the behavior of real colonies.

Ramos et al. analyzes the role the environment and negative or positive feedbacks play in the workings of ant sorting. [20] Yet, the most significant attempt to date to explore the problem is by Parunak and Brueckner. [18] Their key observation is that ant-like systems involve multiple coupled levels and that global (macro) self-organization is fueled by the entropy increase at the local (micro) level. (This issue is analyzed formally by Bar-Yam, who also finds that the sum of the complexity at all scales of a system with a fixed degree of freedom is constant and independent of the particular system. [1]) Parunak et al.'s interpretation of macro-level entropy is based on ant movement, while they consider the configuration of pheromone molecules for micro entropy. Although, according to this approach, our measurements in this paper are all at the global level, the results of our second set of experiments also support their explanation. Parunak and his colleagues also study the more general problem of achieving global objectives by programming local decisions. [17] Observing that *"much current work on constructing systems of this sort is more art than science"*, they present a simple model of adaptive walk (a minimal version of ant sorting behavior) and illustrate how important properties of three practical applications can be derived from the analysis of this model. Our work is another step in this direction by providing insights into the workings of the ant foraging algorithm.

Another attempt to address similar issues, in the context of ant sorting, is by Gutowitz. [10] His focus is on local criteria (ant behaviors) necessary for global efficiency. He compares 'basic' and 'complexity seeking' ants, to find that the latter are more suitable for the task. In contrast to Parunak et al., he argues that disorder is 'pumped' into the system by the energy consumption of the ants, which balances the increased order-level in the environment. Gutowitz's focus is thus on energy efficiency, measured as the time dedicated to information processing by the ant prior to moving decisions. This departs from our approach to relate the order-level of the environment to that of ant colony behavior.

The issues addressed in this paper are also related to collective robotics. In their pioneering work Denebourg et al. suggest that sorting and clustering ants may serve as a behavioral model for mobile robots. [7][2] A series of subsequent works investigate the performance of ant-clustering. Martinoli et al. measure the dynamics of average cluster size depending on the number of cooperating robots. [15] Holland et al. experiment with arena size, probability of retention, and sensor characteristics. [12] In a more general framework, Handl et al. compare the performance of ant-based clustering to traditional clustering methods on specific data sets. [11] Wilson et al. analyze three different annular sorting mechanisms with respect to separation, compactness, shape, and completeness. [25] Contrary to our approach, however, none of these works analyze the dependence of the algorithm's performance on the aggregate properties of the input. Similarly, Krieger et al. experiment with a group of robots solving an ant foraging-like task, but do not address performance's dependence on the properties of the task to be solved. [13]

Our work is also motivated by that of Boer, albeit at a more general level. Boer argues that information retrieval and processing of a stochastic system can be captured by measuring its entropy. Applying this idea to the process of operating a machine, Boer discusses the relation between the level of control and the entropy of movements using the machine's levers. [3]

4.1 Measuring Order and Disorder

Several of the works discussed above consider the entropy, information-level or (dis)order of various systems. However, they use a variety of measures to quantify these properties. Parunak et al. discuss the inherent problem of terminology related to such endeavors: namely, the dichotomy of the term 'entropy' in thermodynamics and information theory. [18] While the latter, as defined by Shannon, even has a strong formal similarity to the former, their intrinsic relationship is unclear. [22] Parunak et al. opt for a spatial version of information entropy, and observe problems in its use, like the dependency on the (artificial) grid's size used to model space. On the other hand, Gutowitz applies two different measures at the micro and macro levels. In the former case, complexity means the density of items at and around a certain location. In the latter, he considers spatial entropy and also discusses the results' dependence on grid resolution.

In preparation for the experiments reported in this paper, we also considered several options to measure the complexity of both the food and the ant society. For theoretical soundness, Shannon's original definition of information entropy was a strong candidate. Ecologists and demographers also use this measure to determine the homogeneity of an area, regarding the diversity of certain species or residential segregation. [21][24] However, as discussed by both Gutowitz and Parunak et al., this measure brings a strong (and artificial) dependency on resolution, which we wanted to avoid. Moreover, we were seeking a measure that would also express the difficulty of the food collection problem.

Another, commonly used option to measure the (dis)order of behavior in higher dimensions is to compare the trajectory of the system to a fixed baseline case. For example, this approach has been used to measure the entropy of saccadic eye movements during the recognition of a face. [14] In our case this option would mean to fix a food or colony configuration and calculate the relative difference between what is actually displayed and this 'ideal case'. However, due to the parallel changes in the configuration of food and that of the ants, as well as to the dependence of the baseline case on the actual location of the food source, we voted against this option.

5 Conclusions and Future Work

Algorithms inspired by the behavior of social insects became popular over the last decade. This popularity is due to the growing need to 'engineer emergent phenomena' in order to cope with today's and tomorrow's software engineering problems. [26] A growing number of applications have been put forward based on the 'ant colony' approach, as well as a generalized and well-formalized metaheuristic under the name of Ant Colony Optimization (ACO). [5] However, most of these algorithms and applications follow closely one of the well-known and widely discussed insect models, like ant foraging, ant sorting, or task differentiation. ACO generalizes the foraging model, making it applicable to a truly wider set of problems, but tells us nothing about why exactly the heuristic works and under what specific circumstances. As discussed above, a limited number of papers dealt with this issue, but the question still remains essentially open.

In this paper we proposed a disorder measuring approach to analyze this issue. As a first step, we investigated how the foraging ant colony's performance depends on the (dis)order in the initial configuration of food in the environment (as a proxy for the difficulty of the task at hand). We found that execution time depends about linearly on the initial disorder. We also studied the time-trajectory of food disorder together with the level of coordination in the ant colony in case of a single food source. Our main finding is that the ant colony reaches its minimum disorder about the same time when the food disorder peaks. This is when the ants established the 'optimized' trail between the source and the nest. We also found that, in case of a single food source, increasing the disorder of the initial food configuration makes the colony's performance more sensitive to the stochastic elements governing its behavior.

These preliminary results show that this type of analysis has a potential for success in understanding the 'driving force' of stigmergetic algorithms. Given this understanding one would be in the position to design completely novel 'insect-like' distributed algorithms for complex problems. This is the long term goal of our work, but before getting there we intend to perform a series of further experiments. We would like to extend our study to the analysis of the two pheromone fields. Since these fields convey information about food placement to the ant colony, these measurements are expected to shed light on the correspondence between the order of the ant colony and the order of the environment and on the efficiency of information transmission in this stigmergetic system. Similarly, we will revisit the use of classic spatial entropy to determine our finding's dependence on the particular measure used. Finally, at a later stage, we also plan to extend our approach to other stigmergetic algorithms, e.g., to ant sorting.

Acknowledgements

The partial support of the GVOP-3.2.2-2004.07-005/3.0 (ELTE Informatics Coopera-tive Research and Education Center) grant of the Hungarian Government and the National Grant for Research in Higher Education FKFP No. 0018/2002 is gratefully acknowledged. We would like to thank for Prof. Lajos Izso, for the inspiration to start this project.

References

[1]   Y. Bar-Yam, "Multiscale Complexity/Entropy", *Advances in Complex Systems*, Vol. 7, No. 1 (2004), pp. 47-63.

[2]   R. Beckers, O. E. Holland, and J.-L. Deneubourg, "From local actions to global tasks: Stigmergy in collective robotics" In R. Brooks and P. Maes, editors, *Proc. 4th Int. Work-shop on the Sythesis and Simulation of Living Systems (Artificial Life IV)*, pp. 181-189. Cambridge, MA: MIT Press, July 1994.

[3]   E. R. Boer, "Behavioral Entropy As A Measure Of Driving Performance", in the *Pro-ceedings of International Driving Symposium on Human Factors in Driving Assessment, Training and Vehicle Design*, 2001.

[4]   D. R. Chialvo, M. M. Millonas, "How Swarms Build Cognitive Maps", *The Biology and Technology of Intelligent Autonomous Agents*, L. Steels (ed.), NATO ASI Series, Series F: Computer and Systems Sciences, Vol. 144, Springer 1995, pp. 439-450.

[5]   O. Cordón, F. Herrera, T. Stützle, "A Review on the Ant Colony Optimization Metaheu-ristic: Basis, Models and New Trends", *Mathware & Soft Computing* (9), 2002.

[6]   J.-L. Deneubourg, S. Aron, S. Goss, and J.-M. Pasteels, "The self-organizing exploratory pattern of the argentine ant", *Journal of Insect Behavior*, 3:159–168, 1990.

[7]   J. L. Deneubourg , S. Goss , N. Franks , A. Sendova-Franks , C. Detrain , L. Chrétien, "The dynamics of collective sorting robot-like ants and ant-like robots", In *Proceedings of the first international conference on simulation of adaptive behavior on From animals to animats*, p.356-363, February 1991, Paris, France

[8]   M. Dorigo, G. D. Caro, L. M. Gambardella, "Ant algorithms for discrete optimization", *Proceedings of Artificial Life 5*, pp. 137—172, 1999.

[9]   P. P. Grassé, "La reconstruction du nid et les coordinations interindividuelles chez belli-cositermes natalensis et cubitermes sp., La théorie de la stigmergie: essai d'interprétation du comportement des termites constructeurs", *Insectes Sociaux*, 6:41–81, 1959.

[10] H. A. Gutowitz, "Complexity-Seeking Ants", In *Proceedings of 3rd European Conference on Artificial Life*, 1993.

[11] J. Handl, J. Knowles, and M. Dorigo, "On the performance of ant-based clustering", *Design and application of hybrid intelligent systems*, pp. 203-213, 2003.

[12] O. Holland and C. Melhuish, "Stigmergy, self-organisation, and sorting in collective robotics", *Artificial Life*, 5:173--202, 2000.

[13] Krieger, M.J.B., Billeter, J-B. & Keller L., "Ant-like task allocation and recruitment in cooperative robots", *Nature* 406: 992-995., 2000.

[14] T. S. Lee and S. X. Yu, "An Information-Theoretic Framework for understanding Saccadic Eye Movements", *Neural Information Processing Systems*, Denver, Colorado, USA, 29 Nov - 4 Dec 1999.

[15] A. Martinoli and F. Mondada. "Collective and Cooperative Group Behaviours: Biologically Inspired Experiments in Robotics", In *Proceedings of the Fourth Symposium on Experimental Robotics ISER-95*, Stanford, USA, June 30- July 2 1995.

[16] C. Papadimitriou, *Computational Complexity*, Addison Wesley, 1994.

[17] H. Van Dyke Parunak, S. A. Brueckner, J. A. Sauter, R. Matthews, „Global Convergence of Local Agent Behaviors", in *Proceedings of the 4th International Joint Conference on Autonomous Agents and Multi-Agent Systems (AAMAS05)*, Utrecht, Netherlands, July 2005, pp. 305-312.

[18] H. Van Dyke Parunak, S. A. Brueckner, "Entropy and Self-Organization in Multi-Agent Systems", in *Proceedings of the International Conference on Autonomous Agents (Agents 2001)*, pp. 124-130, 2001.

[19] V. Ramos, F. Almeida, "Artificial Ant Colonies in Digital Image Habitats–A Mass Behaviour Effect Study on Pattern Recognition", *Proceedings of ANTS'2000-2nd International Workshop on Ant Algorithms (From Ant Colonies to Artificial Ants)*, M. Dorigo, M. Middendorf, T. Stützle (Eds.), pp. 113-116, Belgium, 7-9 Sep. 2000.

[20] V. Ramos, C. Fernandes, A. C. Rosa, „Social Cognitive Maps, Swarm Collective Perception and Distributed Search on Dynamic Landscapes", submitted to *Brains, Minds & Media, Journal of New Media in Neural and Cognitive Science*, 2005.

[21] S. F. Reardon, D. O'Sullivan, "Measures of Spatial Segregation", *Sociological Methodology* 34:121-162, 2004.

[22] C. E. Shannon, "A mathematical theory of communication", *Bell System Technical Journal*, vol. 27, pp. 379-423 and 623-656, July and October, 1948.

[23] H. A. Simon, *The Sciences of the Artificial*, The MIT Press, 1996. pp. 51-52.

[24] H. Theil, *Statistical decomposition analysis*. Amsterdam: North-Holland Publishing Company, 1972.

[25] M. Wilson, C. Melhuish, A. B. Sendova-Franks and S. Scholes, "Algorithms for Building Annular Structures with Minimalist Robots. Inspired by Brood Sorting in Ant Colonies", *Autonomous Robots* Vol. 17, No. 2-3 Sep-Nov 2004. pp. 115-136.

[26] F. Zambonelli, H. Van Dyke Parunak, "Signs of a Revolution in Computer Science and Software Engineering", *Engineering Societies in the Agents World III (ESAW 2002)*, Madrid, Spain, September 16-17, 2002, Revised Papers in LNCS-2577, P. Petta, R. Tolksdorf, F. Zambonelli (Eds.) Springer 2003, pp. 68-81.

Dynamic Decentralized Any-Time Hierarchical Clustering

H. Van Dyke Parunak[1], Richard Rohwer[2], Theodore C. Belding[1],
and Sven Brueckner[1]

[1] NewVectors LLC, 3520 Green Ct, Ste 250, Ann Arbor, MI 48105
{van.parunak,ted.belding,sven.brueckner}@newvectors.net
[2] Fair Isaac Corporation, 3661 Valley Centre Drive, San Diego, CA 92130
richardrohwer@fairisaac.com

Abstract. Hierarchical clustering is used widely to organize data and search for patterns. Previous algorithms assume that the body of data being clustered is fixed while the algorithm runs, and use centralized data representations that make it difficult to scale the process by distributing it across multiple processors. Self-Organizing Data and Search (SODAS) inspired by the decentralized algorithms that ants use to sort their nests, relaxes these constraints. SODAS can maintain a hierarchical structure over a continuously changing collection of leaves, requiring only local computations at the nodes of the hierarchy and thus permitting the system to scale arbitrarily by distributing nodes (and their processing) across multiple computers.

1 Introduction

Clustering is a powerful, popular tool for discovering structure in data. Classical algorithms [17] are static, centralized, and batch. They are static because they assume that the data and similarity function do not change while clustering is taking place. They are centralized because they rely on data structures (such as similarity matrices) that must be accessed, and sometimes modified, at each step of the operation. They are batch because they run their course and then stop.

Some applications require ongoing processing of a massive stream of data. This class of application imposes several requirements that classical clustering algorithms do not satisfy.

Dynamic Data and Similarity Function.—Because the stream continues for a long time, both the data and users' requirements and interests may change. As new data arrives, it should be able to find its way in the clustering structure without the need to restart the process. If the distribution of new data eventually invalidates the older organization, the structure should reorganize. A model of the user's interest should drive the similarity function applied to the data, motivating the need to support a dynamic similarity function that can take advantage of structure compatible with both old and new interests while adapting the structure as needed to take account of changes in the model.

S. Brueckner et al. (Eds.): ESOA 2006, LNAI 4335, pp. 66–81, 2007.

Decentralized.—For massive data, the centralized constraint is a hindrance. Distributed implementations of centralized systems are possible, but the degree of parallel execution is severely limited by the need to maintain the central data structure. One would like to use parallel computer hardware to scale the system to the required level, with nearly linear speed-up.

Any-time.—Because the stream is continual, the batch orientation of conventional algorithms, and their need for a static set of data, is inappropriate. The clustering process needs to run constantly, providing a useful (though necessarily approximate) structuring of the data whenever it is queried.

Biological ants cluster the contents of their nests using an algorithm that meets these requirements. Each ant picks up items that are dissimilar to those it has encountered recently, and drops them when it finds itself among similar items. This approach is dynamic, because it easily accommodates a continual influx of new items to be clustered without the need to restart. It is decentralized because each ant functions independently of the others. It is any-time because at any point, one can retrieve clusters from the system. The size and quality of the clusters increase as the system runs.

Previous researchers have adapted this algorithm to practical applications. Like natural ants, these algorithms only partition the objects being clustered. A hierarchical clustering structure would enable searching the overall structure in time logarithmic in the number of items, and permit efficient pruning of large regions of the structure if these are subsequently identified as expendable.

Our hierarchical clustering algorithm is inspired by previous ant clustering algorithms. Nodes of the hierarchy climb up and down the emerging hierarchy based on locally sensed information. Like previous ant clustering algorithms, it is dynamic, decentralized, and any-time. Unlike them, it yields a hierarchical structure. We designate the items being clustered as leaves, characterized by feature vectors. In our original application, they are documents characterized by keyword vectors.

The acronym "SODAS" promises self-organizing search as well as self-organizing data. This paper describes only the self-organization of the data. The search process has two components. First, foraging agents based on a semantic model of the user [1] continually traverse the hierarchy. As they descend, they make stochastic choices at each node weighted by the similarity between the agent and each possible route. When they encounter a leaf, they assess its relevance, and then ascend the hierarchy, depositing a digital pheromone [6] on each node. Aggregated over many foragers, this pheromone field identifies the subset of the tree most likely to satisfy queries. The second component consists of real-time queries, which sense the pheromone field to move even more directly to relevant leaves. In the absence of foragers, search in a hierarchy requires time $O(k \ log_k \ n)$, where k is the average number of children per node and n is the total number of leaves subsumed. The foragers effectively reduce the factor of k.

Section 2 summarizes previous relevant research in cluster analysis, swarm intelligence, and swarming clustering. Section 3 outlines our algorithm, while Section 4 provides mathematical details on decentralized similarity computations. Section 5 reports on the behavior of the system. Section 6 concludes.

2 Previous Research

SODAS rests on two bodies of previous research: clustering, and swarm intelligence. We review relevant work in both areas, as well as previous attempts to synthesize them.

2.1 Clustering

Clustering as a method of data analysis has been extensively studied for the last forty years. For a general survey, see [17].

Clustering algorithms fall into two broad categories: those that partition the data (such as K-means) and those that yield a hierarchy. We wish to construct and maintain a hierarchy. [11] offers a detailed survey of five approaches to this task.

The most common approach is *agglomerative* clustering, which repeatedly identifies the closest two nodes in the system and merges them until the hierarchy is complete.

Divisive algorithms begin with all leaves in a single cluster. At each stage a cluster is selected and divided into subclusters in a way that maximizes the similarity of the items in each cluster.

Incremental algorithms add leaves one by one to the growing structure. This approach supports a certain degree of dynamism in the data, but in work up to now, the emergent structure is strongly dependent on the order in which the leaves are presented, and cannot adjust itself if the distribution of data changes over time.

Optimization algorithms adjust the hierarchy's structure to minimize some measure of distance between the similarity matrix and the cophenetic distances induced from the hierarchy. Current versions of this approach are centralized.

Parallel methods attempt to distribute the computing load across multiple processors. Olson [25] summarizes a wide range of distributed algorithms for hierarchical clustering. These algorithms distribute the work of computing inter-object similarities, but share the resulting similarity table globally. Like centralized clustering, they form the hierarchy monotonically, without any provision for leaves to move from one cluster to another. Thus they are neither dynamic nor any-time.

SODAS includes both agglomerative and divisive operations. It is incremental in allowing continuous addition of data, but in the limit the structure that emerges is independent of the order in which leaves are presented. It can be interpreted as a hill-climbing optimizer, and runs on multiple processors, without the requirement for centralization in previous work.

2.2 Swarm Intelligence

SODAS' basic mechanisms fall in the category of swarm intelligence [4, 27], and are inspired by biological mechanisms that enable coordination among highly populous, distributed processing entities with only local knowledge of their environment [7]. The particular example that underlies SODAS is nest sorting in ants.

An ant hill houses larvae, eggs, cocoons, and food. The ant colony keeps these items sorted by kind. When an egg hatches, the larva does not stay with other eggs, but is moved to the area for larvae. Biologists have developed an algorithm that is compatible with the capabilities of an ant and that yields collective behavior comparable to what is observed in nature [5, 9]. Each ant executes the following steps continuously.

1. Wander randomly around the nest.
2. Sense nearby objects, and maintain a short memory (about ten steps) of what has been seen.
3. If an ant is not carrying anything when it encounters an object, decide stochastically whether or not to pick up the object, with probability that decreases if the ant has recently encountered similar objects.
4. If an ant is carrying something, at each time step decide stochastically whether or not to drop it, with probability that increases if the ant has recently encountered similar items in the environment.

The Brownian walk of individual ants guarantees that wandering ants will eventually examine all objects in the nest. Even a random scattering of different items in the nest yields local concentrations of similar items that stimulate ants to drop other similar items. As concentrations grow, they tend to retain current members and attract new ones. The stochastic nature of the pick-up and drop behaviors enables multiple concentrations to merge, since ants occasionally pick up items from one existing concentration and transport them to another.

2.3 Previous Work on Swarming Clustering

Several researchers have applied the biological algorithm to engineered systems. These implementations fall into two broad categories: those in which the digital ants are distinct from the objects being clustered, and those that eliminate this distinction. All of these examples form a partition of the objects, without any hierarchical structure.

2.3.1 Distinct Ants and Objects
A number of researchers have emulated the distinction in the natural ant nest between the objects being clustered and the "ants" that carry them around. All of these examples cluster objects in two-dimensional space.

Lumer and Faieta [21] present what is apparently the earliest example of such an algorithm. The objects being clustered are records in a database. Instead of a short-term memory, their algorithm uses a measure of the similarity among the objects being clustered to guide the pick-up and drop-off actions.

Kuntz et al. [19] apply the Lumer-Faieta algorithm to partitioning a graph. The objects being sorted are the nodes of the graph, and the similarity among them is based on their connectivity. Thus the partitioning reflects reasonable component placement for VLSI design.

Hoe et al. [16] refine Lumer and Faieta's work on data clustering by moving empty ants directly to available data items. Handl et al. [12] offer a comparison of this algorithm with conventional clustering algorithms.

Handl and Meyer [13] cluster documents returned by a search engine, to generate a topic map. Documents have a keyword vector of length n, thus situating them in an n-dimensional space. This space is then reduced using latent semantic indexing, and then ant clustering projects them into two dimensions for display. This multi-stage process requires a static document collection.

These efforts use only leaf similarity to guide clustering. Ramos [30] adds a pheromone mechanism. Ants deposit digital pheromones as they move about, thus attracting other ants and speeding up convergence.

Walsham [33] presents a useful summary of the Lumer-Faieta and Handl-Meyer efforts and studies the performance of these algorithms across their parameter space.

Oprisen [26] applies the Deneubourg model to foraging robots, and explores convergence speed as a function of the size of the memory vector that stores the category of recently encountered objects.

Monmarché [23] clusters data objects on a two-dimensional grid, basing drop-off probabilities on fixed similarity thresholds. Inter-object distance is the Euclidean distance between the fixed-length vectors characterizing the objects. To speed convergence, once initial clusters have formed, K-means merges stray objects. Then the sequence of ant clustering and K-means is applied again, this time to whole clusters, to merge them at the next level (without retaining hierarchical structure). Kanade and Hall [18] use a similar hybrid process, employing fuzzy C-means instead of K-means as the refinement process. The staged processing in these models has the undesirable consequence of removing them from the class of any-time algorithms and requiring that they be applied to a fixed collection of data.

Schockaert et al. [31] also merge smaller clusters into larger ones (without retaining hierarchical structure), but using a real-time decision rule that tells an ant whether to pick up a single object or an entire cluster. Thus their algorithm, unlike Monmarché's, can accommodate a dynamic population.

2.3.2 Active Objects

A natural refinement of these algorithms eliminates the distinction between ant and object. Each object is active, and can move itself. These methods are less explicit in acknowledging their relationship to the underlying biological mechanism.

Beal [2] discovers a hierarchical organization among processors in an amorphous computing system. The nodes have fixed locations, but efficient processing requires grouping them into a hierarchy and maintaining this hierarchy if the medium is divided or merged or if some processors are damaged. Processors form groups based on their distance from each other: they find neighbors and elect leaders. These leaders then repeat the process at the next level. The similarity function is implicit in the RF communication connectivity and conforms to a low-dimensional manifold, very different from the topology induced by similarity between arbitrary feature vectors.

Ogston et al. [24] consider a set of agents distributed over a network, initially with random links to one another. Agents form clusters with their closest neighbors, and share their own links with those neighbors to expand the set of agents with whom they can compare themselves. The user specifies the maximum desired cluster size, to keep clusters from growing too large. This system is naturally distributed, any-time, and could reasonably be applied to dynamic situations, but it creates a partition, not a hierarchy.

Chen et al [8] apply the active object model to clustering data elements on a two-dimensional grid. The dissimilarity of data objects is the distance measure that drives clustering. They seek to manage the processor cycles consumed by the leaf agents (a concern that is managed in the systems of the previous section by limiting the number of ants). Their solution is to have leaves fall asleep when they are comfortable with their surroundings, awakening periodically to see if the world has changed.

We have implemented [29] a flat clustering mechanism with active objects. The other algorithms discussed so far form clusters on a two-dimensional manifold, but our algorithm clusters them on a graph topology reflecting the interconnections between processors in a computer network. The nodes of the graph are places that can hold a number of documents, and documents move from one place to another. Each document is characterized by a concept vector. Each element of the concept vector corresponds to a subsumption subtree in WordNet [10, 22], and has value 1 if the document contains a lexeme in the WordNet subtree, and 0 otherwise. Similarity between documents is the cosine distance between their concept vectors. Each time a document is activated, it compares itself with a sample of documents at its current node and a sample of documents at a sample of neighboring nodes, and probabilistically decides whether to move. This algorithm converges exponentially fast [29], even when documents are added while the process runs. To manage the computational cost of the active objects, each one uses pheromone learning [28] to modulate its computational activity based on whether recent activations have resulted in a move or not.

2.3.3 Synopsis
All previous work on ant clustering other than our own clusters documents spatially on a two-dimensional manifold. In addition, some of these algorithms are multi-stage processes that cannot be applied to a dynamically changing collection of documents, and even those that could be applied to such a collection have not been analyzed in this context.

Previous ant clustering on arbitrary feature vectors (thus excluding [2]), including our own, produces a flat partition and thus does not offer the benefits of a hierarchical clustering. SODAS yields a searchable hierarchy to speed retrieval, and can function dynamically with a changing population.

3 Local Operations Achieve Global Structure

We first consider the nature of the data structure we want to achieve, and next propose some simple operations that can construct and maintain it. Then we provide further details on our decision logic, and finally deal with some housekeeping measures.

3.1 Objective: A Well-Formed Hierarchy

In our hierarchies, all data lives in the leaves. We constrain neither overall depth nor the branching factor of individual nodes. The set of all nodes $\mathcal{N} = \mathcal{R} \cup L \cup I$ has three subclasses:

1. The set of root nodes $\mathcal{R}$ has one member, the *root*, which is an ancestor of all the other nodes, and has no distinct parent. (For simplicity in describing the algorithm, it is convenient to consider the root as its own parent.)

2. The set of *leaf nodes* L represents the data items being clustered. Leaves have no children.
3. All other nodes are *internal* nodes, elements of I. Each internal node has exactly one parent, and one or more children that may be either leaves or other internal nodes.

We define two set-valued functions of a node. $children(i) \subset L \cup I$ includes all the nodes that are children of node i, and $desc(i) \subset L$ is the set of leaves that descend (directly or indirectly) from node i. $children(i) = desc(i) = \varnothing$ (the empty set) if $i \in L$. We envision a search process that selects among the children of a node in time proportional to the number of children.

Each node i is characterized by a measure called "homogeneity," $H(i)$, which estimates the collective similarity among $desc(i)$. Later we will consider possible measures for homogeneity, but for now we observe the following constraints that any reasonable measure should satisfy.

1. $H(i) \in [0,1]$, where $H(i) = 0$ indicates that $desc(i)$ are completely dissimilar from one another, and 1 indicates that they are completely similar to one another. "Dissimilar" and "similar" are defined with respect to the user's interests. In our work, they are defined by functions grounded in feature vectors associated with each leaf.
2. For any leaf i, $H(i) = 1$. A leaf is perfectly homogeneous.
3. For any non-leaf node j, $H(j)$ is a function of the complete set of leaves currently subsumed by the node, and ideally does not depend on the internal structure of the hierarchy. Because we require only that $H(j)$ estimate the similarity among leaf nodes, in practice $H(j)$ may vary with the structure, but we prefer measures that minimize such dependency.
4. In a well ordered hierarchy, if n, p, and c are the indices of a node, its parent, and one of its children, we expect $H(p) \leq H(n) \leq H(c)$. That is, homogeneity should increase monotonically as one descends the hierarchy. We call this characteristic of a well-ordered hierarchy, the Homogeneity Monotonicity Condition (HMC). Deviations from HMC indicate regions of the hierarchy that are not well ordered, and that should be restructured.

The HMC is necessary for a well-formed hierarchy, but not sufficient. In addition, all of the children of a node should be similar to one another. One way of quantifying this condition is to require that the removal of any one child from a node should have minimal impact on its homogeneity.

To be more concrete, let $j = parent(i)$, and let $j \backslash i$ represent a node having all the children of j except for i. Then we can define the *contribution* of node i to the homogeneity of its parent $cont(i) \equiv H(j) - H(j \backslash i) \in [-1, +1]$. (It is not the intent that $H(j) = \Sigma cont(i)$ over j's children.) We would like the difference between the maximum and minimum values of $cont(i)$ for $i \in children(j)$ to be minimal. Call this difference (which is between 0 and 2) a node's "dispersion." We seek hierarchies that minimize the dispersion at each node, a condition we call the Dispersion Minimization Condition, or DMC. (The difference between homogeneity and dispersion is analogous to the difference between the average of a set of numbers and their variance. Low homogeneity is consistent with either high or low dispersion, but high homogeneity requires low dispersion.)

3.2 Operations: Promote and Merge

In view of the desired "any-time" property, we consider a hierarchy that has already formed, and define decentralized processes that can improve it incrementally. The spirit of our operations is anticipated by Hartigan [15], who defines a global quality metric over a tree with respect to a similarity matrix, and then explores combinations of local modifications to the tree (*rebranch*, which reconnects a node; *kill*, which deletes a node, and *make*, which introduces a new node) that will improve this metric. This promising approach (which

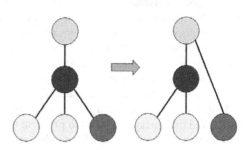

Fig. 1. Promoting.—A node chooses a child and makes it the child of its parent

is centralized and relies on global knowledge) is strangely absent from subsequent clustering research, and is not expounded in his subsequent book on the subject [14], perhaps because in the universe of centralized methods it is computationally costly.

The unit of processing in SODAS is a single non-leaf node, the active node. This node knows its parent and its children. (Since the active node is the parent of its children, the word "parent" is ambiguous. We use "grandparent" to refer to the parent of the active node.) It can estimate the local quality of the hierarchy by comparing its homogeneity with that of its children, and by computing its dispersion, as described in the next section. It seeks to improve these qualities by manipulating them with two operations, Promote and Merge. The only nodes involved in the operation are the active node and its parent and children. Because of its shape (left side of Fig. 1), we refer to this complex as a "crow's foot."

In Promoting, a node chooses one of its children and makes it a child of the grandparent (Fig. 1). If the node is the root, Promoting has no effect. Otherwise Promoting flattens the hierarchy. It moves misplaced nodes up the hierarchy until they meet other nodes with which they are more suitably associated. Promoting is an instance of Hartigan's *rebranch*, and is a local version of the basic step in divisive hierarchical clustering.

In Merging, a node chooses some of its children and combines them into

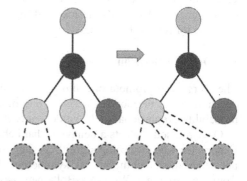

Fig. 2. Merging.—A node joins two highly similar children

a single node (Fig. 2). (For the sake of concreteness we describe the merging of two children, but a larger set of children could be merged at a single step.) If either of the nodes being merged is internal, their children are combined (a combination of Hartigan's *rebranch* and *kill*). A new internal node is added (Hartigan's *make*) only when two leaves are merged. Merging makes the hierarchy deeper. It is a local version of the basic step in agglomerative hierarchical clustering.

The general dynamic of SODAS is that subtrees climb upward, out of branches where they do not belong, and then merge back down into more appropriate branches. This vision of nodes moving up and down the tree in response to homogeneity estimates is analogous to the movement of ants in ant clustering on the basis of item similarity, and motivates our comparison of the two methods.

Promoting and Merging are sufficient to support the basic characteristics of Any-Time, Dynamic, Distributed hierarchical clustering.

Distributed.—Because a node can estimate H locally, it can sense the HMC and DMC, and thus make decisions to promote or merge its children without affecting any nodes other than its parent and its children. Thus many nodes in the hierarchy can execute concurrently on different processors. We envision the nodes (root, internal, and leaves) being distributed across as many processors as are available.

Dynamic.—Classical algorithms for hierarchical clustering presume that the structure is correct at every step. Promote and Merge assume that it is incorrect, and take local actions to improve it. Promoting moves nodes that are in an inappropriate branch of the hierarchy higher up, to a more general level. Merging joins together nodes that are very similar, thus growing hierarchical structure downward. As these processes execute concurrently over the nodes of the hierarchy, nodes continually climb up and down the hierarchy, finding their best place in the overall structure. New leaf nodes can be added anywhere to the structure, and will eventually find their way to the right location. If the similarity measure changes, nodes will relocate themselves to account for the changed measure, while taking advantage of any of the existing structure that is still appropriate.

Any-Time.—Because the algorithm dynamically corrects errors, it never needs to be restarted. The longer it runs, the better the structure becomes. Empirically, it converges exponentially after a short initialization period, and its characteristics are very similar to those of our flat clustering algorithm, for whose exponential convergence we have a theoretical analysis [29]. Thus one can consult the structure at any time for retrieval purposes.

3.3 Detailed Decision Logic

The merge and promote operations are local atomic behaviors of the node. In each decision cycle, the node will select one of its atomic behaviors for execution with probability proportional to the value that each behavior offers at the moment.

Once the node selects a behavior, that behavior decides whether in fact to execute. Experience with swarming algorithms suggests that this decision should be stochastic, not deterministic, both to break symmetries that might otherwise arise, and to escape from local extrema. We use a Boltzmann distribution whose temperature is a tuning parameter of the system. High temperatures encourage more search, while low ones lead to rapid (though often suboptimal) convergence. The use of stochastic decisions based on local information rather than deterministic ones based on global information is a major distinction between our work and [15], and enables us to handle dynamically changing sets of leaves in distributed processing environments.

Both behaviors follow the same generic scheme for computing their value. Each behavior affects an entity made up of one or more of the node's children, and has a

Table 1. Calculating a Behavior's Value

Behavior	Affected Entity	Merit
Merger	Pair of Children	Pairwise similarity, $m_{merge} = h(c_1 + c_2) - h(n)$. Promotes HMC.
Promotion	Single Child	Increase in node's homogeneity if child is removed, $m_{promotion} = h(n \backslash c) - h(n)$. Promotes DMC.

"figure of merit" m." Table 1 summarizes the behaviors, the affected entities, and the computation of the figure of merit for an entity.

Execution of a behavior depends on two conditions.

1. The behavior must enhance the increase of homogeneity as one descends the tree. Promotion must increase the homogeneity of the active node. The node resulting from a merger must have greater homogeneity than its parent. If this condition is not satisfied, the behavior is not permitted.
2. The merit of taking the behavior on an entity must be significantly greater than the merit of taking it on another entity in the same node. If merit for all entities in a node are about equal, we do not have adequate guidance to select one entity over another. An entity's merit must lie above a threshold (currently, the third quartile of all entities) for the behavior to be enabled.

To assess the second condition, we need figures of merit for at least three entities. If the greatest is much larger than the others, we favor the action, but if all of the figures of merit are close together, we do not. We can apply this test with all the entities under a node, or (if the complete set of children is too large to compute the figures of merit efficiently) with a randomly chosen subset that includes three or more. The entities are pairs of children (in the case of merger) or individual children (in the case of promotion). In both cases we need at least three children, which generate $_3C_2 = 3$ pairs.

We order the entities' figures of merit from largest to smallest, and compute the median and the quartiles. All entities with figures of merit greater than zero and above the upper quartile are candidates for action. In principle, we can select stochastically among them, weighted by merit, but currently we use the largest. If no entities have positive figures of merit, or if all figures of merit are between the quartiles, the behavior under consideration is not taken.

We now focus on three figures of merit:

1. mc is the maximal figure of merit, associated with the candidate.
2. mm is the median figure of merit.
3. md ("diameter") is the inter-quartile spread.

We use md to measure how far the candidate is from the median. We can consider either $(mc - mm)/md$ or the inverse. Because we are interested in cases where this ratio is large, and to keep the quantity bounded, we focus on the inverse, $md/(mc - mm)$, which we call the candidate's *proximity*. The node learns the maximum proximity value it has seen, *proxMax*, and then computes the candidate's separation as *1 − proximity/proxMax*.

We learn a separate *proxMax* for each behavior.

We use the separation in two ways. It is the value that the node uses to select which behavior to perform, and also to compute the probability of performing the selected action (via the Boltzmann function).

3.4 Housekeeping

When a node is activated, and before it decides to merge or promote, it does some housekeeping. First, if it has only one child, it is superfluous, so it deterministically promotes its child and dies. Second, if it has exactly two children, either promote or merge would leave it with only one, so it does neither. Third, it compares its homogeneity with that of its parent, and if it violates HMC, it promotes its children deterministically and then dies.

4 A Local Homogeneity Measure

A critical requirement for implementing the algorithm outlined in the previous section is the availability of a homogeneity measure that a node can compute based only on a fixed length-summary available at its immediate children. Notionally, a node's homogeneity is a measure over all of the leaves that it subsumes. A straightforward way to estimate homogeneity, consistent with the definition in Section 3.1, would be an appropriately normalized average pairwise similarity of all leaves subsumed by a node, using one's favorite measure of similarity between feature vectors, such as cosine distance, Euclidean distance, or Hamming distance. However, such a computation would require either that we access all of a node's leaves for each such evaluation (impairing our ability to distribute the algorithm), or else that we store the feature vectors for all leaves in each ancestor internal node (which would greatly expand the required storage requirements for large populations of leaves, particularly for nodes high in the tree).

We use a homogeneity function derived from the mutual information between the leaves and the elements of their feature vectors. This measure can be computed from three constant-length variables stored at each node of the tree.

Let C be a cluster of leaves subsumed by a node, and $C' \subset C$ a subset of that cluster, subsumed by a child of the node. Let (X, Y) be a joint random variable over leaves x and features y, with marginal probability $p_{\bullet x}$ on leaf x. (assumed to be uniform). We can now define $p_{\bullet C'} \equiv \sum_{x \in C'} p_{\bullet x}$, the marginal probability of the cluster C', which for a cluster with only one leaf x is just $p_{\bullet x}$. For higher-level clusters,

$$p_{\bullet C} = \sum_{C' \subset C} p_{\bullet C'} \tag{1}$$

$P_{yx} \equiv P_{y|x} P_{\bullet x}$ is the joint probability of finding feature (e.g., word) y in leaf (e.g., document) x, so $p_{yC'} \equiv \sum_{x \in C'} p_{yx}$ is the joint probability of finding word y in cluster

C'. Then $p_{y\bullet|C'} \equiv p_{yC'}/p_{\bullet C'}$ is the cluster-conditioned marginal probability of a given feature y, and for a single-leaf cluster is just $p_{y|x}$. For higher-level clusters,

$$p_{y\bullet|C} = \sum_{C' \subset C} p_{y\bullet|C'} \frac{p_{\bullet C'}}{p_{\bullet C}} \qquad (2)$$

This quantity permits us to compute the cluster-conditional information content of the feature set, $I_{Y|C} = -\sum_y p_{y\bullet|C} \ln p_{y\bullet|C}$

Let $I_{(Y|X)C} \equiv -\sum_{x \in C} p_{\bullet x|C} \sum_y p_{y|x} \ln p_{y|x}$ be the marginal information of Y given X, conditioned on C. For a cluster with a single word, this is just the entropy of the conditional probability $p_{y|x}$, $I_{(Y|X)C} \equiv -\sum_y p_{y|x} \ln p_{y|x}$. For higher-level nodes,

$$I_{(Y|X)C} \equiv \sum_{C' \in C} \frac{p_{\bullet C'}}{p_{\bullet C}} I_{(Y|X)C'} \qquad (3)$$

$p_{\bullet C'}$, $p_{y\bullet|C'}$, and $I_{(Y|X)C'}$ are the three constant-length values (of length 1, $|Y|$, and 1, respectively) that each node stores. They can be updated by a node from its children with Equations 1, 2, and 3, thereby locally updating

$$M_{YX|C} = I_{Y|C} - I_{(Y|X)C} \qquad (4)$$

$M_{YX/C}$ is the cluster-conditional mutual information, the average amount of information one would gain towards identifying a leaf x in C given a feature y.

$M_{YX/C}$ is the basis for the similarity computations that drive SODAS. If the feature distributions in the various leaves in a cluster are very similar ($M_{YX|C} \approx 0$), one learns very little from a given feature. If they are very different ($M_{YX|C} \approx I_{X|C}$), one learns much. We modify this measure in two ways to define the *homogeneity* of a cluster.

First, we normalize it by a (not necessarily least) upper bound $I_{X/C}$, which under our assumptions is just $ln(/C/)$. It turns out that normalizing each cluster by its size (the number of leaves it subsumes) leads to severe nonlinearities in the similarity measure, so we compute $I_{X/C}$ based on the size of the entire population as our normalizing factor. This normalization (as well as the marginal probability $p_{\bullet x}$) depends on knowledge of the size of the population of leaves being clustered. If old leaves are deleted at the same rate as new ones are added, the size is constant. Otherwise an estimate of the size needs to be propagated throughout the hierarchy.

Second, because we want a measure of homogeneity, not of diversity, we subtract the normalized mutual information from 1.

Thus our homogeneity measure for a node n that subsumes a cluster of leaves C is

$$h(n) \equiv 1 - \frac{M_{YX|C}}{I_{X|D}} \qquad (5)$$

where D is the entire set of leaves.

5 Experimental Results

The behavior of SODAS is most clearly seen using synthetic data with feature vectors randomly selected from $[0,255]^3$. By interpreting each vector as an RGB color, a treemap [3] clearly displays the increasing organization of the data over time.

To avoid the expense of printing color, we do not show these plots here. Instead, we report the behavior of an order-based version of the cophenetic correlation coefficient (CCC) [32]. To avoid undue influence by outliers, we use the Spearman rank correlation coefficient instead of the conventional correlation coefficient. We demonstrate the algorithm in three steps.

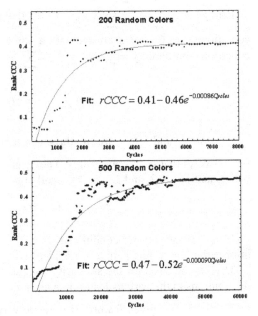

First, as a baseline, we cluster populations of random color data of size 200 and 500, using a version of standard agglomerative clustering under the similarity metric of Equation 5. At each step, we deterministically merge the two nodes for which the resulting new node has maximal homogeneity under Equation 5, breaking ties randomly. Though the clustering step is deterministic, the generation of the colors and the breaking of ties are both random, so we explore 13 replications of each experiment. The mean (standard deviation) of the CCC for 200 leaves is 0.53 (0.05), and for 500 leaves, 0.52 (0.03). The difference is statistically indistinguishable, as confirmed by the Mann-Whitney rank sum test: the sum of ranks for the two

Fig. 3. Convergence of 200 (top) and 500 (bottom) random color vectors

populations are 181 (for 200) and 170 (for 500), within about a quarter of a standard deviation (19.5/4) of the expected mean of 175.5. By construction, clustering n items in this way requires n − 1 steps.

Second, we exercise our algorithm on a random tree with k = 5. This configuration requires the algorithm to exercise both merging and promoting, and emulates an application in which the data begin on different processors. If we began with a flat tree, the behavior of the algorithm would differ little from conventional agglomerative clustering. We plot the CCC every 100 cycles until convergence. Fig. 3 shows the dynamics for representative runs. Because flat ant clustering exhibits very strong exponential convergence, we also show exponential fits, though they are not as close as in the flat case.

The mean (standard deviation) asymptotes for SODAS are 0.47 (0.07) for 200 leaves and 0.48 (0.04) for 500, again indistinguishable; the Mann-Whitney rank sums are 173 and 178, respectively. These are lower than the baseline. The Mann-Whitney rank sums for all 26 baseline runs compared with all 26 SODAS runs are

875 and 503, which are 3.40 standard deviations from the mean of 689, significant at the 0.1% level.

In ant-based partitional clustering, the exponent is inversely proportional to the size of the population [29]. SODAS qualitatively follows this trend, with an exponent on the order of 10-3 for 200 leaves and 10-4 for 500. The stochastic element in SODAS requires many more cycles to achieve convergence than does the deterministic baseline (for 200 leaves, about 1200 cycles to increase the CCC by a factor of $1 - 1/e$, compared with 200 to completion for the baseline algorithm). This disadvantage is offset by the ability to distribute the computation over many concurrent processors, the availability of partial results at any time during the clustering, and the algorithm's ability to handle dynamic data. Such trade-off is common in swarming algorithms: "Gottes Mühlen mahlen langsam, mahlen aber trefflich klein"[1] [20].

To show SODAS' ability to handle dynamically changing data, we begin the process with a random tree of 200 color leaves, and add one additional color leaf every 100 time steps. Fig. 4 shows the convergence when the additional leaves are added at randomly selected nodes, along with a (admittedly rough) fit. Consistent with our experience in partitional clustering, the asymptote drops, and the continual addition of new leaves keeps the dynamics from settling down.

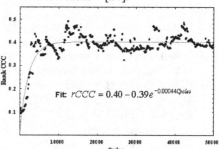

Fig. 4. Dynamic addition of leaves

6   Conclusion and Prospectus

Hierarchical clustering is a powerful tool for data analysis, but has hitherto been restricted to applications in which the data being analyzed is relatively static, and small enough to be handled on a single processor. By adapting mechanisms inspired by social insects, SODAS generates and maintains a hierarchical clustering of a dynamically changing body of data, scaling to arbitrarily large amounts of data by distributing the processing across multiple processors. It supports a twofold information retrieval process, in which foraging agents continuously maintain markers on subtrees that have high relevance to a model of the user, enabling efficient processing of individual queries. While its convergence is slower than conventional deterministic algorithms, it can provide any-time organization of massive, changing data in a distributed environment, an important class of application for which conventional algorithms are ill-suited.

Acknowledgments

This study was supported and monitored in part by the Advanced Research and Development Activity (ARDA) and the National Geospatial-intelligence Agency

---

[1] Approximate translation: God's mills grind slowly but exceedingly fine.

(NGA) under contract number NMA401-02-C-0020. The views, opinions, and findings contained in this report are those of the author(s) and should not be construed as an official Department of Defense position, policy, or decision, unless so designated by other official documentation. This research was sponsored in part by the Air Force Research Laboratory, Air Force Materiel Command, USAF, under Contract number MDA972-03-9-0001. The views and conclusions contained herein are those of the authors and should not be interpreted as necessarily representing the official policies or endorsements, either expressed or implied, of AFRL or the U.S. Government.

References

[1] R. Alonso and H. Li. Model-Guided Information Discovery for Intelligence Analysis. In Proceedings of CIKM '05, 2005.
[2] J. Beal. Leaderless Distributed Hierarchy Formation. AIM-2002-021, MIT, Cambridge, MA, 2002. http://www.swiss.ai.mit.edu/projects/amorphous/papers/AIM-2002-021.ps.
[3] B. B. Bederson, B. Shneiderman, and M. Wattenberg. Ordered and Quantum Treemaps: Making Effective Use of 2D Space to Display Hierarchies. ACM Transactions on Graphics, 21(4):833-854, 2002.
[4] E. Bonabeau, M. Dorigo, and G. Theraulaz. Swarm Intelligence: From Natural to Artificial Systems. New York, Oxford University Press, 1999.
[5] E. Bonabeau, G. Theraulaz, V. Fourcassié, and J.-L. Deneubourg. The Phase-Ordering Kinetics of Cemetery Organization in Ants. Physical Review E, 4:4568-4571, 1998.
[6] S. Brueckner. Return from the Ant: Synthetic Ecosystems for Manufacturing Control. Thesis at Humboldt University Berlin, Department of Computer Science, 2000.
[7] S. Camazine, J.-L. Deneubourg, N. R. Franks, J. Sneyd, G. Theraulaz, and E. Bonabeau. Self-Organization in Biological Systems. Princeton, NJ, Princeton University Press, 2001.
[8] L. Chen, X. Xu, Y. Chen, and P. He. A Novel Ant Clustering Algorithm Based on Cellular Automata. In Proceedings of International Joint Conference on Web Intelligence and Intelligent Agent Technology (WI'04 and IAT'04), 2004.
[9] J. L. Deneubourg, S. Goss, N. Franks, A. Sendova-Franks, C. Detrain, and L. Chretien. The Dynamics of Collective Sorting: Robot-Like Ants and Ant-Like Robots. In J. A. Meyer and S. W. Wilson, Editors, From Animals to Animats: Proceedings of the First International Conference on Simulation of Adaptive Behavior, pages 356-365. MIT Press, Cambridge, MA, 1991.
[10] C. Fellbaum, Editor. WordNet: An Electronic Lexical Database (Language, Speech, and Communication). Cambridge, MA, MIT, 1998.
[11] A. D. Gordon. Hierarchical Classification. In P. Arabie, L. J. Hubert, and G. DeSoete, Editors, Clustering and Classification, pages 65-121. World Scientific, River Edge, NJ, 1996.
[12] J. Handl, J. Knowles, and M. Dorigo. Ant-based clustering: a comparative study of its relative performance with respect to k-means, average link and 1d-som. TR-IRIDIA-2003-24, IRIDIA, 2003. http://wwwcip.informatik.uni-erlangen.de/~sijuhand/TR-IRIDIA-2003-24.pdf.
[13] J. Handl and B. Meyer. Improved ant-based clustering and sorting in a document retrieval interface. In Proceedings of Parallel Problem Solving from Nature (PPSN VII), Springer, 2002.
[14] J. Hartigan. Clustering Algorithms. New York, NY, John Wiley and Sons, 1975.

[15] J. A. Hartigan. Representation of Similarity Matrices by Trees. Journal of the American Statistical Association, 22:1140-1158, 1967.

[16] K. M. Hoe, W. K. Lai, and T. S. Y. Tai. Homogeneous Ants for Web Document Similarity Modeling and Categorization. In Proceedings of Ants 2002, 2002.

[17] A. K. Jain, M. N. Murty, and P. J. Flynn. Data Clustering: A Review. ACM Computing Surveys, 31(3), 1999.

[18] P. M. Kanade and L. O. Hall. Fuzzy Ants as a Clustering Concept. In Proceedings of the 22nd International Conference of the North American Fuzzy Information Processing Society (NAFIPS03), pages 227-232, 2003.

[19] P. Kuntz and P. Layzell. An Ant Clustering Algorithm Applied to Partitioning in VLSI Technology. In Proceedings of Fourth European Conference on Artificial Life, pages 417-424, MIT Press, 1997.

[20] F. v. Logau. Deutscher Sinngedichte drei Tausend. 1654.

[21] E. D. Lumer and B. Faieta. Diversity and Adaptation in Populations of Clustering Ants. In Proceedings of Third Conference on Simulation of Adaptive Behavior (SAB94), MIT Press, 1994.

[22] G. A. Miller. WordNet: A Lexical Database for the English Language. Web Page, 2002. http://www.cogsci.princeton.edu/~wn/.

[23] N. Monmarché. HaNT Web Site. Web Site, 2001. http://www.hant.li.univ-tours.fr/webhant/index.php?lang=fr&pageid=24.

[24] E. Ogston, B. Overeinder, M. V. Steen, and F. Brazier. A Method for Decentralized Clustering in Large Multi-Agent Systems. In Proceedings of Second International Joint Conference on Autonomous Agents and Multi-Agent Systems, pages 789-796, 2003.

[25] C. F. Olson. Parallel Algorithms for Hierarchical Clustering. Parallel Computing, 21:1313-1325, 1995.

[26] S. A. Oprisan. Task Oriented Functional Self-Organization of Mobile Agents Team: Memory Optimization Based on Correlation Feature. In Proceedings of Ant Colony Optimization and Swarm Intelligence (ANTS 2004), pages 398-405, Springer, 2004.

[27] H. V. D. Parunak. 'Go to the Ant': Engineering Principles from Natural Agent Systems. Annals of Operations Research, 75:69-101, 1997.

[28] H. V. D. Parunak, S. A. Brueckner, R. Matthews, and J. Sauter. Pheromone Learning for Self-Organizing Agents. IEEE SMC, 35(3 (May)):316-326, 2005.

[29] H. V. D. Parunak, S. A. Brueckner, J. A. Sauter, and R. Matthews. Global Convergence of Local Agent Behaviors. In Proceedings of Fourth International Joint Conference on Autonomous Agents and Multi-Agent Systems (AAMAS05), pages 305-312, 2005.

[30] V. Ramos and A. Abraham. Evolving a Stigmergic Self-Organized Data-Mining. In Proceedings of 4th Int. Conf. on Intelligent Systems, Design and Applications (ISDA-04), pages 725-730, 2004.

[31] S. Schockaert, M. de Cock, C. Cornelis, and E. E. Kerre. Efficient Clustering with Fuzzy Ants. In Proceedings of Ant Colony Optimization and Swarm Intelligence (ANTS 2004), pages 342-349, 2004.

[32] R. R. Sokal and F. J. Rohlf. The comparison of dendrograms by objective methods. Taxon, 11:33-40, 1962.

[33] B. Walsham. Simplified and Optimised Ant Sort for Complex Problems: Document Classification. Thesis at Monash University, Department of School of Computer Science and Software Engineering, 2003.

Behaviosites: A Novel Paradigm for Affecting Distributed Behavior

From a Healthy Society to a Wealthy Society

Amit Shabtay, Zinovi Rabinovich, and Jeffrey S. Rosenschein

School of Engineering and Computer Science
The Hebrew University, Jerusalem, Israel
ashabtay@gmail.com,
{nomad,jeff}@cs.huji.ac.il

Abstract. In this paper we present the Behaviosite paradigm, a new approach to affecting the behavior of distributed agents in a multiagent system, which is inspired by biological parasites with behavior manipulation properties. Behaviosites are special kinds of agents that "infect" a system composed of agents operating in that environment. The behaviosites facilitate behavioral changes in agents to achieve altered, potentially improved, performance of the overall system. Behaviosites need to be designed so that they are intimately familiar with the internal workings of the environment and of the agents operating within it, and behaviosites apply this knowledge for their manipulation, using various infection and manipulation strategies.

To demonstrate and test this paradigm, we implemented a version of the El Farol problem, where agents want to go to a bar of limited capacity, and cannot use communication to coordinate their activity. Several solutions to this problem exist, but most yield near-zero utility for the agents. We added behaviosites to the El Farol problem, which manipulate the decision making process of some of the agents by making them believe that bar capacity is lower than it really is. We show that behaviosites overcome the learning ability of the agents, and increase social utility and social fairness significantly, with little actual damage to the overall system, and none to the agents.

1 Introduction

Biology-based technology (biomimetics) often provides insight into ways of improving technology based on biological metaphors [1]; nature and evolution have worked hard at finding solutions to many problems that are also present in artificial environments. Parasites have been examined in the biomimetic context, in particular for their special abilities (such as safe navigation inside the human body, needed for microendoscopy [2]).

However, one of the most interesting abilities of biological parasites has received little attention in technological contexts — their ability to manipulate and alter their host's behavior. Usually, parasites alter host behavior so as to

S. Brueckner et al. (Eds.): ESOA 2006, LNAI 4335, pp. 82–98, 2007.

transmit themselves to the next host, as in the case of rabies (by generating aggressive host behavior). In rare cases, biological parasites can actually benefit the host or the host's society. The word "parasite" [3] derives from the Greek word *parasitos*, which means "beside the grain", and originally had a positive connotation; a parasite was a fellow guest who ate beside you at the dinner table. Only later did it receive the meaning of someone eating at the expense of another.

In the computer science literature, the term "parasite" is used in three different contexts, none dealing with behavior manipulation: parasites in simulations of evolution, parasites as a driving force in genetic algorithms, and parasites as a common name for malware (computer viruses, trojan horses, etc.).

1.1 The Behaviosite Paradigm

In this paper, we present a novel paradigm that employs a special kind of agent (called a *behaviosite*) that manipulates the behavior of other agents so as to achieve altered, possibly improved, performance of the entire system. The behaviosite (by definition) is not itself necessary for the normal conduct of the system; thus, it is termed a kind of "parasite".

Within the field of MultiAgent Systems (MAS), the behaviosite is closely related to the idea of adjustable autonomy (AA) [4], although it approaches issues of autonomy in a novel way. AA is about agents varying the level of their own autonomy based upon the situation (thus leveraging three alternative modes of operation, fully autonomous, semi-autonomous, and teleoperated). AA often deals with agents transferring control to human users [5] in cooperative settings. In the context of the Behaviosite paradigm, an agent transfers some of its autonomy to the behaviosite (usually unwittingly, and in any case the agent is better described as *ceding autonomy*). The behaviosite manipulates the agent's behavior to achieve altered performance of the system. In this way, the behaviosite may create improved performance of the overall system (as we will demonstrate in the parasitized El Farol problem [6]), or it may facilitate new behaviors of the system.

Introducing behaviosites into a system may be either planned as part of the overall system design, or added (after the fact) to an already working system. When planned as part of the overall system, it is possible to choose between applying *internal behaviosites* (design hooks inside agents, so that behaviosites can attach to the agent and manipulate them) or *external behaviosites* (which manipulate only the input/output of the agent, vis-à-vis the environment). When applied to an already working system, external behaviosites are usually the only option. Both internal and external behaviosites are discussed in Section 3.

Internal behaviosites require cooperation at the level of agent designer(s), so that the appropriate hooks are in place for them to run (and alter agent behavior). Centrally-designed MAS systems, of course, may include behaviosite hooks because overall system performance can be improved. However, even in systems of self-interested, heterogeneous agents, inclusion of a behaviosite hook may be mandated as a requirement for operation within a given environment — thus giving the environment designer an additional tool for improving overall system behavior.

1.2   A Distributed Approach to Altered Behavior

One of the major strengths of the Behaviosite paradigm is that it is a distributed solution to issues raised in a distributed environment. Consider, for example, the El Farol problem [6] as an example of such a distributed environment. All agents want to go to a bar called El Farol, but it has limited (comfortable) capacity. If there are more attendees at the bar than that capacity, all attendees suffer from the crowdedness. With no option for communication or collusion, an agent must learn the behavior of other agents *en masse*, in order to reach a decision: go to the bar, or stay at home.

With very simple agent behavior, the system reaches an equilibrium around the given capacity. Unfortunately, personal and social utilities are extremely low, since about half the time the bar is overcrowded. To this setting, we introduce behaviosites, and the problem becomes the "parasitized El Farol" problem. We show that with simple infection and manipulation strategies of these special agents, it is possible to dramatically increase personal and social utilities, and even improve social fairness.

Although the El Farol problem is artificial, it has implications for many fields, including game theory, congestion problems in networking, logic, and economics [7]. In most, if not all, of these areas, the Behaviosite paradigm is applicable. There are, in addition, other possible applications for behaviosites, as will be discussed in Section 5.

The rest of the paper is organized as follows. In Section 2 we present a formalization of the Behaviosite paradigm. In Section 3, we discuss the El Farol problem, and how behaviosites could be employed in its solution. In Section 4 we briefly overview the concept of "parasite" in biology and computer science. We conclude in Section 5 with an overall discussion of our approach and of future work.

2   Behaviosite Formalization

2.1   Overall Structure

The Behaviosite paradigm is composed of three parts: the environment, agents (also referred to as hosts), and behaviosites. Environment, agents, and behaviosites will be referred to collectively as "the system" (as in ecosystem). See Figure 1 for an illustration of the environment/agent relationship.

Environment: Encapsulates all of the external factors, conditions, and influences that affect a community of agents and behaviosites. For example, during the course of a program run, it stores the runtime state of the system, and it is discarded when the program ends. In some cases, the environment can be a degenerate instance, as in the case where agents only influence one another. In

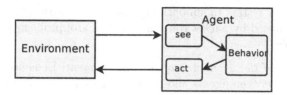

Fig. 1. The environment/agent relationship

other cases, it may have an important role in the conduct of the system, as in the parasitized El Farol problem.

Agent society: A society of agents is a system composed of multiple, interacting, possibly cooperating agents (see [8]). As there are many definitions of agency, we use the one suggested by Franklin and Graesser [9]: *An autonomous agent is a system situated within and as part of an environment that senses that environment and acts on it, over time, in pursuit of its own agenda and so as to effect [sic] what it senses in the future.*

Behaviosite: Most basically, a specialized type of agent. A behaviosite is an additional property/information added to a system with a society of agents, and is not (and should not be) a property of the agent or the environment. The behaviosite is not required for the system, but should be beneficial in some sense; too many behaviosites can degrade some aspects of the system. Below, we present specific definitions regarding behaviosite elements. These definitions are further clarified in Section 3, which presents (in the context of the El Farol problem) what behaviosites are, and their advantages within a system.

2.2 Behaviosite Specifics

Required Traits

Benefiting the system: Behaviosites come with costs to the system, as will be discussed below. The design and use of behaviosites is unnecessary, unless they are beneficial to the system in some respect. Behaviosites may influence a system in two desired ways: they may increase social utility, or they may create new features in a working system. Both are accomplished by altering the behavior of some of the agents. Note that in the behaviosite paradigm, unlike with parasites in nature, the utility of the behaviosite itself is not important when declaring them successful.

System knowledge: A behaviosite must be designed with deep understanding of how the system works: agent-agent interactions, agent-environment interactions, and also internal workings of the agents in some cases. Such knowledge is essential for the success of the behaviosites in improving the system. One type of system in which behaviosites can be beneficial is a system that works in a suboptimal equilibrium. When building a system, usually suboptimality is caused by the need to make it robust against failure. However, there are examples in which sub-optimality results from the inherent structure of the system. The internet is one example of a system in suboptimal equilibrium, with regard to the congestion problem caused by packet routing. The El Farol problem presents another, similar example.

Not a property of the agent nor of the environment: Behaviosites exist in the middle ground between agents and the environment, and should not be a property of either of them.

Optional Traits

Hidden or apparent infection: We usually will not want agents to know who is infected by the behaviosite. Such knowledge may help individual agents exploit the situation, harnessing its own behaviosite or some other parasitized agent to its own needs and thereby damaging the designed mechanism of environment-agents-behaviosites. However, there are some settings in which such knowledge can benefit the system (as also occurs in nature), for example, the elimination of ill-functioning agents (a process known as "apoptosis" in cells).

Finding the host: In many cases in nature, finding the host is essential for the parasite. In the Behaviosite paradigm, it may also be an issue. A behaviosite designer may endow the environment with the responsibility of infecting agents in the system using some strategy (like in the parasitized El Farol problem), or it may leave the task of infection to the behaviosites themselves, thus making the behaviosites more autonomous. In certain contexts, hosts may also be equipped with defense mechanisms against infection.

Behaviosite communication: Behaviosites may communicate with one another within a host (the host may be infected with more than one behaviosite), or across hosts. The latter enables formation of a network of parasitized hosts, which may act in some kind of parasite-induced coalition. This may enable the behaviosites to be a catalyst for the creation of norms or social laws.

2.3 Placing the Behaviosite

To alter host behavior, the behaviosite designer must decide where to place the behaviosite in the flow of the system, as can be seen in Figure 2.

In general, behaviosites can be divided into two main groups, external behaviosites, and internal behaviosites. External behaviosites can alter the input or output of the agent vis-à-vis the environment (Figure 2a). In this way, the host designer(s) need not know of the possible existence of a behaviosite now or in the future. Moreover, the behaviosite designer may introduce them into an existing system.[1]

On the other hand, internal behaviosites usually require the system to be designed "plug and play" for the behaviosite (Figure 2b). The host designer(s) will leave a (sufficiently protected) hook, into which behaviosites can be plugged, possibly created by another designer. Allowing the behaviosite internal access may seem dangerous, but it holds many advantages.

---

[1] Of course, these external behaviosites affect inter-agent communication only if it, too, travels via the environment.

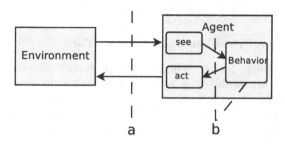

Fig. 2. (a) marks where an external behaviosite can alter the host's behavior, by altering its input/output. (b) marks where an internal behaviosite can alter the host's behavior, by altering internal data or by partial or full replacement of behavior modules.

Internal behaviosites can have two main manipulation methods: changing the host's internal data (Figure 2b, interaction between see-behavior-act modules) or replacing some or all of its behavioral modules (Figure 2b, behavior module). In the first form of manipulation, only relevant data will be changed, and in some scenarios, it can actually solve the problem of dealing with noise resulting from the transduction of input from the environment.[2]

The hook for the second manipulation method is very easy to program, by using the behavioral design patterns suggested by the "gang of four" [11]. Introducing a new behaviosite to a well-designed system may at times be much like programming a new, special behavior for an agent (though it should not be a regular property of the host). In specific systems, if needed, security measures will have to be taken to protect the host from malicious parasites, which could exploit the existence of the hook. Such security measures are abundant; one easy-to-implement example is public/private key encryption (further consideration of these security issues is beyond the scope of this paper).

2.4   Cost of Manipulation

In different scenarios, behaviosites have different types of costs. The first cost that should be considered is the cost to the system designer, for there is the immediate issue of designing behaviosites and testing them. Analyzing system behavior can be very complex, and analysis of a system in which behaviosites are integrated is even more complex. This is because their impact on the system is usually hard to predict without extensive testing. Other costs of behaviosites are system specific, such as balancing behaviosite complexity and number with the benefit they give to the system, cost of possibly increased variation in the society, oscillations, run-time costs, and so forth. Despite all of the above, there are many scenarios in which behaviosites prove themselves very useful.

---

[2] This is somewhat reminiscent of Brooks' subsumption architecture [10], in which various levels can be designed to suppress input/output on other levels.

3   Parasitized El Farol Problem

3.1   The El Farol Problem and Related Work

The El Farol problem (or the Santa Fe bar problem) was introduced by Brian Arthur [6] as a toy problem in economics for using inductive reasoning and bounded rationality. In this problem, N (e.g., 100) agents decide independently each week whether to go to the El Farol bar or not. Comfortable capacity is limited, and the evening is enjoyable only if the bar is not overcrowded (specifically, fewer than 60 agents out of the possible 100 attend).

In the original problem, no communication or collusion is possible, and the only information available to the agents is the number of attendees in the past. An agent will go if it predicts less than 60 agents will go, and will stay home otherwise. Arthur suggested that bounded rationality, together with learning, can yield solutions to problems of resource allocation in decentralized environments, using the El Farol problem as an example [12]. At this point, the problem in the research literature diverged into two branches, differentiated by their utility functions. The first branch was as in Arthur's paper:

$$Util(ag[i]) = \begin{cases} x & attended\ and\ undercrowded \\ 0 & did\ not\ attend \\ -y & attended\ and\ overcrowded \end{cases}$$

The second branch used another kind of utility function:

$$Util(ag[i]) = \begin{cases} x & part\ of\ minority\ group \\ -y & not\ part\ of\ minority\ group \end{cases}$$

In this paper, we use the first utility function, where $x = y = 0.5$.[3] Arthur showed [6] that if each agent uses a set of personal basic deterministic strategies (such as going if more than 55 agents went last time), combined with a simple learning algorithm, then the system converges to the capacity after some initial learning time. Moreover, membership kept changing, and some degree of fairness was maintained. Arthur described the emergent ecology as almost organic in nature. In his work, Edmonds [14] took this analogy a step further by using genetic algorithms for learning, and allowing communication. Edmonds showed that these were sufficient for the development of different, interesting social roles.

However, both solutions produced systems that fluctuated chaotically around the capacity, resulting in low personal and social utility. High variation in the system was one reason for suboptimality. The second was that at many times the bar was overcrowded (above capacity), thus giving negative utility to attending agents.

Bell [15] tried to deal with the overcrowdedness problem by a simple adaptive strategy used by all agents, which led to an outcome close to the socially optimal attendance. Bell's solution holds two pitfalls. The first is that the same strategy must be used by all agents, perhaps too strong a requirement in a distributed

---

[3] For a review of the minority problem, see [13].

system with different designers. The second is that in his simulations most of the attendees were "regulars" who came all of the rounds, thus making for social injustice with the "casuals".

Greenwald [7] also tackled this suboptimality problem, but using a different method. Agents that attended El Farol were required to "pay" some of their utility, and this payoff was distributed among all agents that did not attend. Not surprisingly, the optimal payoff for optimal social utility converged to a 40% attendance fee, for the scenario of 100 agents and bar capacity of 60. Again, this solution may also be problematic in many distributed systems, since it requires a central "utility distributer" that can reach all agents.

The learning algorithm used in the parasitized El Farol simulation was the additive updating learning algorithm, introduced in [12]. Basically, each agent has a pool of simple, personal deterministic strategies. Each such behavior has a weight, initially distributed uniformly. The weights of all these basic strategies are updated in an additive manner once a round, according to the number of attendees in that round, above or below capacity (0.5 or -0.5 utility to attendees, respectively, or zero if it chooses not to attend).

3.2   Using Behaviosites in the Parasitized El Farol Problem

The El Farol bar problem presents a distributed system, with suboptimal social and personal utility. The main idea of the parasitized El Farol problem is to increase social utility with as few side effects as possible, using behaviosites. The main problem was that agents learn and adapt themselves to new situations. If the behaviosites are not carefully crafted, then either their effect will soon vanish, and the system will return to the equilibrium around the capacity with suboptimal social utility, or in each round behaviosites will need to make a stronger impact to achieve the same effect.

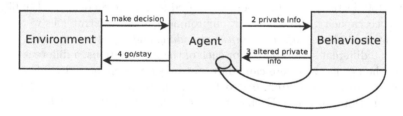

Fig. 3. An illustration of the environment/agent/behaviosite relationship

The system is composed of environment, agents (hosts) and behaviosites (Figure 3). Each agent has an internal behaviosite field that is always occupied, usually with the null behaviosite (see [11]) which has no effect over its host's behavior. Each round, the environment infects some of the agents according to an infection strategy (as will be discussed below), and infection lasts only one round. Agents are asked to provide a decision (whether they will go to the bar or not). Then, the agent gives its behaviosite private information before making the decision. If the behaviosite is not the null behaviosite, it alters the relevant host's data (the behaviosite is placed between "see" and "behavior" of Figure 2). In this way, the agent comes to a decision not using the data received from the environment, but rather by using manipulated data.

Environment infection strategies: In this simulation, the environment had three strategies of infection, which were not mixed. In the first strategy, all agents were candidates for infection (*infect all*). In the second, only attending agents in the given round were candidates for infection (*infect attending*). In the third, candidates for infection were all attending agents at the given round, but only when the bar was overcrowded (*infect overcrowded*). In each strategy, only a percentage of the candidates for infection actually got infected (responsibility of the behaviosite design), depending on the infection rate (0%-100%).[4]

Behaviosite manipulation strategies: The chosen manipulation strategy was quite simple. The behaviosite replaced the parasitized agents' belief regarding the current capacity with a lower one, common to all behaviosites. Since capacity information was kept as the private history of the agent, this decrease was also considered in future rounds by the agent. If a parasitized agent decided to attend the bar and the number of attending agents was higher than the capacity the agent currently believed, it suffered a utility decrease, even if the bar was actually undercrowded. This was intended to enforce a stricter approach; agents were affected by the world according to their personal beliefs, and not according to some global truth.

3.3   Parasitized El Farol Simulation Results

The parasitized El Farol problem was simulated for 2000 rounds, assuming 100 agents in the system. Three different capacities were tested: 50, 60, and 80, where the behaviosite manipulation strategy was to decrease capacity for parasitized agents (50 decreased to 40, 60 also decreased to 40, and 80 decreased to 60). For each such capacity, three different environment infection strategies were tested, as mentioned above: *infect all*, *infect attending*, and *infect overcrowded*, giving a total of 9 different simulations. For each of the 9 simulations, a different percentage of the agents who were candidates for infection were actually infected, with infection rates ranging from 0% to 100% with jumps of 10% (total of 11 different simulations for each). Each of these 99 different simulations was repeated 50 times.

Mean Attendance. As was mentioned above, agents' mean attendance in the El Farol problem converges to the capacity of the bar. In the parasitized El Farol problem, we would like to increase the social utility, without lowering by too much the mean attendance. From the bar owner's point of view, this is one of the most important parameters. From a social utility point of view, decreased mean attendance takes us further away from an optimal solution.

---

[4] Another possible design is that the entire infection strategy is a property of the behaviosite, but this was not implemented.

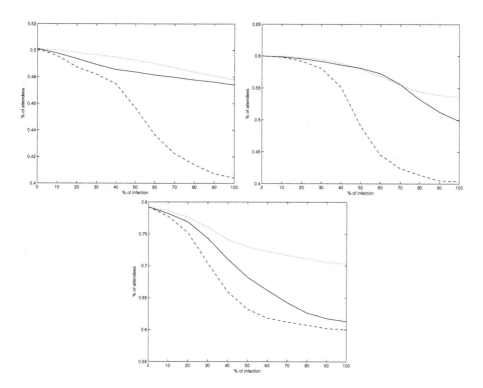

Fig. 4. Mean attendance for capacities of 50, 60, 80, respectively. Legend: .... :Infect All, —:Infect Attending, - - - :Infect Overcrowded.

Figure 4 shows how different infection strategies affected the mean attendance. For all three different capacities, the *infect all* strategy decreased the mean attendance severely, as a function of the behaviosites' infection rate. For 100% infection rate of potential agents (in this case, all agents), the system converged to the capacity induced by the behaviosites. For example, for capacity of 60, infection rate of 100% of course resulted in convergence to 40, since the behaviosites' manipulation strategy is to make the host believe that the capacity is 40.

The *infect overcrowded* strategy resulted in a relatively low effect on the mean attendance, since behaviosites infect agents only in a most particular situation — only attendees, and only when the bar is overcrowded. The outcome of the *infect attending* strategy depended on the bar's capacity. For capacity of 80, the *infect all* and *infect attending* strategies yielded very similar results, since most of the agents are candidates for infection. For the capacities of 50 and 60, *infect attending* strategy's effect resembles the *infect overcrowded* strategy, since it affects only a relatively small portion of the agent society.

Mean Utility. The main objective in the parasitized El Farol problem simulation was to show that it is possible to increase social utility using behaviosites.

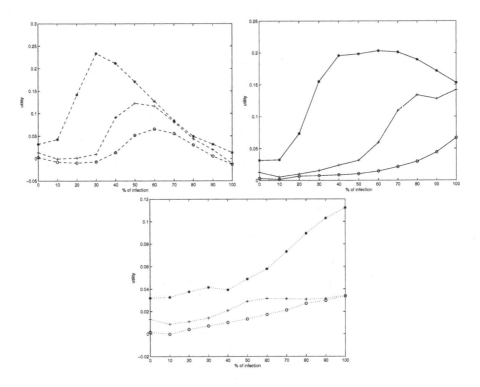

Fig. 5. Mean utility for Infect All, Infect Attending, Infect Overcrowded strategies, respectively. Capacity legend: o–o: 50, +–+:60, *–*:80.

This can be seen clearly in Figure 5, which compares the effect of different capacities for each strategy. Another goal, with roughly the same importance, was not to cause too much harm to the system, namely social injustice, which will be discussed later.

infect all: Infecting all agents resulted in a similar graph shape for all three capacities, differing in the position of the peak, with impressive improvement of mean utility. For capacities of 60 and 80 the improvement was 7–9 times the minimal received in a system without behaviosites, and relatively close to the optimal (0.12 utility out of possible 0.3 for capacity of 60, and 0.23 utility out of possible 0.4 for capacity of 80). For capacity of 50, improvement was 27 times the minimal, though still near zero (0.065 out of possible 0.25).

infect overcrowded: For all three different capacities, the mean utility increase was moderate, with respect to other strategies. For capacities of 60 and 80, the maximal mean utility was about 2.5–3.5 times the minimal mean utility, received by a system with no behaviosites. For the capacity of 50, the maximal mean utility was 22 times better than the minimal mean utility received for a system with no behaviosites, but still near zero (0.034). For capacity of 80, the

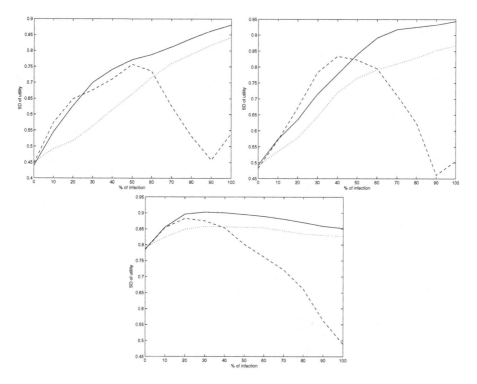

Fig. 6. System's fairness for capacities of 50, 60, 80, respectively. Legend: - - - :Infect All, —:Infect Attending, ... :Infect Overcrowded.

maximal mean utility (0.112) was not significantly lower than the optimal possible (0.4), especially when compared to a system without behaviosites (utility of 0.032).

infect attending: The outcome of this strategy depended heavily on the level of the used capacity. For high capacities (specifically 80), the strategy's behavior was very much like *infect all*, because infecting all attending agents is very much like infecting all agents. For low capacities (specifically 50), the strategy's outcome was very much like *infect overcrowded*, because it affected only a relatively small portion of the society, and the actual effect of the behaviosite was mild. In between (specifically 60), the behavior of this strategy combined features of both.

Forced Justice. As was described earlier, two previous attempts to increase social utility resulted in two proposed solutions, both with undesirable features in certain settings. One feature was the need to charge utility from attending agents [7], which basically kept the social utility within the system. Another led to the creation of bullies [15] — regulars and casuals. In the original El Farol problem, the membership of the agents kept changing, thus keeping some level of social fairness. Social fairness is an important parameter when characterizing

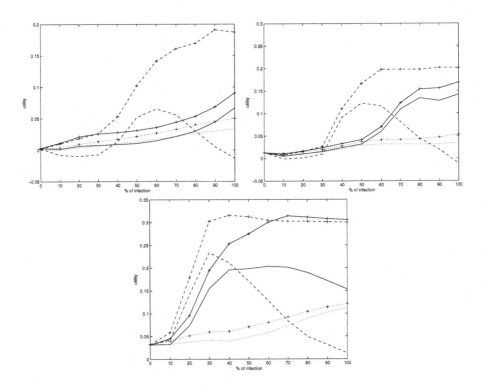

Fig. 7. Mean utility with and without harming behaviosites for capacities of 50, 60, 80, respectively. Legend: - - - :Infect All, —:Infect Attending, ... :Infect Overcrowded. + is for behaviosites that do not cause harm.

the effect of behaviosites on the system, since we do not wish to create regulars and casuals. This is especially true if agents are self-interested, and have no prior incentive to allow behaviosites to infect and affect them. Social fairness was calculated by the following formula:

$$1 - \frac{1}{\#trials} \sum_{t \in trials} \frac{Personal \ \ Attendance \ \ SD[t]}{Mean \ \ Attendence[t]}$$

Social fairness is captured by the mean of standard deviation, normalized according to the mean of a specific iteration. In Figure 6, we can see that for capacities of 50 and 60, *infect attending* and *infect overcrowded* strategies constantly increase the social fairness as a function of infection rate. For capacity of 80, they improved social fairness only a small amount, since already the vast majority of agents go to the bar. However, the *infect all* strategy increased social fairness as a function of infection rate until a certain maximum was reached, and then decreased again. For capacity of 80, it reached exactly the level of social fairness of capacity 60, as would be expected.

Cost of Manipulation. In the specific design of this parasitized El Farol problem, behaviosites caused actual damage to the received utility of agents. If an agent came to an undercrowded bar, but believed it was overcrowded, it would suffer utility loss that unparasitized agents would not — thus imposing a cost upon agents. From the Designer Perspective, behaviosites in the parasitized El Farol problem have several types of costs — run time, integration time of behaviosites, and testing time of various infection and manipulation strategies.

Reflections About Design. The behaviosite in the parasitized El Farol problem presented above is an example of an internal behaviosite, in a system designed to accommodate behaviosites. However, it is also possible to create an external behaviosite, one that the agents need know nothing about. The behaviosite can reside in the interface between the environment and the agent (Figure 2a). Parasitized agents can receive manipulated information from the environment regarding the current capacity, or manipulated information of number of attendees in a specific round. The effect of such altered data should be the same as presented above, and social utility should, again, increase.

4   Related Work

4.1   Related Work in Biology

In nature, most common recorded behavior manipulations are done by parasites with a complex life cycle, as it ensures host-to-host transmission. For example, in the case of *Dicrocoelium* [16], parasitized ants' behavior (the upstream hosts) is modified so that they crawl up grass stalks, thus improving chances of being ingested by a passing cow (the downstream host). Although most parasite manipulations are harmful to the host, there are examples in which parasites are beneficial, either to the host or to the society.

Increasing the fitness of the hosts' society can usually be seen in the case of close kin, such as ants or bees. Bumblebees have successfully mastered the use of parasite-induced altered behavior to their own advantage [17]. A parasitized worker bee prolongs its life span by changing its behavior and staying in the cold of night at the field (the cold retarded parasitoid development). This way, the entire colony benefits from this infection, due to increased foraging.

4.2   Related Work in Computer Science

The term "parasite" is used in various contexts in the computer science literature. However, in each context its meaning is substantially different from its use in the Behaviosite paradigm. Host-parasite paradigm in computer science previously existed in three main roles: for simulations of evolution such as Ray's Tierra computer program [18], as a driving force in genetic algorithms (usually in the context of predator-prey and co-evolution [19]), and as malware in the electronic world. None talked about using parasites to change the behavior of individual agents, to shift the equilibrium of the entire society.

In their work, Mamei, Roli and Zambonelli [20] presented an idea closely related to that of the Behaviosite Paradigm, within the context of cellular automata. They presented a method for controlling the global behavior of cellular automata using local influences. In their approach, a subset of the cellular array was selected on which to introduce a beneficial signal, either compatible or destructive of some global pattern. This signal was then diffused within the cellular system due to asynchronous time lines and globally effective random perturbation. The Behaviosite Paradigm can be viewed as having a similar structure — behaviosites infect an agent (with an infection strategy more sophisticated than just perturbation), and change its output behavior (the "special" cellular automata). However, Behaviosites' effect is local in time and space, in contrast to what is discussed in [20]. The former also do not rely on an existing diffusion effect, but rather rely on their mobility and infection strategies to seek key control points.

Computer Agents' Behavior. Behaviosites affect behavior, but what constitutes "behavior", both the agent's and the system's, is quite difficult to define; there are numerous ways of approaching the issue. Two of the most common are logic-based behavior and Brooks' [10,21] emergent behavior and subsumption architecture. Behavior is considered as an aspect of the individual agent, of an agent in a society, and of the whole society. Much research explores the creation of agents with defined behavior, or analyzes an existing system's behavior. For our purposes, we do not attempt to define exactly what behavior is, but rather use Brooks' view, that behavior results from the agent's interaction with the environment.

5   Discussion and Future Work

In this paper, we presented the Behaviosite paradigm in the spirit of biomimetics — parasites manipulating their hosts' behavior. Although the term "parasite" is not new in computer science, it has been used in different contexts than the Behaviosite paradigm describes. We specified the behaviosite concept, which in essence is a special type of agent, which infects and manipulates other agents to achieve altered performance of the system. We described the parasitized El Farol problem, and showed that social and personal utilities and social fairness can be increased using behaviosites; in some cases, mean attendance deviates from the capacity by only a small amount.

The behaviosites used were internal behaviosites with a fixed, unchanging influence over the agents (though it is equally possible to use external behaviosites, or those with dynamic influence). The parasitized El Farol problem simulated self-interested agents. However, behaviosites could also be integrated into a cooperative society to form new norms or social laws, or to eliminate ill-functioning agents.

In our view, the major contribution of the Behaviosite paradigm is conceptual — thinking of a system composed of environment and agents as whole, something that can be manipulated using external forces (behaviosites) that employ local changes (affecting agents' individual behaviors) to bring about altered behavior of the entire system. However, as users of this paradigm, we do not consider ourselves omnipotent — we just use existing capabilities of the (possibly self-interested) agents and environment. Hence this is not simply mechanism design, but rather augmenting the system, or parasitizing it. It also differs from existing research in adjustable autonomy, because of this holistic view, which AA is lacking.

After understanding what the Behaviosite paradigm is, one might wonder if the term "parasite" is appropriate. There are, indeed, significant differences. The behaviosite is not an autonomous agent in and of itself. Moreover, in nature the utility gain of behavior manipulation is of the parasite, and not the host; is it not an important part of being a parasite? However, we intend parasitic activity to be a metaphor, and need not require an exact match between nature and behaviosites. The key analogy is the fact that behaviosite actions constitute behavior manipulation of the host.

Behaviosites are not just a way of propagating false information within a system. The intimacy of agent-behaviosite induces far more powerful effects. Lies can be disregarded or overcome by agents. However, when a host is parasitized, the behaviosite is considered an almost integral part of the agent. Agents can doubt external information, but rely on their internal beliefs — as was shown in the parasitized El Farol problem, not acting on the basis of personal belief did not help "shake" the influence of the behaviosite.

As with the agent metaphor itself, the Behaviosite paradigm can be very appealing, but could also conceivably be overused. It is certainly the case that it is possible to use solutions other than behaviosites — behavioral change can be entirely inside the agent (e.g., random coin flips inside agents in the El Farol problem, with strategies similar to the ones applied by the behaviosites), or it can be totally a property of the environment. The analogy with agents is clear, for although sometimes an agent-like approach is inappropriate (and solutions can theoretically always be engineered in other ways), the key question is "what is the best solution?". In some cases, the Behaviosite paradigm presents conceptual advantages.

In the future, we would like to further strengthen the Behaviosite paradigm by showing it is applicable and desirable in other scenarios. One example is using external behaviosites in an already-built real-time environment, namely the internet, for dealing with the packet congestion problem. The solution should be similar to that of the parasitized El Farol problem with some modifications. Another application is the automatic generation of stories; it is a rapidly growing field, with high potential in the gamer community. Behaviosites are an excellent solution for altering stories by changing some of the characters' behavior and adding new, unpredictable system behavior in a distributed manner.

Acknowledgment

This work was partially supported by Israel Science Foundation grant #039-7582.

References

1. Vincent, J.F.V., Mann, D.L.: Systematic technology transfer from biology to engineering. Phil. Trans. R. Soc. Lond. A **360**(1791) (2002) 159–174
2. Menciassi, A., Dario, P.: Bio-inspired solutions for locomotion in the gastrointestinal tract: background and perspectives. Phil. Trans. R. Soc. Lond. A **361**(1811) (2003) 2287–2298
3. Miller, J.H.: The critic as host. Critical Inquiry **3**(3) (1977) 439–447
4. Nickles, M., Rovatsos, M., Weiss, G., eds.: Post-proceedings of the First International Workshop on Computational Autonomy — Potential, Risks, Solutions. In Nickles, M., Rovatsos, M., Weiss, G., eds.: Agents and Computational Autonomy. Volume 2969 of Lecture Notes in Computer Sciences., Springer-Verlag (2003)
5. Scerri, P., Pynadath, D.V., Tambe, M.: Towards adjustable autonomy for the real world. Journal of Artificial Intelligence Research **17** (2002) 171–228
6. Arthur, W.B.: Inductive reasoning and bounded rationality (the El Farol problem). Amer. Econ. Review **84**(406) (1994)
7. Grace Hopper Celebration of Women in Computing: Fair and Efficient Solutions to the Santa Fe Bar Problem, Grace Hopper Celebration of Women in Computing, A. Greenwald, J. Farago and K. Hall (2002)
8. Weiss, G.: Multiagent systems: A modern introduction to distributed artificial intelligence. MIT Press (1999)
9. Franklin, S., Graesser, A., eds.: Is it an agent, or just a program?: A taxonomy for autonomous agents. (1996) In Proceedings of the Third International Workshop on Agent Theories, Architectures, and Languages.
10. Brooks, R.A.: Intelligence without reason. In: Proceedings of the 12th International Joint Conference on Artificial Intelligence, Sydney, Australia (1991) 569–595
11. Gamma, E., Helm, R., Johnson, R., Vlissides, J.: Design Patterns: Elements of Reusable Object-Oriented Software. Addison-Wesley Professional Computing Series (1994)
12. Greenwald, A., Mishra, B., Parikh, R.: The Santa Fe Bar problem revisited: Theoretical and practical implications. Festival on Game Theory: Interactive Dynamics and Learning, SUNY Stony Brook (1998)
13. Moro, E.: The minority game: an introductory guide. Advances in Condensed Matter and Statistical Physics (2004)
14. Edmunds, B.: Gossip, sexual recombination and the El Farol Bar: Modelling the emergence of heterogenety. Journal of Artificial Societies and Social Simulation (1999)
15. Bell, A.M., Sethares, W.A.: The El Farol problem and the internet: Congestion and coordination failure. Computing in Economics and Finance 1999 812, Society for Computational Economics (1999)
16. Poulin, R.: Evolutionary Ecology of Parasites — From individuals to communities. Springer (1997)
17. Muller, C.B., Schmid-Hempel, P.: Exploitation of cold temperature as defense against parasitoids in bumblebees. Nature **363** (1993) 65–67
18. Ray, T.: Tierra. http://www.his.atr.jp/ ray/tierra (1990)
19. Hillis, W.D.: Co-evolving parasites improve simulated evolution as an optimization procedure. Artificial Life II (1992)
20. Mamei, M., Roli, A., Zambonelli, F.: Emergence and control of macro-spatial structures in perturbed cellular automata, and implications for pervasive computing systems. IEEE Transactions on Systems, Man, and Cybernetics, Part A: Systems and Humans **35**(3) (2005) 337–348
21. Brooks, R.A.: Intelligence without representation. Artificial Intelligence **47** (1991) 139–159

Programming Modular Robots with the TOTA Middleware

Marco Mamei and Franco Zambonelli

Dipartimento di Scienze e Metodi dell'Ingegneria,
University of Modena and Reggio Emilia
Via Allegri 13, 42100 Reggio Emilia, Italy
{mamei.marco,franco.zambonelli}@unimore.it

Abstract. Modular robots represent a perfect application scenario for multiagent coordination. The autonomous modules composing the robot must coordinate their respective activities to enforce a specific global shape or a coherent motion gait. Here we show how the TOTA ("Tuples On The Air") middleware can be effectively exploited to support agents' coordination in this context. The key idea in TOTA is to rely on spatially distributed tuples, spread across the robot, to guide the agents' activities in moving and reshaping the robot. Three simulated examples are presented to support our claims.

1 Introduction

A modular (or self-reconfigurable) robot is a flexible robot made up of a collection of (typically simple) autonomous elements connected with each other with some degree of freedom in their relative movements [1,2,3,4,5,6].

The key idea underlying a modular robot is to have its components execute distributed control algorithms so as to coordinate their actions and let the robot assume a specific shape or move according to some specific motion pattern (i.e., gait).

The flexibility of modular robots is highly desirable for tasks to be performed in hostile environments, such as fire fighting, search and rescue after an earthquake, and battlefield reconnaissance [7,8,9,10]. In these cases, robots can encounter unexpected situations and obstacles, hard to overcome for fixed-shape monolithic robots. A modular robot, instead, could shape itself depending on needs. For example, to pass through a hole, the robot can transform itself into a sort of snake; to move through a downhill slope, it can assume a circular shape and roll; to enter a room through a closed door, a modular robot may disassemble itself into a set of smaller units, crawl under the door, and then reassemble itself in the room.

Modular robots represent a perfect application scenario for multiagent systems. On the one hand, the modules constituting the modular robot should be autonomous and running agent applications. This, in fact, avoids single point of failure and bottlenecks. If one module breaks down the other can reorganize

S. Brueckner et al. (Eds.): ESOA 2006, LNAI 4335, pp. 99–114, 2007.

their activities leaving the broken element behind. Autonomy enables also disconnected operations: modules can disassemble, move along different paths and reassemble subsequently. On the other hand, the main task the modules have to undertake is *coordination*. The agents governing the modules must coordinate their respective activities to enforce a specific global shape or a coherent motion gait in the whole robot (i.e., multiagent system).

For the purpose of supporting agent coordination, in our research, we developed a general middleware called "Tuples On The Air" (TOTA). TOTA supports the creation of distributed overlay data structures spread across a distributed network. Up to now, TOTA has been proved useful in developing a number of multiagent applications in distributed computing systems including: motion coordination in pervasive computing scenarios, on-demand routing protocols in MANET, P2P protocols and swarm intelligence algorithms [11,12]. Implementing all these applications becomes relatively simple when suitable overlay data structures can be spread across the network to guide agents' coordination activities.

In this paper, we want to further test the TOTA's generality by implementing some advanced mechanisms required for the control of a modular robot. In particular, our goal is to show that TOTA enables to easily and flexibly express and program biologically-inspired control algorithms (i.e. hormone-based [5]) for modular robots' coordination.

The rest of the paper is organized as follows. Section 2 briefly presents the main concepts at the core of the TOTA middleware and its programming model. Section 3 focuses on a specific hormone-based approach to control modular robots (as adopted by [5]) and shows how it can be implemented by means of the TOTA middleware. Moreover, we explain the advantages of our implementation and discuss some related works. Section 4 presents three examples of modular robot's coordination using TOTA. The examples have been implemented on the Polybot modular robot simulator [4]. Finally, Section 5 presents some concluding remarks.

2   The Tuples on the Air Approach

TOTA is a general-purpose middleware for multiagent coordination, in distributed computing scenarios [12]. In TOTA we assume the presence of a network of possibly mobile nodes, each running an agent application. Each agent is supported by a local version of the TOTA middleware. Nodes are connected by only short-range network links; there are not long backbones in the network. Each agent has only a local (one-hop) perception of its environment. Long range interactions must be mediated by other agents. Upon the distributed space identified by the dynamic network of TOTA nodes, each agent is capable of locally storing tuples [13] and letting them diffuse through the network. Tuples are injected in the system from a particular node, and spread hop-by-hop accordingly to a specified propagation rule (see Figure 1(top)). In the modular robot scenario, this reflects in having each agent installed in a module of the robot. The

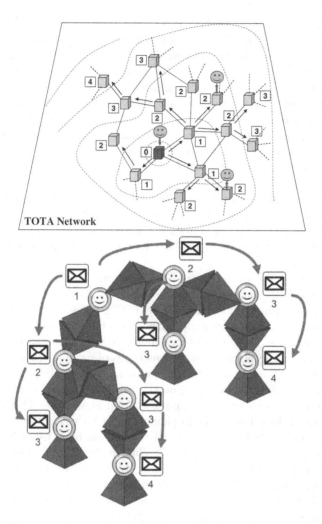

Fig. 1. (top) The general scenario of TOTA: application components live in an environment in which they can inject autonomously propagating tuples and sense tuples present in their local neighborhood. The environment is realized by means of a peer-to-peer network in which tuples propagates by means of a multi-hop mechanism. (bottom) TOTA in modular robots.

modules (and thus the agents) are connected according to the topology of the robot. Tuples are injected and propagate across the robot's body (see Figure 1(bottom)).

In TOTA, distributed tuples $\mathbf{T}=(\mathbf{C},\mathbf{P},\mathbf{M})$ are characterized by a content $\mathbf{C}$, a propagation rule $\mathbf{P}$ and a maintenance rule $\mathbf{M}$. The content $\mathbf{C}$ is an ordered set of typed fields representing the information carried on by the tuple. The propagation rule $\mathbf{P}$ determines how the tuple should be distributed and propagated in the network. This includes determining the "scope" of the tuple (i.e. the distance at which such tuple should be propagated and possibly the spatial direction of propagation) and how such propagation can be affected by the presence or the absence of other tuples in the system. In addition, the propagation rules can determine how tuple content should change while it is propagated to actually create distributed data structures. The maintenance rule **M** determines how a tuple's distributed structure should react to events occurring in the environment. For instance, when new nodes get in touch with a network, TOTA automatically checks the propagation rules of the already stored tuples and eventually propagates the tuples to the new nodes. Similarly, when the topology changes due to nodes' movements, the distributed tuple structure changes to reflect the new topology.

From the application components' point of view, executing and interacting basically reduces to define and inject tuples in the network (*inject* method) and to read local (*read* method) and one-hop neighbor (*readOneHop* method) tuples via a pattern-matching mechanism. TOTA provides a compact API to perform these operations.

We developed a first prototype of TOTA running on Linux IPAQs equipped with 802.11b WLAN and Java (J2ME, CDC, Personal profile). Moreover, we have implemented an emulator to analyze TOTA behavior in presence of hundreds of nodes [11]. To perform experiments with modular robots, we connected our TOTA simulator with the Polybot modular robot simulator [4]. This program can simulate the behavior of various types of modular robots, taking into account both the characteristics of the joints connecting different parts of the robot and the physical forces acting on the robot (e.g., gravitation), and offers a 3D view of the robot's actual configuration and movements. Distributed algorithms to control the robot can be implemented with this simulator. Specifically, each module of the robot is provided with an API enabling us to drive the module actuator, and to sample and possibly change the way in which the robot is connected to the other modules. To connect this simulator with the TOTA one, we created an object having access both to the TOTA API and to the modular robot API. This object "runs," at the same time, in the TOTA simulator and in the modular robot simulator, connecting the two.

3   Multiagent Coordination in Modular Robots

From a multiagent perspective, the main challenge in modular robots is the design of decentralized coordination mechanisms enabling autonomous agents (i.e., modules) to coordinate their actions to achieve a specific global shape, or a specific motion gait. Some of the most innovative approaches to control a modular robot adopt the biologically inspired idea of hormones. These approaches have been used to control the CONRO modular robot and directly inspired our work [5]. Hormone signals are actually sort of messages, spread across the robot and triggering the individual actuator's bending. For example, a "head" module in a modular robot (see later for details) can inject in the robot a sequence of hormone signals. All the other modules can be programmed to react to the income of such signals by bending their actuator by a specified angle. A motion gait would be encoded by means of a specific sequence of hormones to be injected in the robot and by means of specific reactions triggered by these hormones, changing the bending angles.

The idea of hormones is a perfect match for TOTA distributed tuples and our approach has been to re-implement hormones with the support of our middleware. With this regard, it is fair to remark that we do not propose a novel approach for modular robot coordination. We just take advantage of the TOTA middleware to implement (with some changes) the hormone-based approach [5]. In particular, the main subject of our research has been the chain-type modular robot. This kind of robots is characterized by the fact modules are connected in a line configuration (e.g., snake-like), or - eventually - in a tree-like configuration (e.g., robot with legs), see the figures in next pages. In our experiments, we assumed that the robot is composed of very simple equal modules (i.e., joint actuators). Each module has a "front" side and a "back" side. On each side there are two docking points and an infrared network link. The two docking points enable a module to physically connect with other ones. This is of course fundamental to actually building the chain constituting the modular robot. The infrared (IR) link enables communication between connected modules (see Figure 3). Modules connect by their IR links in a network, resembling the robot topology.

Each module runs the TOTA middleware and an agent in charge of driving the module joint. The agent, looking at the active IR links, is able to infer whether it is the "head," the "tail," or a part of the "body" of the robot. Specifically, the "head" agent is the one with only the back IR link active, the "tail" agent is the one with only the front IR link active, a "body" agent is one having both the IR links active. The process of assessing whether an IR link is active or not can be based on "ping" messages and can be executed iteratively to take into account topological reconfigurations and module breakdown.

From a methodology point of view and in very general terms, the proposed approach consists in codifying a motion gait by means of a *Gait* tuple. Such a tuple has the structure depicted in Figure 2. Once this tuple is injected in the modular robot, it propagates hop by hop across all the modules changing its content to the desired gait. For the upcoming discussion – where we will present concrete code samples – it is important to remark that the, in TOTA, tuples are implemented by means of objects. The TOTA middleware executes the tuple's methods to "animate" it. In particular the *changeTupleContent* method allows a tuple to change its content and the *move* method actually propagate the tuple to neighbor nodes where it will be executed again.

When an agent installed on a module senses the income of a tuple of this kind, it reacts by bending the module joint by the angle specified in the tuple. So, for example, if in a robot composed of N modules a tuple having in its content a fixed angle of about $(360/N)°$ is spread, the robot closes into a loop. More specifically, the presented approach (that is strongly inspired by [5]) is based on the following key points.

Abstract GaitTuple
C = (id, angle)
P = (propagate hop-by-hop, changing the content so as to encode in the "angle"-distributed data structure the shape the robot has to assume)
M = (if the network topology changes, restart propagation according to new head, body and tail position)

Fig. 2. Structure of the abstract *GaitTuple*. This tuple encodes in its distributed shape (i.e., angle field values) the form we want the robot to assume.

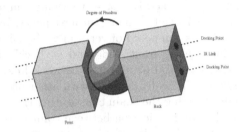

Fig. 3. A single module composing the modular robot. In our research we focus on simple module having just two docking points and two IR network links one for each side (front and back) of the module.

1. The head agent injects in the network (i.e., in the robot modules) a specific GaitTuple, representing the shape (or a step of the gait) the robot has to assume.
2. The tuple propagates from the head to the tail letting the robot bend accordingly.
3. When the tail receives the tuple, it injects another tuple (with constant value) for the purpose of notifying the head that the Gait Tuple completed its travel.
4. When the head receives the above constant tuple it can inject another *Gait-Tuple* implementing the second configuration the robot has to assume (i.e., second step in a motion gait). Or, alternatively, the constant tuple can automatically trigger a change in the content of the *GaitTuple* to let the robot assume the second configuration.
5. The process continues iteratively.

3.1   Related Approaches

As already introduced, the research on CONRO modular robot [5] directly inspired our experiments. However, the control mechanism, based on TOTA, extends the original hormone-based approach. TOTA tuples are active data structures and can change while being stored in the modular robot. Thus, even a complex gait can be obtained by using just one TOTA tuple that changes to let the robot assume different configurations. On the contrary original hormones are passive and modules have to use several hormones to create a single gait.

In another research [2], each module of the modular robot runs a simple finite state automaton in which state transitions are driven by the local state, the state of neighbor modules, their locations, and some external information. Communications are limited to the immediate neighborhood and a limited number of bits are exchanged at each time step. The goal is not to create an exact predefined shape, but a structure with the correct properties (structural, morphological, etc.). Any stable "emergent" structure that exhibits the desired properties is considered satisfactory, with no regard for the "optimality" or details of the resulting geometry. This approach is very similar to ours, although our goal is to actually create engineered shapes and gaits, and not just purely emergent ones. The works [14,3] goes further and introduces a compiler to automatically derive local rules from an high-level shape description.

The research in [15,6] presents an interesting approach oriented toward self-reconfiguration and shape formation. In this approach, the desired configuration is grown from an initial seed agent. The initial seed produces growth by creating a gradient (similar to a TOTA distributed tuple), which attracts other agents. Once positioned, the agents become seed to let the shape grow again. The growth is guided by a representation of the desired configuration, which can be automatically generated from a 3D CAD model. Although very powerful, this approach focuses on shape formation and almost disregards gait coordination. Moreover, the approach assumes the presence of individual modules, more complex than the ones presented here.

Another thread of research, in modular robots, involves conceptually centralized control mechanisms [16]. In these approaches, a control table, specifying how each module must bend its actuator, is compiled off-line and then uploaded into the modules. The main advantage of this approach is that it allows us to design even complex motion gaits rather easily. The main drawback is that the control table is built for a specific robot configuration, and if the robot changes (e.g., new modules get connected), the table must be rebuilt from scratch. The research in this area is mainly oriented to devising new languages to build the control table. One of the most advanced proposals is PARSL (Phase Automata Robot Scripting Language) [4]. PARSL is a scripting language based on XML syntax, designed to express motion gaits for chain-type modular robots. In PARSL it is possible to design a motion gait by means of abstract "waves of activity" traveling across the robot. Such high-level description is then automatically compiled to create the control table.

4   Experiments

In the rest of this section we will use TOTA to support three motion gaits in modular robot: the "caterpillar gait" (that lets the robot proceed by mimicking the motion of a snake) and the "rolling gait" (that lets the robot close in a loop,

---

CaterpillarGait Tuple
C = (state, angle)
P = (propagate hop-by-hop, storing on intermediate nodes changing the content accordingly to the table in Figure 5)
M = (If on the head node and upon the receipt of a gait-tuple, re-apply propagation)

Fig. 4. The structure of the *CaterpillarGaitTuple* tuple

Current State	New State	New Angle
INIT	A	$+45°$
A	B	$+45°$
B	C	$-45°$
C	D	$-45°$
D	A	$+45°$

Fig. 5. This table shows how the content of the *CaterpillarGaitTuple* changes

and then roll). Finally, we will present a gait for legged robots where agents coordinate legs' movements to proceed forward. It is worth noting that while the mechanisms underlying the former two gaits are well known in modular robot research [5,16], the latter one has been designed from scratch.

4.1 Caterpillar Gait

To implement the caterpillar gait, the head agent starts the movement by injecting a caterpillar tuple (i.e., a TOTA tuple of the class *CaterpillarGaitTuple*). The general structure of such a tuple is depicted in Figure 4, it propagates across the robot letting it bend accordingly. Once the tail agent receives the tuple, according to the general description given above, it injects another tuple to notify the head that a new step is ready to be executed. At this point, the head agent updates the *Caterpillar GaitTuple* accordingly to the Table 5 and injects it again. Once spread, this tuple lets the gait proceed by another step. Useful insights to understand how the caterpillar gait works and how the Table 5 has been compiled can be found in Figure 6. The code implementing the *CaterpillarGaitTuple* tuple can be found in Figure 7. This process is iterated letting the whole robot move performing the caterpillar gait (see Figure 8).

4.2 Rolling Gait

The idea of this gait is to let the robot close in a loop and then roll. Unfortunately, the modular robot simulator we employed does not allow structures with loops. Structures with loops are overconstrained. The simulation does not solve the constraint satisfaction problem. The simulation does not detect self-collision either. To overcome this problem, we let the robot bend in an open loop (something like a 'C' shape) and then roll. Although this complicates the rolling

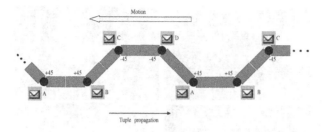

Fig. 6. The caterpillar gait works by letting a pattern of activity travel along the robot, letting it going forward

```
public class CaterpillarGaitTuple extends GaitTuple {
/* constant declaration as in caterpillar gait table */
/* tuple sates: INIT, A,B,C,D and respective angles
degA,degB,degC,degD are defined */

public int state = INIT;
public int angle = 0;

protected void changeTupleContent()
{
 switch(state)
 {
  case INIT : state = A;
              angle = degA;
              break;
  case A     : state = B;
              angle = degB;
              break;
  case B     : state = C;
              angle = degC;
              break;
  case C     : state = D;
              angle = degD;
              break;
  case D     : state = A;
              angle = degA;
              break;
 }
 }
}
```

Fig. 7. The code realizing the *CaterpillarGaitTuple* TOTA class

procedure, it allows us to maintain the general approach described before. In fact, we still have a "head" and a "tail" agent that would be otherwise removed if the loop were actually closed (i.e., with only "body" agents). The *RollingGait-Tuple* is the tuple employed to let the robot roll. In general terms, it can have two states, T (turn) and F (flat). Consider, for example, a robot composed of 12 modules and assuming a turning angle of 45°. A tuple spread in the robot with a distributed shape like "FTTFTTFTTFTT" (see Figure 9) closes in a loop. Then, if the tuple changes its content by "rolling" the above string (like the ROL assembler command), the robot performs the rolling gait. From the single tuple point of view, this consists in changing its content to assume values

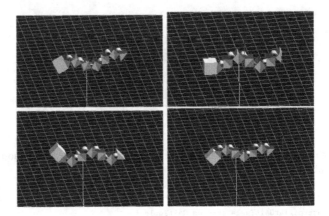

Fig. 8. Some stages of a caterpillar gait, in a chain-typed modular robot, composed of six actuators

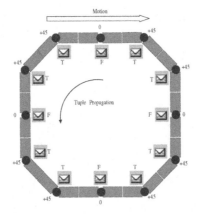

Fig. 9. In the rolling gait, the robot moves in one direction by shifting the turning modules (T) to the opposite direction

---

Rolling Gait Tuple

C = (state, angle)

P = (propagate hop-by-hop, cycling between the states F - T - T. Set the angle to 45deg if the state is T. Set the angle to 0 if the state is F)

M = (if the network topology changes, restart propagation according to new head, body and tail position)

Fig. 10. The rolling gait tuple

```
public class RollingGaitTuple extends GaitTuple {
// number of modules composing the robot
private static final int N_MODULES;
// number of turning points
private static final int N_TURNS;
// radius of the turn
private static final int RADIUS ;
// turning angle in deg
private static final int TURN;

public int state = 0;
public int angle = 0;

protected void changeTupleContent()
{
  if(this.getSourceFromId().equals(tota.toString()))
    state = (state + 1)% N_MODULES;

  int mod = Integer.parseInt(tota.toString().substring(1));

  boolean cond = false;
  for(int i=0;i<N_TURNS;i++)
  {
    boolean cond1 =
    ((state+(i*N_MODULES)/N_TURNS) % N_MODULES) == mod;
    boolean cond2 =
    ((state+(i*N_MODULES)/N_TURNS) % N_MODULES) ==
    ((mod + RADIUS)% N_MODULES);
    if(cond1 || cond2)
    {
      cond = true;
      break;
    }
  }

  if(cond)
    angle = TURN;
  else
    angle = 0;
}
}
```

Fig. 11. The code realizing the *RollingGaitTuple* TOTA class

F - T - T iteratively. It is worth noting that such a kind of content change critically depends on the number of modules composing the robot and the number of turns we want to implement to let the robot close in a loop. For example, three turns of 60° each create a triangular track, four turns of 90° each create a rectangular track, etc. Moreover, it depends on the number of modules involved in each turn. For example, in Figure 9, two modules bend by 45° to create a 90° turn. Despite all these parameters, it is rather easy to build a general algorithm enabling a tuple to create dynamically, at runtime, the sequence of F and T states it has to cycle (e.g., F - T - T) to enable the rolling gait. A general description of the *RollingGaitTuple* enabling the rolling gait in the case of a robot composed of 12 modules and assuming four turns of 90° each, split between two modules bending by 45°, is illustrated in Figure 10. The code realizing the *RollingGaitTuple* can be found in Figure 11. Some snapshots showing the rolling gait in action are in Figure 12.

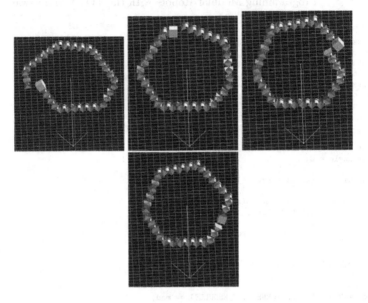

Fig. 12. Some stages of a rolling gait in a chain-typed modular robot composed of 32 actuators

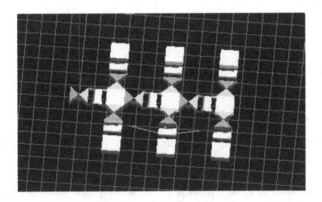

Fig. 13. A modular robot arranged in a 6-legged configuration

4.3 Walking Gait

We performed this experiment on a "legged" robot that can move by coordinating legs movements. The idea of this experiment is to have the modules of the robot connected in a 6-legs configuration (see Figure 13), and then coordinate the actions of these modules so as to let the legged robot walk. In this example, the robot is built from two types of modules (both available from the Polybot simulator): joints and connectors. Among the several possible configurations

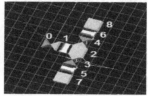

Fig. 14. (left) Detail of a robot leg. The pitch-yaw orientation between the two modules allows high flexibility. (right) Different neighbor connections allow each module to estimate its role within the robot (0 = HEAD, 1 = SPINE, 3 = LEFT-SHOULDER, 4 = RIGHT-SHOULDER, 5 = LEFT-LEG, 6 = RIGHT-LEG).

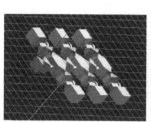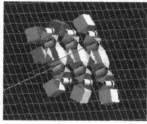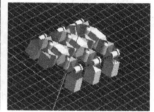

Fig. 15. A 6-legged robot stands up

```
public class StandUpTuple extends GaitTuple {

  // bend degree
  private static final int Deg = 90;
  public int angle;

  protected void changeTupleContent()
  {
    int role = (RoleTuple)tota.read(new RoleTuple()).role;
    if (role == RIGHT-LEG) angle = -Deg;
    else if (role == LEFT-LEG) angle = Deg;
    else angle = 0;
  }
}
```

Fig. 16. The code realizing the *StandUpTuple* TOTA class

upon which it is possible to build a legged robot, the one we choose presents three key advantages:

- The adopted configuration is very modular. In order to crate a robot with more legs it is sufficient to add other legs (in multiples of two) at the end of the previous robot.
- The robot is highly flexible. It can swing in pitch and yaw both the backbone and the legs.

```
public class WalkerGaitTuple extends GaitTuple {
 //states
 private static final int FORWARD = 0;
 private static final int REVERSE = 1;

 public int state = FORWARD;
 public int angle = 0;

 protected void changeTupleContent()
 {
  int role = (RoleTuple)tota.read(new RoleTuple()).role;

  if (role == RIGHT-LEG) angle = -45;
  if (role == LEFT-LEG) angle = 45;
  if (role == SPINE) angle = 0;

  if (state == FORWARD)
  {
   if (role == LEFT-SHOULDER) angle = 0;
   if (role == RIGHT-SHOULDER) angle = -45;
   state = REVERSE;
  }
  else
  {
   if (role == LEFT-SHOULDER) angle = 45;
   if (role == RIGHT-SHOULDER) angle = 0;
   state = FORWARD;
  }
 }
}
```

Fig. 17. The code realizing the *WalkerGaitTuple* TOTA class

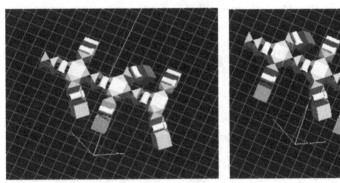

Fig. 18. The legged robot walks by coordinating legs movements

- Most importantly for the upcoming discussion, modules have a direction (front-rear) and they can distinguish both the kind of module to which the are attached (i.e., joint or connector) and the orientation of the connection (i.e., pitch-pitch, yaw-yaw, or pitch-yaw), see Figure 14(left). Thus each module can infer its position within the robot. Since connectors have no degrees of freedom – they are passive components – they do not need to localize. In particular it is possible to identify the following six important *roles* for modules: HEAD, SPINE, LEFT-SHOULDER, RIGHT-SHOULDER, LEFT-LEG, and RIGHT-LEG (see Figure 14(right)).

The robot in Figure 13 is in the rest mode. The first tuple we envisioned is the one forcing the robot to stand up (see Figure 15). The code of this *StandUpTuple* tuple (reported in Figure 16) is really simple. It basically forces all leg modules to turn 90°. More precisely, the way in which modules are connected implies that left legs should bend by 90°, while right legs by −90°. Once the robot is standing up, it can start moving the legs to proceed upward. This again is realized by letting the head of the robot inject another tuple that propagates across the modules. This *WalkerGaitTuple* tuple is very simple: it alternatively lets the left and right robot legs swing 45° forward. The code of this tuple is reported in Figure 17, while some screen-shots of the actual robot movement are presented in Figure 18.

5 Conclusions

In this paper we applied the TOTA middleware to support agents' coordination in a modular robot application scenario. As illustrated with concrete code examples, TOTA distributed tuples represent a valid abstraction to guide agents' activities. Despite the simplicity of the experiments reported in this paper, we are confident that the capability of distributed tuples (and of TOTA middleware) will have an important role in future research. However, we are also aware that the widespread exploitation of the proposed mechanisms will require the identification of proper methodologies to help designers in the development of complex applications (e.g. complex shape or articulated motion gait). In addition to that, we must also recognize that additional mechanisms – not dealt with by this paper – may also have an important role in this field. These include game-theoretic approaches [17] and cellular automata approaches [18,19]. Part of our future work is about studying how these other approaches can be integrated with ours.

Acknowledgments

Work supported by the project CASCADAS (IST-027807) funded by the FET Program of the European Commission.

References

1. Balch, T., Parker, L.: Robot Teams: From Diversity to Polymorphism. A K Peters (2002)
2. Bojinov, H., Casal, A., Hogg, T.: Emergent structures in modular self-reconfigurable robots. In: Proceedings of the Intlernational Conference on Robotics and Automation. IEEE CS Press, San Francisco, California, USA (2000)
3. Jones, C., Mataric, M.: From local to global behavior in intelligent self-assembly. In: Proceedings of the Conference on Robotics and Automation. IEEE Press, Taipei, Taiwan (2003)

4. Modular Reconfigurable Robotics at PARC:
   http://www2.parc.com/spl/projects/modrobots ( )
5. Shen, W., Salemi, B., Will, P.: Hormone-inspired adaptive communication and distributed control for conro self-reconfigurable robots. IEEE Transactions on Robotics and Automation **18** (2002) 1 – 12
6. Stoy, K., Nagpal, R.: Self-reconfiguration using directed growth. In: 7th International Symposium on Distributed Autonomous Robotic Systems. Springer-Verlag, Toulouse, France (2004)
7. Noda, I., Takahashi, T., Morita, S., Koto, T., Tadokoro, S.: Language design for rescue agents. In Tanabe, M., van den Besselaar, P., Ishida, T., eds.: Digital Cities II. Springer (2002) 371–383
8. Rybski, P., Stoeter, S., Papanikolopoulos, N., Burt, I., Dahlin, T., Gini, M., Hougen, D.F., Krantz, D.G., Nageotte, F.: Sharing control: Presenting a framework for the operation and coordination of multiple miniature robots. Robotics and Automation Magazine **9** (2002) 41 – 48
9. Svennebring, J., Koenig, S.: Building terrain-covering ant robots. Autonomous Robots **16** (2004) 313 – 332
10. Tambe, M., Bowring, E., Jung, H., Kaminka, G., Maheswaran, R., Marecki, J., Modi, P., Nair, R., Okamoto, S., Pearce, J., Paruchuri, P., Pynadath, D., Scerri, P., Schurr, N., Varakantham, P.: Conflicts in teamwork: Hybrids to the rescue. In: Proceedings of the International Conference on Autonomous Agents and Multi-Agent Systems. ACM Press, Utrecht, Netherlands (2005) 415 – 422
11. Mamei, M., Zambonelli, F.: Programming pervasive and mobile computing applications with the tota middleware. In: Proceedings of the International Conference On Pervasive Computing (Percom). IEEE CS Press, Orlando, Florida, USA (2004)
12. Mamei, M., Zambonelli, F.: Programming stigmergic coordination with the tota middleware. In: Proceedings of the International Conference on Autonomous Agents and Multi-Agent Systems. ACM Press, Utrecht, Netherlands (2005) 415 – 422
13. Gelernter, D., N.Carriero: Coordination languages and their significance. Communication of the ACM **35** (1992) 96 – 107
14. Butler, Z., Kotay, K., Rus, D., Tomita, K.: Generic decentralized locomotion control for lattice-based self-reconfigurable robots. International Journal of Robotics Research **23** (2004) 919 – 938
15. Nagpal, R., Kondacs, A., Chang, C.: Programming methodology for biologically-inspired self-assembling systems. In: Proceedings of the Spring Symposium on Computational Synthesis. AAAI Press, Stanford, California, USA (2003)
16. Yim, M., Zhang, Y., Duff, D.: Modular robots. IEEE Spectrum (2002)
17. Wolpert, D., Wheeler, K.R., Tumer, K.: General principles of learning-based multi-agent systems. In: Proceedings of the International Conference on Autonomous Agents. ACM Press, Seattle, Washington, USA (1999)
18. Wolfram, S.: A New Kind Of Science. Wolfram Media (2002)
19. Mamei, M., Roli, A., Zambonelli, F.: Emergence and control of macro spatial structures in perturbed cellular automata, and implications for pervasive computing systems. IEEE Transactions on Systems, Man, and Cybernetics **35** (2005) 337 – 348

ASOS: An Adaptive Self-organizing Protocol for Surveillance and Routing in Sensor Networks

Jorge Simão

LIACC — Departamento de Ciência de Computadores
Faculdade de Ciências da Universidade do Porto,
R. do Campo Alegre, 823, 4150-180 Porto
jsimao@dcc.fc.up.pt

Abstract. We present a simple model of self-organization for sensor networks that addresses two conflicting requirements: hazard situations should be reported to a *sink node* with as little delay as possible, even in highly dynamic regimes; and power consumption by individual nodes should be as low as possible and balanced. The model includes a surveillance protocol that explores correlation between source location and event types, and a variation of *gradient-based routing* that adapts continuously to energy available at selected routers and to changes in topology. Simulation runs provide support to the heuristics we implemented to select routers and nodes to report events, since network longevity increases when compared to other solutions for sensor networks. The performance increase is particularly accentuated when the correlation between event types at neighboring nodes is significant.

1 Introduction

The effectiveness of wireless sensor networks — networks of low-cost, low-power devices capable of sensing the physical world and communicating over a wireless medium, is largely dependent on the ability of sensor nodes to self-organize and relay messages in a power efficient manner [1].

Consider the following model: 1) the sensor nodes are displaced (quasi) randomly in space, and nodes are allowed to be installed and started at different times; 2) each node is assumed to be capable of monitoring its immediate environment, detected hazard situations (e.g. temperature raising above a safety threshold), and broadcasting data messages to other nodes within a communcation range; 3) the communication range is assumed to be much smaller than the diameter of the deployment area; 4) nodes are capable of receiving data messages sent by nearby nodes, process the information received, and relay data messages to other nodes.

Our goal is to design a set of protocols for the sensor network that cope with two conflicting requirements:

- Hazard situations should be reported to a *sink node* with as little delay as possible, even in highly dynamic regimes.

S. Brueckner et al. (Eds.): ESOA 2006, LNAI 4335, pp. 115–131, 2007.

- Power consumption by individual nodes should be as low as possible and balanced.

The first requirement implies that a low-latency routing mechanism must be available to relay messages between nodes further away from the sink node and nodes near the sink[1]. In particular, message caching and aggregation techniques should not be used to reduce traffic because they increase the latency of event notifications [2,3]. Since node batteries may have short lifetimes, communication may be unstable, and new nodes may be added to the network to increase coverage, density, or replace dead nodes, the protocols should be adapted to highly dynamic regimes.

The second requirement implies that coordination protocols should use as few messages as possible, and energy usage should be balanced among nodes within a local neighboorhood. This is a distinctive feature of sensor networks since energy available at nodes is limited. Considering this aspects from start allows the network to operate for longer periods of time, reducing the rate at which power sources or node need to be replaced. If battery reload is supported (e.g. using solar energy), this will also give more time for power sources to reload. Balancing power consumption mitigates the possibility that key nodes be prematurely drown out of energy, and normal operation of the network be disrupted (e.g., due to partitioning).

An additional requirement is that the operation of the network does not depend on the working of one or several central nodes. Thus, the mode of operation should be fully distributed. Furthermore, individual nodes should not require specially tailored configurations. This means, that sensor nodes should self-organize to establish roles, priorities, and other forms of coordination. Additionally, to handle dynamics and large networks, nodes should use local rules (or heuristics) that do not require global information.

The contribution we present has two innovations compared to existing self-organizing approaches to sensor network design. First, message routing continuously adapts to available energy at selected routers without generating extra traffic or requiring global link cost information to be collected at nodes [4]. Minimum hop count paths are discovered, even in the presence of network dynamics and with minimal increased message traffic. Secondly, the surveillance protocol uses source location, events descriptions, and awareness of available energy to decide if hazard notifications should be reported to the sink. Namely, nodes may select neighboring nodes that have more critical information to report, that are closer to the sink, or that have higher energy levels to represent them at the sink. The representation role is canceled if critical information, not known by the sink, needs to be reported. This is motivated by the fact that reporting less critical information about a region near a more critical information provides little information gain. Moreover, if two surveillance points are physically located near each other, a single notification is needed to trigger localized intervention by the

---

[1] The sink node is defined as a special node in the network whose role is to maintain a global view of network (e.g., to make a report to a human operator, or to publish collected data in the Internet).

staff and/or systems processing the information that arrives at the sink (e.g., sending rescue to the affected area). This may reduce traffic without incurring in significant loss of information.

We delay the review of related work to section 4. The rest of this paper is organized as follows: in section 2, we present our model design (ASOS) in detail. In section 3, we evaluate the model by simulating a sensor networks with some dynamics. Section 4 discusses the results, compares our approach with other approaches to self-organization on sensor-networks, and points directions for future research. Finally, section 5 presents our conclusions.

2   Model Design

Our network model comprises a collection of sensor nodes $S(t) = \{n_i\}$ displaced in space. Nodes can be added and removed from the network dynamically. That is, $S(t+1)$ is not necessarily the same as $S(t)$. Each node n_i is configured with a fixed unique identifier $id(n_i)$, that is used to discriminate between nodes. We assume that the sink node is able to map the identifiers of nodes to physical locations in some coordinate system. Two possibilities solutions to implement this are: node location is pre-registered in a data-base at deployment time, or identifiers include location information directly (e.g., obtained from a GPS receiver installed in each node). We also assume that control programs on the nodes can read the current energy level from the hardware (e.g., percentage full). For node n_i, we designate such value as $energy(n_i)$. This is used to tailor network operation in such a way that the standard deviation of energy available at nodes $\sigma(\{energy(n_i)\})$, $n_i \in S(t)$, is reduced.

The main task of each node is to monitor its immediate environment and detect possibly hazard situations. We assume that each node can detect several types of hazards (e.g. inferred from polled conditions in different sensors of the node, such as a thermometer and/or a smoke detector). A type identifier, common to all nodes, is used to identify the specific type of hazard. Once a hazard situation is detected the node may proceed to notify a sink node using an alarm message (ALARM). To allow several types of hazards to be notified in a single message, type identifiers are defined as integer powers of two. This way, a combined hazard can be coded using the logical operation OR[2]. As a working definition, we say that an hazard type t_1 is *more encompassing* than hazard type t_2, if t_1 reports all individual hazard situations reported in t_2 and at least one more not reported in t_2.

We propose two simple protocols: A surveillance protocol and a routing protocol. The surveillance protocol is used to determine which nodes in a local neighboorhod are responsible for sending ALARM messages. The protocol works by allowing a node to select a neighboor, its leader, as its representative to the sink. A node only sends ALARM messages if it has information that is more critical than its leader (i.e. with additional hazard types). In selecting leaders, nodes reporting more hazards, closer to the sink, or higher in energy supply take

---

[2] The sink node uses appropriate masks to retrieve the individual types.

precedence over others. This reduces the average and standard deviation of the consumed energy, thus fostering network longevity.

The routing protocol is used to push messages from sensor nodes to a sink node. This is done using a variation of *gradient-based routing* (GBR) [3]. In GBR, each node selects as its router one or more of its neighboring node whose distance to the sink is lower. If a node has more than one router, then energy aware heuristics are used to spread routing workload. We take this energy aware heuristics approach one step forward, by using a new heuristic that always selects the router with higher energy level. Additionally, GBR is a data centric protocol which requires flooding of *interest* messages sent by a sink to establish routes. This can be costly if the network is very large and very dynamic. ASOS uses an efficient scheme to handle topology changes by having nodes overhear neighboor activity and possible changes in distance information. Because our version of GBR incorporates several new improved features, we describe it in detail. Below, we present the routing protocol first and next the surveillance protocol because the later depends on the former. The two protocols are, nevertheless, intertwined.

2.1   Routing Protocol

When a node is started, its first task it to estimate the distance to the sink node. The distance metric we use is simply the minimal number of hops required to reach the sink. For node n_i, we represent such distance estimation as $dist(n_i)$.

For a node to obtain its distance to the sink, it starts by broadcasting a WHO message and wait for nearby nodes to respond with a DIST message. DIST messages contain the distance to the sink and the energy level of the sending node. If node n_j replies to node n_i with a DIST message specifying $dist(n_j) = d$, and $dist(n_i)$ is unknown, then node n_i sets its $dist(n_i)$ value to $d+1$. This captures the fact that $k+1$ hops are required to reach the sink from node n_i — one to reach n_j from n_i, and d to reach the sink from n_j. Henceforth, n_j is considered by n_i as one of its routers; this information is saved in a router list $routers(n_i)$. A node only sends a WHO message with a DIST message if it has at least one router.

If DIST messages, sent by a node n_j, are received by n_i when $dist(n_i)$ is known, then the following cases are considered: if $dist(n_j) < dist(n_i) - 1$, $dist(n_i)$ is set to $dist(n_j)+1$, $routers(n_i)$ is cleared, and n_j is added to $routers(n_i)$. This is the case where a better router (closer to the sink) is found. If $dist(n_j) \geq dist(n_i)$ and $n_j \notin routers(n_i)$, then the message is ignored, because a better router is known. If $dist(n_j) = dist(n_i) - 1$ then n_j is added to $routers(n_i)$ as an additional router (unless n_j is already a router for n_i, in which case the message is ignored). If $dist(n_j) \geq dist(n_i)$ and n_j is the only router for n_i then $dist(n_i)$ is updated to $dist(n_j) + 1$. If $dist(n_j) \geq dist(n_i)$, but n_i has other routers, then n_j is removed from $routers(n_i)$. The rules described allow the nodes to keep distance information consistent as the network topology changes. The rules are also applied when ALARM messages are received (see below), since they also include distance information. As can be inferred from the rules, all routers of a node are estimated (by that node) to be at the same distance from the sink

$(dist(n_i) - 1)$. Whenever node n_i changes $dist(n_i)$, it sends a DIST message so neighboring nodes can learn about the new value. In table 1, we present a summary of the rules for the routing and surveillance protocols.

If no DIST message is received by n_i within a time period of t_d duration after it sent a WHO message, then n_i sends a new WHO message. Thus, a node will keep probing its neighborhood until at least one neighboor replies with a DIST message. This permits the network to be started incrementally without *interest* messages being regularly sent by a sink as is done in data-centric models [2]. Figure 1 shows an illustraction of how nodes learn about distance values.

A particular case of the routing initialization procedure is for nodes at minimum distance from the sink node. That is, nodes whose messages can be directly received by the sink node. For these nodes $dist(n_i)$ is always set to 1. This can be done by having the sink node participate in the routing protocol, by sending DIST messages (with distance 0) whenever it receives WHO messages. Alternatively, one or a few special sensor nodes physically located near the sink can be parametrized with distance 1 at start-up.

Nodes keep estimates of the residual energy available to its routers. We write the value of n_j energy level, as estimated by n_i, as $energy(n_j, n_i)$. The router of n_i estimated to have higher energy level is designated the *assigned router* of n_i ($arouter(n_i)$). Formally, $arouter(n_i) = \text{maxarg}_{n_j}(energy(n_j, n_i)), n_j \in routers(n_i)$. This is the router most likely to relay the next message transmitted by n_i.

Whenever a node wants to route a message to the sink node (e.g., an ALARM message), it broadcasts the message including as data field the identity of its assigned router. If node n_j receives a message from a node n_i specifying n_j as the assigned router, and n_j knows $dist(n_j)$, then n_j retransmits the message. Moreover, when n_j retransmits the message it changes the router data field in the message to the identity of its own assigned router ($arouter(n_j)$).

Nodes monitor the activity of their assigned routers. If node n_i broadcast an ALARM message and detects no activity of $arouter(n_i)$ during a time period t_r, then it removes $arouter(n_i)$ from $routers(n_i)$, and chooses another router from $routers(n_i)$ as its assigned router for future transmissions. If $routers(n_i)$ is empty, n_i set $dist(n_i)$ as unknown and restarts the routing initialization protocol by sending a WHO message.

To keep accurate estimates of routers energy level at all times, ALARM and DIST messages always include information about the current energy level of the sending node[3]. If a node $n_j \in routers(n_i)$, announces an energy level $energy(n_j)$ such that $energy(n_j) > energy(arouter(n_j), n_i)$, then n_j becomes the new assigned router for n_i. This scheme allow traffic sent by n_i to be spread among its routers in such a way that variance in residual energy at nodes is reduced. This promotes network longevity by not allowing key nodes to die too soon due to excessive message relay. Figure 2 shows a sketch of the operation of the routing protocol and state maintained by nodes.

---

[3] We assume that adding this extra data field to messages has a negligible energetic cost.

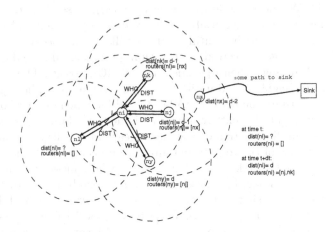

Fig. 1. DIST and WHO messages are exchanged so nodes can learn about distance values: n_i broadcasts request for distance information using a WHO message. n_j and n_k, at distance $d-1$, and n_y at distance d reply with a DIST message. If the message from n_y arrives first at n_i, $dist(n_i)$ is first set to $d+1$ and after set to d. If the message from n_j or n_k arrives first, n_y message is ignored. $routers(n_i)$ is changed accordingly. Once n_i learns its distance value it sends a DIST message so n_l can learn about this.

To enable the sink node to have feedback about the status of all nodes in the network (e.g., to detected mal-functional nodes or nodes with low power), every node sends an ALIVE message sporadically. An ALIVE message is also sent by a node when the routing initialization protocol ends, i.e., when a DIST message is received (e.g., at start up). If the node generates an ALARM message, the timer associated with ALIVE messages is reset. Router monitoring also applies to ALIVE messages. Both ALIVE and ALARM message contain sequence numbers so that delayed messages can be detected by the sink.

2.2 Surveillance Sub-protocol

As mentioned above, the main function of sensor nodes is to detect hazards and notify the sink by broadcasting ALARM messages. However, not all sensor nodes in a local neighborhood need to send ALARM messages at all times and in all situations that they detect hazards. Instead, nodes can monitor the activity of their neighbors and only send an ALARM if critical new information needs to be reported. The heuristic we use is to have nodes with more encompassing hazard types to take priority over other **neighboring** nodes. In the case where neighboring nodes detect the same type of events, nodes closer to the sink take priority.

To implement the surveillance protocol, each node regards one of its neighboring nodes or itself as its *leader*. For node n_i, we designate its leader as $leader(n_i)$. If n_i is leader of itself ($leader(n_i) = n_i$), we say that n_i is a *self-leader*. Only self-leaders send ALARM messages. At start up, a node is always self-leader. Leader

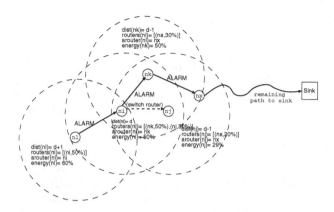

Fig. 2. Message routing from sensor nodes to sink: node n_i has two routers — n_j and n_k, both at $d-1$ distance from sink; n_i currently assigned router is n_k since the estimate energy level of n_k is higher than for n_j ($energy(n_k, n_i) > energy(n_j, n_i)$). The solid line show the probable path of an ALARM message sent by n_l. Dash line notes possible router change in the near future.

identify may change as ALARM messages are received (see below). A node n_i keeps an estimate of the distance to sink of its leader, and its energy level. We represent these values as $dist(leader(n_i), n_i)$ and $energy(leader(n_i), n_i)$, respectively. A node also memorizes the type of hazard last reported by its leader.

A node that is a self-leader broadcasts ALARM messages periodically. If an hazard has been detected, the time period for ALARM messages broadcast is t_a; if no hazard has been detected, the time period is made longer $(t_c > t_a)^4$. This periodic transmission allows the state of the environment be known by the sink at all times, including the detection of a hazard, updates to hazard types, notification of hazard extinctions, corrections to false alarms (caused by errors in sensor reading), and recover from lost ALARM messages. In addition to periodically send ALARM messages, a self-leader also sends an ALARM message whenever its hazard type changes (even if it has recently sent an ALARM message). This allows for novel events to be quickly notified at the sink. The timer associated with ALARM sending is also reset. An ALARM message is also sent whenever a node becomes a self-leader.

If a node n_i overhears an ALARM message sent by node n_j **whose source is also** n_j, it procedes as follows: if n_j is n_i current leader, n_i updates the leader information, and checks if its hazard type become more encompassing than its leader. If so, n_i becomes a self-leader and sends an ALARM message. If n_j is not n_i current leader, than n_i checks if n_j alarm type is more encompassing than its leader. If so, n_j becomes the leader of n_i. If not, n_i selects as its leader the node closer to the sink.

When the hazard type of node n_i that is not a self-leader changes (due to changes in the physical environment), the node also checks if its alarm type

---

[4] The alarm type identifier we use to represent a cleared hazard is 0.

Table 1. Summary of rules for routing and surveillance protocols: n_i receives messages from n_j

Condition $\Longrightarrow$ Action
When $ALARM \lor DIST$ is received:
$dist(n_i) = nil \Longrightarrow dist(n_i) = dist(n_j) + 1, arouter(n_i) = n_j, leader(n_i) = n_i$
$dist(n_j) < dist(n_i) \Longrightarrow routers = \{\}, arouter(n_i) = n_j$
$dist(n_j) \geq dist(n_i) \land n_j \notin routers(n_i) \Longrightarrow$ ignore
$dist(n_j) = dist(n_i) - 1 \Longrightarrow routers(n_i) = routers(n_i) \cup \{n_j\}$
$dist(n_j) \geq dist(n_i) \land routers(n_i) = \{n_j\} \Longrightarrow dist(n_i) = dist(n_j) + 1$
$dist(n_j) \geq dist(n_i) \land |routers(n_i)| > 1 \Longrightarrow routers(n_i) = routers(n_i) - \{n_j\}$
When $ALARM$ is received $\land n_j$ is the source:
$n_j = leader(n_i) \land type(n_i) > type(n_j) \Longrightarrow leader(n_i) = n_i$
$n_j \neq leader(n_i) \land type(n_j) > type(leader(n_i)) \Longrightarrow leader(n_i) = n_j$
$n_j \neq leader(n_i) \land \neg(type(n_j) < type(leader(n_i)) \lor type(j) > type(leader(n_i)))$
$\Longrightarrow leader(n_i) = minarg_{n_k}\{dist(n_j, n_i), dist(leader(n_i), n_k)\}$
$energy(leader(n_i), n_i) < energy(n_i) \cdot f \land dist(n_i) = dist(leader(n_i), n_i)$
$\Longrightarrow leader(n_i) = n_i$
When $type(n_i)$ changes:
$type(n_i) > type(leader(n_i)) \Longrightarrow leader(n_i) = n_i$
$type(n_i) < type(leader(n_i)) \Longrightarrow$ ignore
$type(n_i) = type(n_j) \land dist(n_i) = dist(n_j, n_i) \Longrightarrow leader(n_i) = n_i$
$\langle type(n_i) = type(n_j) \lor type(n_i) > type(leader(n_i)) \lor type(n_i) < type(leader(n_i))$
$\Longrightarrow leader(n_i) = n_i$

become more encompassing than the type of the leader. If so, n_i becomes a self-leader and sends an ALARM message. If the leader's type continues to be more encompassing than n_i than nothing is done. If the hazard types are identical, n_i becomes self-leader if it is closer to the sink. The first two rules allow nodes to overrule current leaders if they hold critical hazard information that is not being reported by the leader (e.g., because its sensors have not detected the hazard yet). The last two rules allow nodes closer to the sink to takes precedence in leadership if hazard types are identical.

A node n_i, that is not a self-leader, also becomes a self-leader and sends an ALARM message, if $energy(leader(n_i), n_i) < energy(n_i) \cdot f$ ($f < 1$), and its distances to the sink is the same as its leader ($dist(n_i) = dist(leader(n_i), n_i)$). This allow nodes at the same distance to the sink to take turns in leadership as energy is dissipated, which contributes to reduce $\sigma^2(\{energy(n_i)\}, n_i \in S(t))$. Often this event makes the previous leader of n_i elect n_i as its new leader (i.e., there is a role reversal).

If a node n_i does not receive an ALARM message from its leader during a $t_w > t_c$ time period, it becomes a self-leader and sends an ALARM message. This is used to recover from crashes and communication failures with leader nodes. When there is a change of the leader the timer associated with leader disconnection is reset. Figure 3 shows an illustration of the operation of the surveillance protocol.

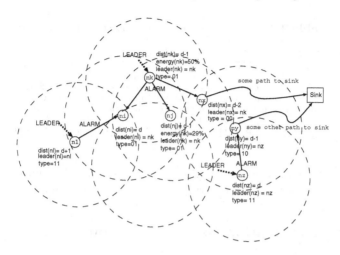

Fig. 3. Leader selection in the surveillance protocol: nodes n_k an n_j have the same hazard types, are at the same distance from sink, but n_k is leader of n_j because it has higher energy level. Node n_k is also leader of n_i, because it is closer to the sink. Node n_l is a self-leader although is further away from the source than its router n_i, because n_i is not a self-leader and n_k ALARM messages can not reach n_l. n_z is a self-leader because its alarm type is more encompassing than the one of its router n_y.

Below, we present the structure of the messages exchanged by sensor nodes while involved in the routing and surveillance protocol. A summary description of the messages' purpose is also shown.

– ALARM[*source id, sender id, router id, type, seq, dist, energy*] — Message routed to sink node to report hazards. Sent when an hazard is detected or as clear message, and periodically resend every t_a time period (if $type \neq 0$), or every t_c time period (if $type = 0$). *source id* is the identifier of the node that first generate the message, *sender id* is the identifier of the node sending the message, *router id* is the identifier of the assigned router for this message, *type* is the hazard type identifier, *seq* is a sequence counter, and *dist* and *energy* are, respectively, the current distance to sink and energy level of the sender.
– WHO[sender id] — Message sent by nodes to query neighboring nodes. Sent when a node is started or connection to all current routers is lost. Repeated periodically every t_w time period until at least one neighboor responds. This kind of message is not routed to the sink.
– DIST[*sender id, distance, energy*] — Message sent in reply to a WHO message sent by neighbooring node; includes information about distance to sink node. It is also sent when the distance to sink of the source changes. This kind of message is also not routed to the sink.
– ALIVE[*source id, sender id, router id, timestamp*] — Message routed to sink node to report active presence of node; sent very rarely (e.g. once a day)

Table 2. Parameters of the routing and surveillance protocol

Parameter	Description
t_d	maximum waiting period before a new WHO message is sent
t_r	maximum idle time for a router
t_l	time period for ALIVE messages broadcast ($t_l \gg t_a$)
t_a	time period before ALARM message is broadcast ($t_a < t_r$)
t_c	time period before ALARM message with *hazard type* = 0 is broadcast ($tc > t_a$)
t_w	maximum idle time for leader node ($t_w > t_c$)
f	maximum percentage difference of energy level of a node and its leader

In table 2, we present the list of parameters used by the routing and surveillance protocols, a summary description of their meaning, and suggested values.

3   Model Evaluation Using Simulation

To evaluate the model design and performance we have built a visual simulator of a sensor network. The simulator does not implement a detailed model of any specific MAC layer or sensor node hardware. Instead, it is a simple environment where the performance and key features of our model can be easily tested. Additionally, we assume that all nodes are identical (possibly with the exception of the sink). In particular, transmission range is made equal for all nodes, and the same number and type of alarms can be raised by all nodes. The sink node is located at the border of the surveyed environment. We model message passing using arbitrary large reception and transmission buffers. Because transmission range is short we assume that message transmission is instantaneous. That is, if a node broadcasts a message it is immediately put in the reception buffer of all nodes within the transmission range. Time is made to evolve synchronously in all nodes, with a time step corresponding, by convention, to 1 second. Each time step is divided in two phases: in the first phase, all messages in sending buffers are put in the reception buffers of nodes within the transmission range; in the second phase, the control code of the nodes is allowed to run (in an arbitrary order).

3.1   Goals, Metrics, and Methodology

In evaluating our model using simulation we have the following goals in mind:

- Compare the performance of our protocol whit other protocols proposed in the literature. In particular, we investigate experimentally how ASOS compares with *gradient-based routing*. Other protocols are informally compared in section 4.
- Evaluate what parameters have more influence in performance gains.
- Study how well the model scales with the size of the network.
- Test if routing mechanisms work efficiently and speedily even if the network topology changes frequently.

For this purpose, we use several metrics:

Hazard cost. This is the average amount of energy that the network uses per hazard event generated at some node. Includes the routing cost, and additional protocol messages overhead.

Network longevity. How long does the network stays functional given some battery capacity for nodes. The metric we use is to consider a network non functional if all nodes that are neighbors of the sink exhaust their power supply. This means that no more messages can arrive at the sink, rendering the network (temporarily) useless. Other alternative metrics are: the time before a fraction of sink neighbors to exhaust their power supply, and the time it takes for information accuracy at sink to drop below some fixed threshold.

Accuracy of information at sink. How accurate is the view that the sink has of the network. The metric we use is the average proportion of correct inferences about the state of hazard type indicators at all active nodes, during the live time of the network.

The methodology we use to realize the above goals is as follows.

Nodes are semi-randomly located in a square environment. Care is taken so that all nodes, with the exception on border nodes, have the same number of neighbors (K). Moreover, no initial partition on the network graph is allowed. In the first experiments, we start all nodes at the same time. In the dynamics regime, we force some fixed percentage of nodes to be down at all times. To simplify analysis of the results, message passing between neighboring nodes is assumed to be reliable. Nevertheless, sensor misreading is accounted by the protocol due to periodic retransmission of ALARM messages.

Message sending and message reception (plus processing) is assumed to cost one unit of energy. All nodes are started with the same amount of energy E. We trigger hazards with the same probability p_a for all nodes, and all N_t hazard types have equal probability of being raised or cleared. When there is a change on the status of an hazard type there is a probability R that the new status is changed to the value of the corresponding hazard type in some random neighbor. With probability $1 - R$ the hazard type is toggled. Thus, R is a measure of the correlation between hazard types at neighboring nodes.

To investigate the performance of ASOS when compared to GBR routing, we have simulated the behavior of GBR by making a few modifications to ASOS: selection between alternative routers is made stochastically, which is one of the heuristics that have been tested in GBR; nodes are always self-leaders, meaning that the surveillance protocol of ASOS is not used and all events trigger alarm messages. On the other hand, distance information in our version of GBR is known using the same mechanism as ASOS, instead of having the sink diffuse interest messages as in standard GBR. We designate this approximation as GBR-S, which is actually an improved version of GBR that handles dynamics effectively. To keep the comparisons fair, we make nodes running GBR-S send ALARM messages every t_a (or t_c) time steps as is done in ASOS. In [3], the authors prove that GBR performs better than the *directed diffusion* protocol, and in [2,5] the authors prove that directed diffusion performs better than *flooding*. Thus, claiming that ASOS performs better than GBR, entails **in principle** that ASOS performs better than flooding and directed diffusion. However, because implementation details and measures used can bias results we are working on additional simulations to compare ASOS with these other protocols.,

When comparing the performance of ASOS and GBR for a given network size, we use exactly the same set of network topology for the two protocols. For each network size, we used 20 different network topologies. This increases the significance of the simulation results. Moreover, we generate exactly the same sequence of hazard event for the two protocols for a given network size (same seed used for random number generator). The network sizes we use range from 50 to 400 nodes, with increments of 50.

3.2   Comparative Evaluation

In running our simulations, we use the following parameter settings for the surveillance and routing protocols: the time before a WHO message is retransmitted t_d was set to 10 seconds (i.e., 10 simulation time steps); the time routers are allowed to remain idle is 60 seconds; the time for ALIVE message transmission is 20 minutes; the maximum time between ALARM transmissions for a self-leader t_a is set to 30 seconds, and 60 seconds for cleared hazards (t_c); the maximum idle time for a self-leader t_w was set to 15 minutes; finally, the fraction of energy reduction for leadership over-ruling f is set to 0.8.

For the simulator parameters we use the following values: $E = 10000$, meaning that a node can send or receive up to 10000 messages. The number of neighbors K was set to 4. Different settings for these two parameters do not change the comparative results we present, although they change the absolute values obtained. The number of alarm types we consider is 2, and the probability of an alarm being raised at a node p_a is set to 0.1. This creates constant activity throughout the networks.

In figure 4(a), we show the average energy cost per hazard for ASOS and GBR-S, when there is no correlation between hazards at neighboring nodes ($R = 0$). The results show that ASOS performs better then GBR-S for the full range of network sizes considered. This is explained by the fact that in ASOS many hazard event do not generate ALARM messages. Namely, events at nodes that are not at that time self-leaders. This includes the cases where the leader of the node is reporting a more encompassing hazard type, or cases where the leader is closer to the sink (and the hazard type of the node is not more encompassing than the one of the leader). Contrary to this, GBR-S always generates ALARM messages whenever an hazard event is generated. Hazard energy cost decreases with network size, because the number of hazards generated until time t grows linearly with the number of nodes and the average distance to the sink grows sub-linearly.

In figure 4(b) we plot the network longevity for ASOS and GBR-S. Here, the results demonstrate the superiority of the ASOS compared to GBR-S, for all network sizes considered. For a network with size 50 there is an increase of about 25% in network longevity. This means that for the same starting energy a sensor network operation with the ASOS protocol is able to deliver surveillance information during longer timer periods than GBR-S. This is explained, in part, because the surveillance protocol considerably reduces the number of ALARM messages sent. Network longevity is also increased because router selection is made to compensate variation in available energy at the routers. We are currently working to disentangle the effects of the two characteristic mechanisms of ASOS — leadership selection and router selection, to see what is the relative contribution of each in explaining the increased network longevity. Note that network longevity is roughly the same for all network size considered. Network longevity is quite sensitive to network topology as indicated by the error bars for standard deviations in figure 4(b).

In figure 4(c) we show the data for the information accuracy at the sink. We have found that the accuracy for ASOS is quite similar to GBR-S. These results are explained, first, because we are considering a small number of hazard types (2), and secondly, because ASOS is quiet conservative in pre-empting event reporting. More aggressive design solutions to explore event correlation are possible, exchanging energy saving for accuracy (e.g., to have node over-rule a leader only if they are reporting a larger quantity of hazard types than their leader). Note that in ASOS non reported events are always less critical than the events at some neighboring node (the leader), thus the slightly drop in information accuracy for ASOS does not correspond to lost information about important hazards. The information accuracy drops with network size. This is explained by the fact that in larger networks partitions, caused by the exhaustion of one or a few nodes, tend to contain more nodes.

In figure 4(d) we make a comparison of the network longevity when nodes are running ASOS for different values of correlation between alarms at neighboring nodes ($R = 0, R = 0.4, R = 0.8$). The plots validate the intuition that higher correlation produces longer longevity of the network. This is the case because higher correlation means that a node is less likely to experience hazards different for its leader and therefore become a self-leader. The increase in network longevity when there is a change from zero correlation to high correlation is about 40%. Comparing ASOS with GBR-S with $R = .8$ gives an advantage to ASOS of more than 80%. Sensitivity analysis have shown that similar comparative results also apply when $K = 8$. This suggests that exploiting event correlation at neighboring nodes to increase network longevity is a viable and useful approach.

3.3   Impact of Dynamics

To study the effects of dynamics in the performance of our model we imposed a failure regime where some D fraction nodes is always down at a given point in time. The network already starts with D nodes down, and with some probability F at each time step a down node is started and a running node is made to fail. Nodes start with a high level of energy so that energy consumption is not relevant in this experiment. Simulations are run for 20000 time steps.

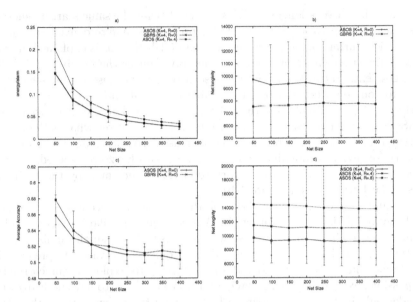

Fig. 4. Simulation results: **a)** energy cost per hazard for ASOS and GBR-S ($R = 0$); **b)** network longevity for ASOS and GBR-S ($R = 0$); **c)** average accuracy of network information at sink ($R = 0$); **d)** network longevity for ASOS for different values of hazard correlation ($R = 0, R = 0.4, R = 0.8$).

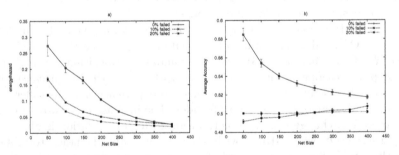

Fig. 5. Simulation results for dynamics: **a)** energy cost per hazard; **b)** information accuracy at sink

In figure 5(a) we plot the average cost per hazard for the dynamic regime with $F = 0.01$, and for 0%, 10%, 20% failed nodes. In figure 5b) we plot the information accuracy at the sink for the same failure regimes. As can be seen from the plots the performance of ASOS measured by hazard cost for the three regimes is comparable. Note that $F = 0.01$ represents a very harsh dynamic regime, beyond the demands of most real world applications (it corresponds to have a node going down and another starting every 100 seconds). The drop in information accuracy up to 10% reflects possible cuts in connectivity for some network sub-graphs, and the time that it takes for nodes to detected lost routers and lost leaders. Reducing the values of parameters t_r and t_w increases information accuracy, at the expense of increased energy cost per alarm (plots not shown).

4 Discussion, Related, and Future Work

Our routing protocol is a variation of *gradient-based routing* (GBR) [3], which is an improvement to the *directed diffusion* model [2,5]. Both GBR and directed diffusion are data-centric model, where sink nodes diffuse *interest* messages to advertise an interest in a piece of named data. Interests are diffused through the network so that relevant nodes can learn about the interest, and allow nodes to trace back routes to the sink [6]. In GBR this is done by using the number of hops to the sink as a distance metric (called *height* in GBR), and relaying event messages through the neighbor closer to the sink.

In our intended application, a sink is always interest in getting information about hazard events, therefore sending interest messages is pointless and costly. We use a different mechanism to keep distance values update from GBR. Instead of diffusing interest messages, nodes exchange DIST and WHO messages to handle network reconfigurations efficiently.

Gradient following methods related to GBR and ASOS have also been used in robotics and autonomous agents research for robot navigation and manipulation — the *artificial potential field* approach [7].

Several heuristics for traffic spreading have been explored in GBR. In the *stochastic scheme*, message routing is assigned randomly to one of the neighboring nodes closer to the sink. This is the heuristic we attributed to GBR when comparing it to ASOS. Two other additional heuristics, are the *energy-based scheme*, that makes nodes low on energy to discourage others to send messages trough it by advertising an increased height value which is propagated down the network, and *stream-based scheme* which assigns a router to specific nodes. The performance difference between these heuristics is small [3]. Contrary to this, the heuristic we used in ASOS provide considerable increases in network longevity. More work is needed to disentangle the relative merit of traffic spreading and leader selection mechanisms in ASOS. Whatever the results of this analysis may be, we have showed that the two mechanisms working together deliver considerable improvements over GBR.

Similar to our approach, the *Maximum lifetime energy routing* protocol uses residual energy information for routing in sensor networks [4]. This protocol compute optimal paths to sink nodes using a distance metric that includes both energy consumed to reach the sink and residual energy at nodes along a path. The protocol uses a graph shortest-path algorithm that requires global information at nodes. Although this approach provides, in principle, better results than a using only local information for routing decision, it may be unfeasible in very large and dynamic networks due to the overhead of maintaining link cost tables updated. Our routing protocol does not consider residual energy at all nodes in a path, only neighbors. This allows the protocols to scale with network size, and perform well in dynamic regimes.

The approach we use in the surveillance protocol has some connections with work on energy-aware routing protocols with hierarchical clustering [8]. For example, in LEACH [9], nodes within a local neighboorhood self-organize to select a cluster header or leader. This cluster head becomes the local router. Cluster leaders turn take, based on a random number generated at each node, so energy dissipation is balanced. Our approach is different. Router selection is not random, but relies on energy awareness. Leader selection in not used for routing purposes but rather to explore correlation of space and events between neighbors. This allows reduction in message traffic in a way not explored previously be other protocols.

Although our protocol pursues strong performance criteria, there is still much space for additional optimizations and services. An obvious improvement is for the retransmission time of WHO messages to increases exponentially when no neighboring node responds with a DIST message (as is done IEEE 802.11 CSMA/CD Ethernet). This may save considerable amount of energy if nodes are started asynchronously.

A drawback of our design is that sensing resolution/precision is made to match the communication range of sensors. However, for many applications this is not a serious issue because sensors communication range is usually small. There are also practical solutions to address this issue. We suggest two: nodes may estimate the spatial distance of neighbors by measuring the power signalling, and not consider as leader a node that is too distant; or nodes may send ALARM messages even if they are not leaders, although less frequently.

Although our base model does not support multiple distributed located sinks, it can be adapted for this. The simplest solution is to have nodes memorize distance and router information independently for each sink. If different sinks can coordinate activity (e.g. using the Internet), then a different subset of nodes can be assigned to each sink. No modification is needed in ASOS to handle this kind of scenario.

In the future, we plan to evaluate our model with a more sophisticate sensor network simulator including detailed models of the radio MAC layer. Furthermore, use of ASOS in a real-world scenario would be an important test to the protocol. Modeling realistic hazard events regimes is also expected to give a better estimate of model performance (e.g., use a cellular automata to model the spreading of a fire in a forest tree surveyed with a sensor network). We are also evaluating how variance in transmission range influences protocol performance. Finally, integration or extension of ASOS to handle mobile sinks and mobile sensor nodes can be pursued [10].

5   Conclusions

In this paper, we have proposed a model of self-organization for sensor networks. The task of each sensor in the network is to report hazard situations to a sink node, and to route messages from nearby nodes. For this purpose we specified two protocols: a surveillance protocol and a routing protocol. The surveillance protocol uses correlation between event types to reduce traffic for hazard notifications. The routing protocol uses a variation of *gradient-based routing* that adapts continuously to energy available at selected routers and handles network dynamics efficiently. We have performed simulations to compare our protocol with gradient-based routing with a modified implementation. Results show that our approach increases network longevity. The effect in more accentuated if correlation between event types at neighboring nodes is high. Our work illustrates how ideas and principles from self-organized adaptive systems can be used for engineering network applications. The implementation of the sensor network test-bed is available from LIACC[5].

References

1. I.F. Akyildiz, W. Su, Y. Sankarasubramaniam, and E. Cayirci. Wireless sensor networks: a survey. *Computer Networks*, 38:393–422, 2002.
2. Chalermek Intanagonwiwat, Ramesh Govindan, and Deborah Estrin. Directed diffusion: A scalable and robust communication paradigm for sensor networks. In *Proc. of the 6th Annual ACM/IEEE International Conference on Mobile Computing and Networking (MobiCom'00)*, 2000.
3. Curt Schurgers and Mani B. Srivastava. Energy efficient routing in wireless sensor networks. In *MILCOM Proc. of Communications for Network-Centric Operations: Creating the Information Force*, 2001.
4. J H Chang and L Tassiulas. Maximum lifetime routing in wireless sensor networks. *IEEE/ACM Transactions on Networking*, 2004.
5. D Estrin, R Govindan, J Heidemann, and S Kumar. Next century challenges: Scalable coordination in sensor networks. *MOBICOM*, 1999.
6. WR Heinzelman, J Kulik, and H Balakrishnan. Adaptive protocols for information dissemination in wireless sensor networks. In *Proc. Annual international conferance in mobile computing and networking*, 1999.
7. Jean-Claude Latombe. *Robot Motion Planning*. Kluwer Academic Publishers: Norwell, MA, USA, 1991.
8. Kemal Akkaya and Mohamed Younis. A survey on routing protocols for wireless sensor networks. *Ad Hoc Networks*, 2005.
9. WR Heinzelman, A Chandrakasan, and H Balakrishnan. Energy-efficient communication protocol for wireless microsensor networks. In *Proc. Hawaii international conference system science*, 2000.
10. A Howard, MJ Mataric, and GS Sukhatme. Mobile sensor network deployment using potential fields: A distributed, scalable solution to the area coverage problem. *Distributed Autonomous Robotic Systems*, 2002.

---

[5] Thanks to the anonymous reviewers for making useful suggestions that improved paper quality, and to Marco Costa for proof reading the final version of the paper.

Towards the Control of Emergence by the Coordination of Decentralized Agent Activity for the Resource Sharing Problem

Frédéric Armetta, Salima Hassas, Simone Pimont, and Olivier Lefevre

LIRIS, Nautibus, 8 Bd Niels Bohr
Université Claude Bernard-Lyon 1
43 Bd du 11 Novembre F-69622
Villeurbanne

Abstract. Explicit and high semantic level communications are not always the best approaches to coordinate the global system activity in the context of Multi-Agent Systems (MAS). Insect societies take advantage of a stigmergic way to communicate which does not require centralized control, but enable insects to coordinate their complex global tasks. In this paper, we describe and motivate a new approach to elaborate Complex Exchanges between Stigmergic Negotiating Agents (CESNA), for the critical resource sharing problem. We describe a negotiating network as a generic and suitable representation of the problem, along with its implemented behaviours. We present some promising results and attempt a first interpretation of how this decentralized system leads local behaviours to a global problem solution.

1 Introduction

In this paper, we propose a Multi Agent approach for the critical resource sharing problem in a dynamic environment. For this problem, a set of consumers try to acquire a set of shared resources to achieve a set of tasks. In this context the resources allocation process is submitted to a set of constraints (such as chronological constraints) related to tasks to be achieved by the consumers. These constraints make the system, obtained by the consumers and the resources, react as a complex system, since intermediate states leading to a solution of the resources allocation problem, are interrelated in a retroactive way: one resource assignment impacts on the remaining possibilities of future assignments of other resources. We propose in this work to address this problem through a decentralized multi-agent negotiation process: each agent elaborates a subpart of the global solution by negotiating with other agents, through complex exchanges, expressing its preferences for potential resources assignments. Doing so, the Multi-Agent System constructs a negotiation network, representing contracts of potential resources repartition/exchange between agents to be validated/invalidated. Agents negotiate to validate/invalidate contracts fitting their needs with respect to the needs of other agents. For this problem, the agents

S. Brueckner et al. (Eds.): ESOA 2006, LNAI 4335, pp. 132–150, 2007.

must coordinate their activity to elaborate a global allocating pattern fitting the complex problem needs. Moreover, the Muti-Agent System has to cover the set of possible states balancing efficiently exploration and exploitation periods. During exploration, the system attempts new possible patterns among the vast set of possibilities. During exploitation, the system reinforces the elaborated combinations it perceives as relevant.

We present in section 2 the critical resource sharing problem from a multi-agent point of view. Section 3 presents some related works. In section 4, we propose a negotiation network through which the characteristics of the problem of critical resources sharing are exhibited. This network serves as a medium for agents negotiation to solve the critical resource sharing problem. The implemented behaviours presented in section 5 provide promising results studied in section 6. We propose in section 7 a first analysis of the system capacity to control its decentralised activity and exhibit some co-relations between the local behaviours of agents and the global activity of the system. Finally, we illustrate in section 8 the interest of our approach by giving some comparing results for the graph coloring problem, and conclude in section 9.

2   The Critical Resource Sharing Problem

2.1   Description of the Problem

In this paper, we address the general resource sharing problem as a dynamic distributed constraint satisfaction problem. For our study, we represent this problem through 3 components as follows:

- A set of consumers : each consumer consumes parts of resource(s) to be satisfied.
- A set of resources : The resources propose a limited quantity of services.
- A set of constrained relations between consumers allocations : Consumers have to respect some allocation patterns allowing the constraints satisfaction.

These components are represented differently following the different instances of the critical resource sharing problem:

- For the manufacturing scheduling problem, one has to schedule the repartition of a set of tasks on a set of machines with respect to a set of constraints : like chronological constraints related to the manufacturing of a product which imposes the execution of a set of task in a specified order. In this context a consumer is a product task to achieve, which consumes a part of time on a resource. The objective of the resources allocation problem here is to provide a planning of the resources use for the different tasks which respects the chronological constraints between the tasks of a same product manufacturing. For this problem, additional constraints like the respect of due dates for products delivery, resource use optimisation, etc.. often make the problem more difficult to solve.

- For the graph coloring problem, each vertex needs to be assigned a color which is different from all the colors assigned to its neighbors. When the number of authorised colors is limited, each color is a critical resource. In this case, allocations must fit the constraints represented by the coloring network structure.
- For the problem of human resources assignment, tasks to be achieved (produce, learn, teach, ..etc) require adequate teams (resource allocation patterns). Each human has some competence (that can evolve) and can contribute to different activities.
- etc.

To solve these problems using a multi-agents approach, we need to make explicit the representation of the problem characteristics. Agents have partial vision of the whole problem, and act locally on the elaboration of partial solutions. Partial solutions are inter-related. Their constructions need to be co-ordinated to reach a satisfying global solution for the problem.

2.2 A Need for Coordination Between Agents

Multi-Agent Systems approach the critical resource sharing problem as a decentralized negotiation problem. The negotiation process is held on the different possible resources assignments, to satisfy the problem constraints. To address this problem we consider the search space, that represent the set of all the combinations of potential problem variables assignments. As in many optimisation problems, the search space size grows exponentially with the problem size (number of variables). Generally, the search space size is considered as an important criterion to define the problem solving hardness. We consider the sparsity of solutions through the search space as a second criterion of difficulty. The rarer the solutions, the more difficult they are to find. Generally, the strongest the constraints applied on a problem, the rarer the solutions tend to be.

In the context of a decentralized negotiation, we wish to explicitly consider a third criterion of difficulty : at what extent relations between a solution sub-parts are constrained? For the resource sharing problem, how much the constrained relations between consumers make the elaboration of patterns difficult to achieve? In [9], Parunak's team describes an hyperactivity phenomena for a resource sharing problem (the graph coloring problem). In our opinion, the hyperactivity of agents arise from a lack of agents ability to co-ordinate their respective activities. In [2], we show that this hyperactivity results from a lack of communication between agents, which prevent them to perceive the complex characteristics of the problem during the solving process, and thus to elaborate complex patterns of negotiation. We show in section 3 that this coordinating problem appears in many situations. This observation leads to the proposal of a new approach for multi-agent systems, in order to efficiently coordinate their negotiating activity.

3   Self-organizing Systems and Resource Sharing

In [4], the authors propose a Multi-Agent System approach to dispatch trucks on painting machines. Their approach is based on the emergent specialisation of painting machines leading to reduce functioning costs. In [5], multi-agent systems seem to be appropriate for the manufacturing problem. An adequate allocation of products on machine queues permits to increase the production system output. Nevertheless, these approaches do not allow to make plannings in advance, and to benefit from anticipating information. The anticipation could provide useful properties like robustness, flexibility, etc. which are required in many production situations (respect of due dates, minimisation of stocks, etc.). For the scheduling problem, anticipating increases the complexity of the solutions to build : each task assignment to a resource must respect a chronological consistency with the assignments of tasks belonging to the same product manufacturing process. Some other problems lead to an inherent complexity of tasks assignments. In our opinion, the presented models do not address perfectly the co-ordination problem of the agents activity in a constrained environment. The multi-agents negotiation process depends upon the medium of agents communication. A first category of works are based on the *Contract Net* protocol. In [11], this protocol permits a consumer agent to bid for supplier agents. We implemented this protocol for a resource sharing problem. In our model, each agent bids for resources fitting its needs. We noticed that this protocol does not permit to reach a solution when the complexity of patterns to elaborate increases. It induces latency within social interactions. Each agent undergoes many constraints which induce several negotiations to manage in parallel. When problems are complex, the latency introduced by each act of negotiation is added to latency introduced by the other negotiations being conducted in parallel and may lead to the global system deadlock. This protocol seems to be adequate for an agent requesting services from other agents (relation cardinality : 1-n) ; But in our case, many agents share the same environment and simultaneously request services from several other agents (relation cardinality : n-n) : we can not validate a contract locally without considering the complex associated negotiating environment. Nevertheless, there are different ways to address these issues (to establish contracts undergoing incertitudes, heuristics to minimize the set of solution to evaluate, etc.). In [1], a way to reduce the difficulties inherent to the *Contract Net* protocol to establish complex contracts, is presented.

The second way for an agent to address this problem is to benefit from a stigmergic communication inspired from social insects : each agent marks tags on the environment to communicate. In [8], a way to coordinate the global activity of agents is presented. While tagging their environment, agents elaborate a schedule for the production chain. Local interactions allow a global solving process. However, the perceived improvement must be significant for an agent to decide to change its resource use. Indeed, the changes blindly impact the overall system, they propagate through the problem constraints. For instance, product tasks must respect a chronological order. If a task agent changes its scheduled time, this can affect its associated product tasks and the global schedule. Changes applied on the current solution propagate through the complex system which produce hyperactivity of agents and lead to a chaotic behavior. In [9], the authors propose to calm hyperactive agents. In [3], a graph coloring problem is addressed through a stigmergic approach. In this work, the emerging system-level performance may decrease when agents consider obsolete information in the context of a large-scale system. Different local patterns emerge and influence the problem solving. The associated abstract representation propagates through the system. Then, the question is : 'how to make agents select locally appropriate actions that lead them to adequate behaviours and permit to reach a global solution? It is difficult to analyze the behaviour of such systems. In [10] an interesting work has been presented in this perspective.

In this section, we have presented some limits for the *Contract Net* protocol to elaborate complex patterns. We believe that stigmergic communication is appropriate to the multi-negotiation (many local negotiations at the same time through a complex environment). Our objective consists in making patterns emerge within social interactions among agents. To do so, we propose to provide a negotiation support structure, on which the complex characteristics of the problem to address as well as the complex agents exchanges could be expressed.

4 Representation of the Resource Sharing Problem Using a Negotiation Network

For this approach, we follow the framework defined in [7]. Reactive and situated agents interact by using the environment as a medium for their actions effects inscription. This allows to express the influence of past and persistent effects issued from past behaviours, on the future behaviours of agents. In order to endow the system with a self-organizing capacity (capacity to make a structure emerge without external control), agents behaviours need to balance exploration and exploitation of the environment. Random exploration allows to diversify the research through the environment in order to find new potential ways. The exploitation enables to reinforce promising ways in a self-catalytic manner (i.e. the more a way is promising, the more it is exploited).

With our model called CESNA (Complex Exchanges between Stigmergic Negotiating Agents), the general problem is represented by a negotiation network, represented by potential contracts to be validated or invalidated by negotiating agents. Each agent acts upon a sub-network that represents the contracts to which the agent participates. Each agent must validate a satisfying sub-set of its associated contracts by negotiating with agents expressing needs that are in conflict with its needs.

More formally, we define a network as a graph $G = < N, R >$ where $N = B \cup C$. Let $A = \{a_1, a_2, a_3, \ldots, a_n\}$ be a set of agents. We associate a node from the set B to each agent. In the rest of this paper, we consider that an agent will be represented in the graph by its associated node ($B = A$).

- Let $B = \{B^{or} \cup B^{and} \cup \ldots\} = \{b_1, b_2, b_3, \ldots, b_n\}$ be a set of connecting nodes standing for logical relations. Theses relations allow to express the agents satisfying configurations according to their associated contracts.
- Let $C = \{c_1, c_2, c_3, \ldots, c_m\}$ be a set of contrat nodes.

- Let $R = \{r_1, r_2, r_3, \ldots, r_p\}$ be a set of edges between the nodes of the network. We denote $suc(w_i) = \{y|(w_i, y) \in R\}$ the set of successors for a node w_i, and $pred(w_i) = \{x|(x, w_i) \in R\}$ the set of predecesors for a node w_i.

This network respects the following rules :

- $\forall a \in A, pred(a) = \emptyset$
- $\forall b \in B, suc(b) \in \{B \cup C\}$
- $\forall c \in C, suc(c) = \emptyset, pred(c) \in B$

Contracts and Agents are linked as described below :

- The set of contracts associated with the agent a is denoted by : $C(a), a \in A, C(a) \subset C$. This set is established by the procedure 1 $getContrats$.
- The set of agents associated with the contract c is denoted by : $A(c), c \in C, A(c) \subset A$.
- The validity state of a contract for an agent is denoted by : $\varphi(c, a), c \in C, a \in A, \varphi(c, a) \in \{true, false\}$. The validity state for a contract is denoted by : $\varphi(c) = \wedge_{a_i \in A(c)} \varphi(c, a_i) = (\forall a_i \in A(c), \varphi(c, a_i) = true), c \in C, \varphi(c) \in \{true, false\}$.

Function 1. getContracts($n \in N$)

$Set\ return \leftarrow emptySet()$
if $n \in C$ **then**
  $return.add(n)$
else
  for all $w \in suc(n)$ **do**
    $return.add(getContracts(w))$
  end for
end if
return return

The whole network expresses the problem in its totality :

- A set of accessible states : with our model, the search space is represented by the set of validity states combinations for the contracts of the network.
- A set of constraints to follow : logical relations from the set B stand for these constraints. They allow to compute the satisfaction agent, with respect to the validity state of its associated contracts, thanks to the procedure 2 $getSatisfaction$.

Finally, this network allows to express the possible satisfying situations for an agent, with respect to a set of selected contracts. Each agent must reach the satisfaction for a subset of its associated contracts so as to find a global solution, that is to find $C_{valid} \subset C| \{\forall c \in C_{valid}, \forall a_i \in A(c), \varphi(c, a_i) = true\}$, $\{\forall a \in A, getSatisfaction(a) = true\}$.

Function 2. $\{true, false\}$ getSatisfaction($n \in N$)

if $n \in C$ then
   $c \leftarrow n$
   return $(\nexists a \in A(c)|\varphi(c, a) = false)$
else if $n \in B^{and}$ then
   return $(\nexists s \in suc(n)|getSatisfaction(s) = false)$
else if $n \in B^{or}$ then
   return $(\exists s \in suc(n)|getSatisfaction(s) = true)$
else if $n \in N^{\cdots}$ then
   ... {specific behaviour for the connecting node}
end if

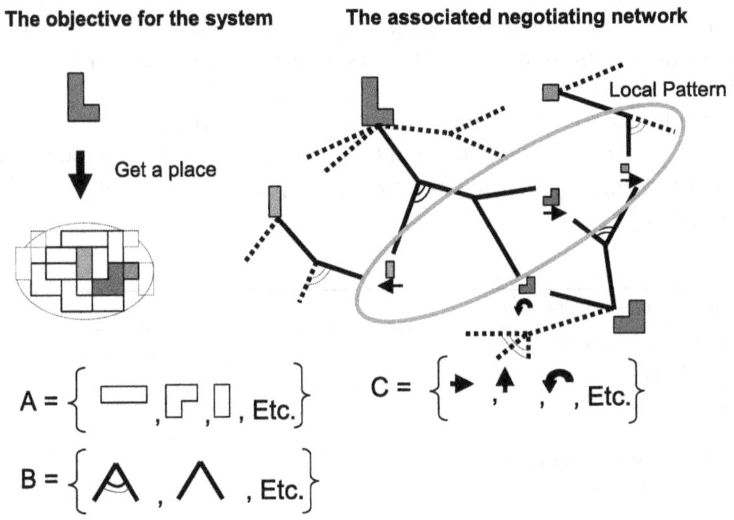

Fig. 1. An illustration of the problem representation

    Thanks to its capacity to represent complex relations between agents, the network can be applied to a spatial negotiation problem, presented on the figure 1, or to critical resource sharing problems. In our model, we do not fix what an agent accounts for (task, resource, etc.), nor the contract types (resource exchange, coordinated move, coherent change, etc.). The network structure can be extended in order to express specific constraints between agents. In this article, we focus on the generic capacity to express relations between agents sharing the same resources.

5   Negotiating Behaviour

While the system evolves, each agent executes a life procedure described in procedure 3. We define an activity period as a life procedure perception/action executed for each agent in a random order. For each activity period, each agent perceives its environment, and influences other agents for the contracts it chooses (figure 2). Each agent benefits from a stigmergic communication : what are the most promising contracts ? Then, each agent makes a reactive choice : it selects a set of satisfying contracts and marks its choices in its environment, influences for its requested contracts.

Function 3. agents Life

while $\exists a \in A | getSatisfaction(a) = false$ **do**
    for all $a \in A$, random order **do**
        $perceiveEnvironment(a)$
        $influenceForContracts(a, a, true)$
    end for
end while

5.1 Perceive Environment

An agent perceives and communicates through the environment. To permit that, each node of the network is associated to a value $\lambda(n | n \in N) \in \mathbb{N}$. For a contract, this value, which express the strength of the attractiveness / repulsiveness, is initialized to zero at the beginning of the resolution process. For the connecting nodes, this value provides a memorization of the perception ; it is updated by the procedure 4.

Function 4. perceiveEnvironment($n \in N$)

if $n \in C$ **then**
    return $\lambda(n)$
else if $n \in B$ **then**
    $List\ buffer \leftarrow emptyList()$
    for all $s \in suc(n)$ **do**
        $buffer \leftarrow buffer + perceiveEnvironment(s)$
    end for
    if $n \in B^{and}$ **then**
        $\lambda(n) \leftarrow average(buffer)$ {return the mean of successors}
    else if $n \in B^{or}$ **then**
        $\lambda(n) \leftarrow maximum(buffer)$ {return the max of successors}
    else if $n \in B^{\cdots}$ **then**
        ... {specific behaviour for the connecting node}
    end if
    return $\lambda(n)$
end if

5.2 Influence for Contracts

From this point, as described in the procedure 5, an agent considers the perceived values to select contracts and request for contracts that could satisfy him.

The ϵ function, not detailed in this paper, allows to give a feedback on the λ value for a contract. If the agent requests the contract, it increases the λ value for the contract in order to raise attention of other associated agents on the contract. On the contrary, when an agent rejects the contract, he decreases the λ value for the contract. Other agents associated with the contract will perceive this communicating act for their next life procedure.

The *exploratoryExpression* function embodies the exploration/exploitation balance for the system. It allows an agent to initiate new contracts. The exploration rate influences the system's performance, as described in section 6.

Function 5. influenceEnvironment($n \in N, a \in A, state \in \{true, false\}$)

---

if $n \in C$ then
    c ← n
    $\varphi(c, a) \leftarrow state$
    $\lambda(c) \leftarrow \lambda(c) + \epsilon(c, state)$ {ϵ , not detailed for this paper, communicate the interest of the agent for the contract}
else if $n \in B^{and}$ then
    for all $s \in suc(n)$ do
        $influenceEnvironment(s, a, state)$
    end for
else if $n \in B^{or}$ then
    if state = true then
        $sucMax = Max_{s \in suc(n)} \lambda(s)$ {Max return a random select among equal max values}
        $sucMax \quad = \quad expressionExploration(sucMax, getSuc(n))$ {exploratoryExpression can change sucMax for an other node, thanks to an exploration parameter described later}
        $influenceForContracts(sucMax, a, true)$
        for all $s \in suc(n) | s \neq sucMax$ do
            $influenceEnvironnement(sucMax, a, false)$
        end for
    else
        for all $s \in suc(n)$ do
            $influenceEnvironnement(s, a, state)$
        end for
    end if
else if $n \in B^{\cdots}$ then
    ... {specific behaviour for the connecting node}
end if

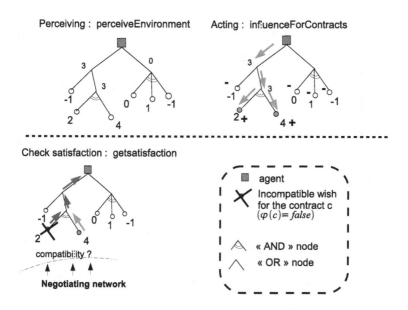

Fig. 2. Perceiving / acting process for an agent

6   Global Coordination Measures

We applied our approach to some randomly generated problems in order to measure the coordination capacity of agents to establish complex contracts. The generated problems contain both N^{or} and N^{and} nodes. We used :

- $\forall n \in B, 1 < suc(n) < 5$
- $\forall a \in A, \forall c \in C, 1 < \delta(a, c) < 6$, with $\delta(c, a)$ the distance between a and c

We guarantee a solution for each generated problem. Whatever the generated problem size, the solving process always reaches the explicitly built solution. For each studied problem, solutions are rare among the set of possible unsuccessful arrangements. It is probable that there is only one solution, that is suitable for the study of the coordination capacity of agents in a constrain environment.

In this section, each collected dot stands for 100 computations. In order to save computing time for our experiments, we stop the solving process after 1000 activity periods. We consider that the process fails, record the failure and count 1000 activity periods for the current measure. In 6.1, we measure the performance of the system with respect to the variation of the exploration parameter value. In 6.2, we measure the influence of the problem size on the time spent before reaching a solution.

6.1   Influence of the Exploration Parameter

On the chart of the figure 3, we represent the influence of the exploration parameter on the average activity period measure. In procedure 5, the function *exploratoryExpression* allows to randomly select a different node from

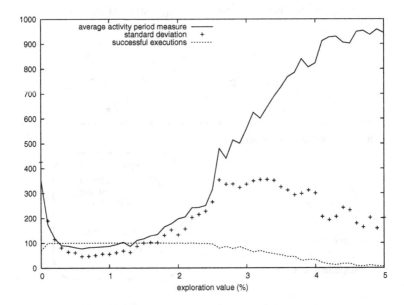

Fig. 3. Impact of the exploration parameter on the resolution time (measures for 100 executions)

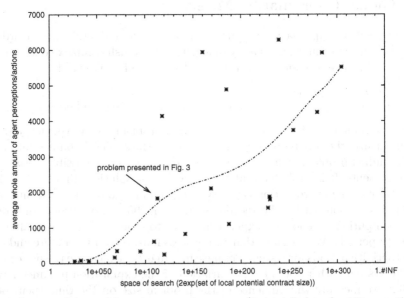

Fig. 4. Impact of the problem size on performances (dots picked up for 100 executions)

the successor perceived as the more promising, with a probability equal to $explorationParameter/100$. We randomly select the following problem : 21 agents must validate 85 contracts (guaranteed solution) among 374 in a 847 nodes graph.

The general aspect of the curve leads to state that the efficient value for the parameter is situated around one percent. In other experiments, like those presented further for the graph coloring problem, the optimal value is located in the same area. It slightly varies according to the graph topology : the exploration depends both on the amount of node from B^{or} and theirs positions in the graph.

We observe that for near zero values, the Multi-Agent System quickly finds the solution, or stands a long time (much than 1000 activity periods) in a bad solving configuration without reaching the solution. Moreover, a large exploration leads to a bad functioning. In this case, it appears difficult to perform complex exchange with a high noise factor. The standard deviation value tends to decrease because the system tends to homogeneously exceed the time limit. The large distance between collected measures point out the necessity for reactive Multi-Agent Systems to ensure a good balancing between exploration and exploitation.

6.2   Influence of the Problem Size

On chart of the figure 4, we show the system response to the increasing of the problem size. We present the average amount of perception/action of agents (= average amount of activity periods * number of agents) according to the size of the search space. For the presented problems, the contracts set size varies from 100 to more than 1000. We represent the search spaces on a logarithmic scale. We set the exploration parameter to 1%.

We notice that the computing time does not depend solely on the problem size. Although consuming time tends to increase with the problem size, we are faced to particularly difficult problems. For the most difficult problems, the solving process never exceeds a few seconds, the success probability is situated around 90%. The linear tendency of the bezier curve approximation represents a logarithmic increasing of the average perception/action done according to the increasing of the addressed problems. For this study, we do not compare the system performance with other approaches for specific problems. We address the problem of agents co-ordination in order to elaborate complex patterns. These satisfying results show that it is possible to coordinate the agent activity in order to build complex exchanges. The proposed negotiation doesn't generate the hyperactivity that we noticed with other models. The previous models react unappropriately to the complexity of patterns, and to the sparsity of the solutions. The proposed multi agent system is successful for constrained problems thanks to its capacity to express the complex characteristics and the choices of agents within the negotiating network. To go further, we attempt a first understanding of the relation between the micro/macro level of the solving process. In section 7, we present other measurements in order to understand the emerging behaviours arising through the negotiation network.

7   Behaviour Analysis

The agent activity allows to cover the accessible states for the system, in order to find a global satisfying pattern. It is difficult to analyze the raw trace arising from the transition state of $\varphi(c) \in \{true, false\}, c \in C$. We do not perceive any coherence on this raw signal which seems to arise from a chaotic behaviour. However, the collected performance measures indicate that the system can address difficult problems. What is the dynamic between order and disorder allowing the coordination of decentralized decisions ? In this section we attempt to show up consistent elements from the raw trace in order to facilitate its study, which allow to partially validate first hypothesis about the emerging behaviour of the system.

7.1   Local to Global and Global to Local Information Propagations

We measure the state transitions for $\varphi(c) \in \{true, false\}, c \in C$ in order to complete the perceived informations, we also memorize and report the state transitions for $\varphi(b) \in \{true, false\}, b \in B$ which stand for the validity state propagated by agents during the procedure 5. On the chart of the figure 5,we propose to foreground deep changes from the raw trace while underlining low transition rate occurrences applied on distinct perimeters :

- deep change measure : Each node is associated with a deep change variable initialized to zero. Each time a node transition occurs (toward satisfied or unsatisfied state) we reset the variable value to zero. Otherwise, we increase the variable value to express the node stability. On the figure 5, we sum this value for nodes belonging of the same perimeter. This allow to observe deep changes over time for each area.
- Distinct perimeters : Starting with a local contract node associated with the perimeter 0, we increase the perimeter each time we cover a connecting node.

While measuring low transition rate occurrences, we can observe a correlation of activity between subparts of the network, from local to global and from global to local. Some of these transitions stand for a branch point for the exploration of the search space. On the chart of the figure 5, we observe the influence of these transitions : they can propagate from local to global (left part) or from global to local (right part). These results comfort our suspicion that the constraints expressed through the network facilitate a non explicit communication between agents, about their state during the solving process. We discuss in the next section the influences between emerging patterns through the network, and the survival conditions for patterns.

7.2   Ability to Memorize

In section 3, we notice that the agent hyperactivity can sometimes prevent the system from reaching a solution. Each time an agent goes on an exploring behaviour, he risks to destroy definitively a pattern that is being constructed. Our model allows agents to perceive the complex characteristics of the problem they are trying to solve and to perceive their state during the solving process. Thanks to this ability, subparts of the negotiating network could influence each others. Nevertheless, how does the system behave face to the demolishing effects of the exploration ? This aspect is related to the capacity of the system to self-organize.

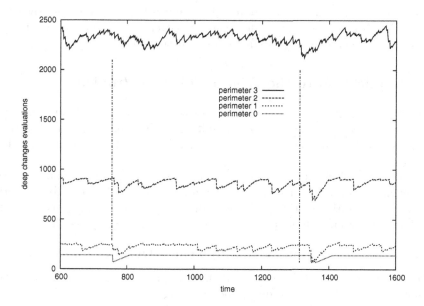

Fig. 5. Deep changes : local to global and global to local

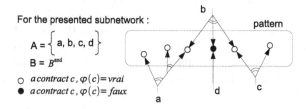

Fig. 6. Pattern memorization

A system self-organizes if it can create and maintain inner stable structures without external control. We represent on the figure 6 a subpart of a network for which an agent d conflicts with a pattern preserved by agents a, b and c. We only represent the B^{and} connection nodes. these nodes are sufficient to represent a pattern (the B^{or} connecting nodes represent alternatives for patterns). Let us study the activity process in this case. The agent d communicates its disagreement, the contract between d and b is invalidated, the agent b perceives it (procedure 4). The agent b also perceives the support given by agents a and c (the agent b perceives from the environment the mean of influences from a, d and c thanks to the procedure 4). The agent b attitude (that is to influence the agent d to take part of the pattern, or discourages the achievement of the pattern supported by the agents a and c) depends on the intensity and on the frequency of the perceived influences. We believe that the survival condition for a pattern depends on its relevance in its environment which represents the state of the problem solving. The system activity allows for the covering of the search space, which is an opportunity for relevant patterns to grow. Two compatibles patterns can merge or be partially adapted if necessary.

8   Application to the Graph Coloring Problem

Graph coloring consists in assigning colours to the graph node in such a way that each directly connected nodes admit different colors. We deal with the *k-coloring* problem. In this context, we know in advance the number of available colours (k).

The graph coloring problem is a very representative complex resource sharing problem. The problem sub-solutions are interdependent. We describe in section 8.1 a representation of this problem in our framework. Then, we compare the performance of our solving process to some other existing approaches.

8.1   A Representation for the Problem in Our Framework

We see on the Figure 7 the network for the graph colouring from the agent point of view. According to our model, each agent is associated with a node of the graph to colour. An agent thus selects a colour. To be satisfied, the selected colour must be coherent with the agent's environment, i.e., the direct neighbours of the considered node in the graph to be coloured (outer consequences of the choice). In addition, the agent communicates its choice in its environment (inner consequences of the choice). Thus, an agent choosing the colour B communicates the fact that it does not carry the colour R : N(R), nor the colour V : N(V). This transverse decomposition allows the agent's of the neighbourhood to check that they are not in conflict, without knowing the precise state of the colouring choice made by the agent.

On the Figure 8, we perceive more precisely the connections between the agents on a complete instance of the model. Each agent expresses its choice

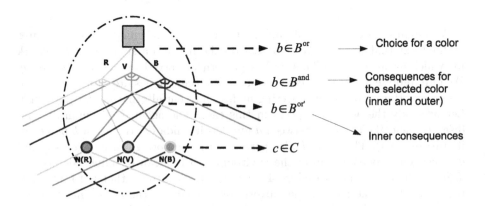

Fig. 7. Colouring network : an agent point of view

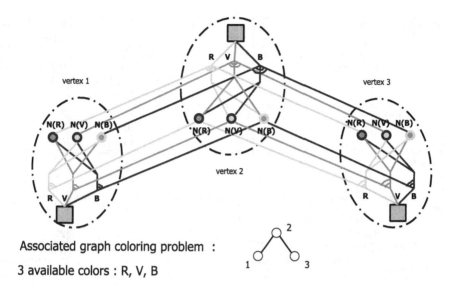

Fig. 8. Coloring network

(inner consequences) and perceives the state of its environment (external consequences). The two channels of communication are however both symmetrical : agents perceive and expresses influences on the two channels of communication. For this representation, we use the most classical nodes of the sets B^{or}, B^{and} and C. An adaptation was carried out for the nodes of the set $B^{or'}$. For this kind of nodes, we broadcast the preferences by flooding (Function 5 *influenceEnvironnement*) according to the colouring information carried out by the nodes of the set B^{and}. Moreover, the node satisfaction is checked by counting as much contract agreements as the number of its neighbours in the colouring graph (Function 2 *getSatisfaction*). Indeed, the agent does not consider the distribution of the agreements between its offspring. Only the number of agreements that allow him to guarantee that he is not contradicting its environment are considered.

8.2   Performance Measures

We applied CESNA to several graph colouring problems with different difficulty levels (Figure 9). For some difficult problems, CESNA quickly converges towards a solution. Solving these problems requires one activity period (AP) on average, even for big size instances (such the graph *miles1000* from Mycielsky which comprises 128 nodes, and requires 42 colors). For these kind of problem, our approach allows to easily perceive the complex characteristics of problems.

In order to study the behaviour of our system on more difficult instances, we used the various graphs studied in [6]. The authors propose a specific EVA algorithm (*Evolutionary Annealing algorithm*) to the problem of scheduling which take profit from a centralized representation of the tackled problems. The hybrid approach presented combines both the genetic algorithm and the

Problem	CESNA approach					EVA Algorithm
	Solved (100 run)	Exploration parameter (%)	AP average	AP Standard deviation	Runtime average (Athlon 3.5 GHz.)	Best time (SUN Sparc 10)
miles1000	100 %	0	1.5	5.1	1.1 s.	N.C.
	100 %	0.1	1	0.3	0.1 s.	N.C.
	100 %	0.2	3.6	13.1	5.6 s.	N.C.
school	100 %	0.1	5.2	36.7	15.7 s.	12 s.
	100 %	0.2	2	1.3	3.6 s.	12 s.
	100 %	0.3	3.2	2.8	8.4 s.	12 s.
school_nsh	99 %	0.1	5.8	29.9	12.9 s.	29 s.
	100 %	0.2	2.1	1.7	3 s.	29 s.
	100 %	0.3	2.8	2.2	5.2	29 s.
le450_5a	0 %	-	-	-	-	366 s.
le450_15c	0 %	-	-	-	-	73392 s.

Fig. 9. CESNA performances for various graph coloring problems

simulated annealing principles for the graph colouring problem. We represent some comparative results on the table of figure 9. The computing times are given as an indication (different machines, language of implementation used for EVA unknown), but permits to have an idea of the solving abilities of the proposed CESNA model.

CESNA gave its best performances with a parameter of exploration bordering 0.1%. The problems such as school1 and school1_nsh studied in [6] are solved without difficulties. Some instances recognized as being difficult (Leighton graphs le450_5a and le450_15c) are currently not solved by the CESNA model. Although the approach does not claim to solve the most difficult problem instances, we did not yet exploit all the capacities of our approach and do not exclude to improve these first results. I

9   Conclusion

In this paper, we have described the critical resource sharing problem as a very complex one, for which we have proposed a MAS negotiation model based on the elaborating of contracts through a network. We have underlined the necessity for the solving process to represent the complex characteristics of the addressed problem in order to allow the coordination of the agent activity. The presented network elaborated and exploited by situated agents, is described as a generic and suitable representation for the problem. We have presented stigmergy as an appropriate communication mechanism in this context. We underline the necessity for the agents to efficiently combine exploitation (reinforcement) and exploration (diversification) behaviours. We have shown that the exploration rate determines the system performances. The analysis of the system behaviour point up a concordance between the local and the global negotiating levels, that allows the coordination process to validate/invalidate emerging patterns. The ability to memorize sub-solutions in order to evaluate them permit to the system to efficiently organize the covering of the search space. Indeed, a pattern (a set of validate coherent contracts on a perimeter) does not disappears because of a bad system decision, but thanks to an extended incompatible activity which describes it as not relevant in its environment, and then not suited for the solution to build. The influences expressed through the network between patterns allow a more relevant covering of the search space and a better convergence speed to a solution.

The good characteristics for this system lead to believe it is self-organized, which mean it make internal structures emerge without external control. We have presented some experimentations to measure the coordination capacity of agents, and have given some first very promising results. We have shown that we can compare CESNA performances to the ones from other specific optimisation methods which benefit from a central representation of the problem.

For the resource sharing domain, there are relatively few reports on the use of reactive behaviours when problem are very constrained. We think that this is due to lack of capacity to consider complex characteristics between contracts during the resolution process with known protocols, and from the associated difficulties to well balance exploration and exploitation in order to find a solution. The presented work contributes to answer those problematics and open a new way to consider the resource sharing problems using multi-agent systems.

References

1. Samir Aknine, Suzanne Pinson, and Melvin F. Shakun. An extended multi-agent negotiation protocol. *Autonomous Agents and Multi-Agent Systems*, 8(1):5–45, 2004.
2. Frédéric Armetta, Salima Hassas, and Simone Pimont. A new protocol to share critical resources by self-organized coordination. In *the Third International Workshop on Engineering Self-Organising Applications (ESOA'05 : AAMAS)*, 2005.
3. Sven A. Brueckner and H. Van Dyke Parunak. Information-driven phase changes in multi-agent coordination. In *AAMAS '03: Proceedings of the second international joint conference on Autonomous agents and multiagent systems*, pages 950–951, New York, NY, USA, 2003. ACM Press.
4. M Campos, E Bonabeau, G Theraulaz, and Deneubourg. Dynamic scheduling and division of labor in social insects. *Adaptive Behaviour*, 8:83–95, 2001.
5. Vincent Cicirello and Stephen Smith. Wasp-like agents for distributed factory coordination. Technical Report CMU-RI-TR-01-39, Robotics Institute, Carnegie Mellon University, Pittsburgh, PA, December 2001.
6. D. A. Fotakis, S. D. Likothanassis, and S. K. Stefanakos. An evolutionary annealing approach to graph coloring. In Egbert J. W. Boers, Stefano Cagnoni, Jens Gottlieb, Emma Hart, Pier Luca Lanzi, Gunther Raidl, Robert E. Smith, and Harald Tijink, editors, *Applications of Evolutionary Computing. EvoWorkshops2001: EvoCOP, EvoFlight, EvoIASP, EvoLearn, and EvoSTIM. Proceedings*, volume 2037, pages 120–129, Como, Italy, 18-19 2001. Springer-Verlag.

7. Salima Hassas. *Systmes Complexes base de Multi-Agents Situs.* Habilitation Diriger des Recherches, Universit Claude Bernard - Lyon 1, Laboratoire d'InfoRmatique en Images et Systmes d'information, Décembre 2003.
8. Hadeli Karuna, Paul Valckenaers, Constantin Bala Zamfirescu, Hendrik Van Brussel, Bart Saint Germain, Tom Holvoet, and Elke Steegmans. Self-organising in multi-agent coordination and control using stigmergy. In Giovanna Di Marzo Serugendo, Anthony Karageorgos, Omer F. Rana, and Franco Zambonelli, editors, *Engineering Self-Organising Applications, First International Workshop, ESOA 2003. Melbourne, Victoria, July 15th, 2003. Workshop Notes*, pages 53–61, 2003.
9. H. Van Dyke Parunak, Sven A. Brueckner, Robert Matthews, and John Sauter. How to calm hyperactive agents. In *Proceedings of the second international joint conference on Autonomous agents and multiagent systems*, pages 1092–1093. ACM Press, 2003.
10. Van Parunak, Sven Brueckner, John Sauter, and R. Matthews. Global Convergence of Local Agent Behaviors. In *The Fourth International Joint Conference on Autonomous Agents & Multi Agent Systems (AAMAS)*, 2005.
11. Reid G. Smith and Randall Davis. Framework for cooperation in distributed problem solving, January 1981.

Reinforcement Learning for Online Control of Evolutionary Algorithms

A.E. Eiben, Mark Horvath, Wojtek Kowalczyk, and Martijn C. Schut

Department of Computer Science, Vrije Universiteit Amsterdam
{gusz,mhorvath,wojtek,schut}@cs.vu.nl

Abstract. The research reported in this paper is concerned with assessing the usefulness of reinforcment learning (RL) for on-line calibration of parameters in evolutionary algorithms (EA). We are running an RL procedure and the EA simultaneously and the RL is changing the EA parameters on-the-fly. We evaluate this approach experimentally on a range of fitness landscapes with varying degrees of ruggedness. The results show that EA calibrated by the RL-based approach outperforms a benchmark EA.

1 Introduction

During the history of evolutionary computing (EC), the automation of finding good parameter values for EAs have often been considered, but never really achieved. Related approaches include meta-GAs [1,6,15], using statistical methods [5], "parameter sweeps" [11], or most recently, estimation of relevance of parameters and values [10]. To our knowledge there is only one study on using reinforcement learning (RL) to calibrate EAs, namely the mutation step size [9]. In this paper we aim at regulating "all" parameters. To position our work we briefly reiterate the classification scheme of parameter calibration approaches in EC after [2,4].

The most conventional approach is *parameter tuning*, where much experimental work is devoted to finding good values for the parameters *before* the "real" runs and then running the algorithm using these values, which remain fixed during the run. This approach is widely practicised, but it suffers from two very important deficiencies. First, the parameter-performance landscape of any given EA on any given problem instance is highly non-linear with complex interactions among the dimensions (parameters). Therefore, finding high altitude points, i.e., well performing combinations of parameters, is hard. Systematic, exhaustive search is infeasible and there are no proven optimization algorithms for such problems. Second, things are even more complex, because the parameter-performance landscape is not static. It changes over time, since the best value of a parameter depends on the given stage of the search process. In other words, finding (near-)optimal parameter settings is a dynamic optimisation problem. This implies that the practice of using constant parameters that do not change during a run is inevitably suboptimal.

S. Brueckner et al. (Eds.): ESOA 2006, LNAI 4335, pp. 151–160, 2007.

Such considerations have directed the attention to mechanisms that would modify the parameter values of an EA on-the-fly. Efforts in this direction are mainly driven by two purposes: the promise of a parameter-free EA and performance improvement. The related methods – commonly captured by the umbrella term *parameter control* can further be divided into one of the following three categories [2,4]. *Deterministic parameter control* takes place when the value of a strategy parameter is altered by some deterministic rule modifying the strategy parameter in a fixed, predetermined (i.e., user-specified) way without using any feedback from the search. Usually, a time-dependent schedule is used. *Adaptive parameter control* works by some form of feedback from the search that serves as input to a heuristic mechanism used to determine the change to the strategy parameter. In the case of *self-adaptive parameter control* the parameters are encoded into the chromosomes and undergo variation with the rest of the chromosome. The better values of these encoded parameters lead to better individuals, which in turn are more likely to survive and produce offspring and hence propagate these better parameter values. In the next section we use this taxonomy/terminology to specify the problem(s) to be solved by the RL-based approach.

2   Problem Definition

We consider an evolutionary algorithm to be a mechanism capable of optimising a collection of individuals, i.e., a way to self-organise some collective of entities. Engineering such an algorithm (specifically: determining the correct/best parameter values) may imply two different approaches: one either *designs* it such that the parameters are (somehow) determined beforehand (like in [10]), or one includes a component that *controls* the values of the parameters during deployment. This paper considers such a control component.

Thus, we assume some problem to be solved by an EA. As presented in [10], we can distinguish 3 layers in using an EA:

- **Application layer:** The problem(s) to solve.
- **Algorithm layer:** The EA with its parameters operating on objects from the application layer (candidate solutions of the problem to solve).
- **Control layer:** A method operating on objects from the algorithm layer (parameters of the EA to calibrate).

The problem itself is irrelevant here, the only important aspect is that we have individuals (candidate solutions) and some fitness (utility) function for these individuals derived from the problem definition. Without significant loss of generality we can assume that the individuals are bitstrings and the EA we have in mind is a genetic algorithm (GA). For GAs the parameter calibration problem in general means finding values for variation operators (crossover and mutation), selection operators (parent selection and survivor selection), and population size. In the present investigation we consider four parameters: crossover rate p_c, mutation rate p_m, tournament size k^1, and population size N. This gives us a paramater quadruple $\langle N, k, p_m, p_c \rangle$ to be regulated. Other components and parameters are the same as for the simple GA that we use as benchmark, cf. Section 4. The rationale behind applying RL for parameter calibration is that we add an RL component to ("above") the GA and use it to specify values for $\langle N, k, p_m, p_c \rangle$ to the underlying GA. Monitoring the behavior of the GA with the given parameters enables the RL component to calculate new, hopefully better, values – a loop that can be iterated several times during a GA run. Within this context, the usefulness of the RL approach will be assessed by comparing the performance of the benchmark GA with a GA regulated by RL.

To this end, we investigate RL that can perform on-the-fly adjustment of parameter values. This has the same functionality as self-adaptation, but the mechanics are different, i.e., not by co-evolving parameters on the chromosomes with the solutions. Here, RL enables the system to learn from the actual run and to calibrate the running EA on-the-fly by using the learned information in the same run.

The research questions implied by this problem description can now be summarized as follows.

1. Is the performance of the RL-enhanced GA better than that of the benchmark GA?
2. How big is the learning overhead implied by using RL?

As for related work, we want to mention that including a control component for engineering self organising applications is not new - the field of autonomic computing recognises the usefulness of reinforcement learning for control tasks [12]. Exemplar applications are autonomous cell phone channel allocation, network packet routing [12], and autonomic network repair [8]. As usual in reinforcement learning problems, these applications typically boil down to finding some optimal *control policy* that best maps actions to system states. For example, in the autonomic network repair application, a policy needs to be found that optimally decides on carrying out costly test and repair actions in order to let the network function properly. The aim of our work is slightly different than finding such a control policy: we assume some problem on the application level that needs to be solved by an EA on the algorithm layer. As explained before, we consider the self organisation to take place on the algorithm level rather than the application level (as is the case for autonomic computing applications).

3 Reinforcement Learning

Our objective is to optimize the performance of an EA-process by dynamically adjusting the control parameters as mentioned above with help of reinforcement learning. The EA-process is split into a sequence of *episodes* and after each

---

[1] Because the population size can vary we use *tournament proportion or tournament rate* (related to the whole population), rather than tournament size.

Table 1. Components of State and Action vectors

Index	State Parameter	Type	Range
s_1	Best fitness	$\mathbb{R}$	0-1
s_2	Mean fitness	$\mathbb{R}$	0-1
s_3	Standard deviation of the fitness	$\mathbb{R}$	0-1
s_4	Breeding success number	$\mathbb{N}$	0-control window
s_5	Average distance from the best	$\mathbb{R}$	0-100
s_6	Number of evaluations	$\mathbb{N}$	0-99999
s_7	Fitness growth	$\mathbb{R}$	0-1
$s_8 - s_{11}$	Previous action vector		
Index	Control Parameter	Type	Range
c_1	Population size	$\mathbb{N}$	3-1000
c_2	Tournament proportion	$\mathbb{R}$	0-1
c_3	Mutation probability	$\mathbb{R}$	0-0.06
c_4	Crossover probability	$\mathbb{R}$	0-1

episode an adjustment of control parameters takes place. The state of the EA-process (measured at the end of every episode) is represented by a vector of numbers that reflect the main properties of the current population: mean fitness, standard deviation of fitness, etc. In a given state an action is taken: new control parameters are found and applied to EA to generate a new episode. The quality of the chosen action, the *reward*, is measured by a function that reflects the progress of the EA-process between the two episodes. Clearly, our main objective is to apply reinforcement learning to learn the function that maps states into actions in such a way that the overall (discounted) reward is maximized. In this paper we decided to represent states and actions by vectors of parameters that are listed in Table 1. The reward function could be chosen in several ways. For example, one could consider improvement of the best (or mean) fitness value, or the success rate of the breeding process. In [9] four different rewarding schemes were investigated and following their findings we decided to define reward as the improvement of the best fitness value.

3.1   The Learning Algorithm

Our learning algorithm is based on a combination of two classical algorithms used in RL: the Q-learning and the SARSA algorithm, both belonging to the broader family of Temporal Difference (TD) learning algorithms, see [14] and [7]. The algorithms maintain a table of state-action pairs together with their estimated discounted rewards, denoted by $Q(s, a)$. The estimates are systematically updated with help of the so-called *temporal difference*:

$$r_{t+1} + \gamma Q(s_{t+1}, a_{t+1}^*) - Q(s_t, a_t)$$

where r, s, a denote reward, state and action, indexed by time, and γ is the reward discount factor. The action a_{t+1}^* can be either the best action in the state s_{t+1} (according to the current estimates of Q) or an action (not necessarily optimal) which is actually executed (in the exploration mode of the learning algorithm). When the best action is chosen we talk about *on-policy TD control* (SARSA learning), otherwise we talk about *off-policy TD control* (Q-learning), [14].

As noticed in [14], both learning strategies have different characteristics concerning convergence speed and ability of finding optima. Therefore, our version of reinforcement learning will be switching between on- and off-policy control at random, with a pre-specified frequency δ.

The approach outlined above works with discrete tables of state-action pairs. In our case, however, both states and actions are continuous. Therefore, during the learning process we will maintain a table of observed states, taken actions and obtained rewards and use this table as a trainig set for modeling the function Q with help of some regression model: a neural network, weighted nearest-neighbour algorithm, regression tree, etc. This, in turn, leads to a yet another problem: given an implicit representation of Q and a current state s, how can we find an optimal action a^* that maximizes $Q(s, a)$? For the purpose of this paper we used a genetic algorithm to solve this sub-problem. However, one could think about using other (perhaps more efficient) optimization methods.

There are two more details that we have implemented in our RL-algorithm: periodical retraining of the Q-function and a restricted size of the training set. Retraining the regression model of Q is an expensive process, therefore it is performed only when a substantial number of new training cases are generated; we will call this number a *batch size*. Using all training cases that were generated during the learning process might be inefficient. For example, "old" cases are usually of low quality and they may negatively influence the learning process. Moreover, a big training set slows down the training process. Therefore we decided to introduce an upper limit on the number of cases that are used in retraining, *memory limit*, and to remove the oldest cases when necessary. The pseudo-code of our training algorithm is presented in Figure 1.

The randomization process that is mentioned in lines 6 and 10 uses several parameters. Reinforcement learning has to spend some effort on exploring the unknown regions of the policy space by switching, from time to time, to the *exploration mode*. The probability of entering this mode is determined by value of the parameter ε. During the learning process this value is decreasing exponentially fast, until a lower bound is reached. We will refer to the initial value of ε, the discount factor and the lower bound as ε-initial value, ε-discount factor and ε-minimal, respectively.

In exploration mode an action is usually selected at random using a uniform probability distribution over the space of possible actions. However, this common strategy could be very harmful for the performance of the EA. For instance, by decreasing the population size to 1 the control algorithm could practically kill the EA-process. To prevent such situations we introduced a new mechanism for exploration that explores areas that are close to the optimal action. As the optimal action is found with help of a separate optimization process, we control

1 Initialize Q abitrarily
2 Initialize ε
3 **Repeat** (for each episode)
4   Ask the controlled system for initial state s
5   Choose an action a' according to the optimization over the function $Q(s, a')$
6   a = randomize a' with ε probability.
7   **Repeat** (for each step of the episode)
8   Do action a, and observe r, s'
9   Choose an action a' that oprimizes the function $Q(s', a')$
10   a'' = randomize a' with ε probability.
11   Add new training instance to Q: $\langle s, a, r + \gamma(\delta Q(s', a') + (1 - \delta)Q(s', a'')) \rangle$
12   Re-train Q if the number of new cases reached the *batch size*
13        $s = s'$
14        $a = a''$
15   (until s is not a terminal state)
16 Decrease ε

Fig. 1. The pseudo-code of our training algorithm

our exploration strategy with a parameter that measures the *optimization effort*. Clearly, the smaller the effort, the more randomness in the exploration process. As mentioned earlier, in this research we used a separate genetic algorithm to find optimal actions. Therefore, we can express the optimization effort in terms of the rate of decrease of the number of evaluations in the underlying genetic process.

3.2   System Architecture

The overall architecture of our learning system is shown in Figure 2. It consists of three components: General Manager, State-Action Evaluator and Action Optimizer.

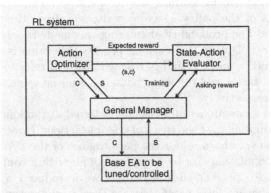

Fig. 2. The architecture of a RL-controller for EA

General Manager is responsible for managing the whole process of RL. It maintains a training set of state vectors, together with taken actions and rewards, activates the training procedure for modeling the Q function and calls Action Optimizer to chose an action in a given state.

Action Optimizer contains an optimisation procedure (in our case: a genetic algorithm referred to as AO-EA) which is responsible for seeking an optimal action (a vector of control parameters). In other words, for a given state s the module seeks an optimum of the function $Q(s, \_)$ that is maintained by the State-Action Evaluator module.

State-Action Evaluator maintains a function that estimates the expected discounted reward values for arbitrary state-action pairs. The function is implemented as a regression model (a neural network, weighted nearest-neigbour, regression tree, etc.) and can be retrained with help of a suitable learning alrgoritm and a training set that is maintained by the General Manager Module.

4   Experiments

The test suite[2] for testing GAs is obtained through the Multimodal Problem Generator of Spears [13]. We generate 10 landscapes of 1, 2, 5, 10, 25, 50, 100, 250, 500 and 1000 binary peaks whose heights are linearly distributed and where the lowest peak is 0.5. The length L of these bit strings is 100. The fitness of an individual is measured by the Hamming distance between the individual and the nearest peak, scaled by the height of that peak.

We define an adaptive GA (AGA) with on-the-fly control by RL. The AGA works with control heuristics generated by RL on the fly. RL is thus used here at runtime to generate control heuristics for the GA.

The setup of the SGA is as follows (based on [3]). The model we use is a steady-state GA. Every individual is a 100-bitstring. The recombination operator is 2-point crossover; the recombination probability is 0.9. The mutation operator is bit-flip; the mutation probability is 0.01. The parent selection is 2-tournament and survival selection is delete-worst-two. The population size is 100. Initialisation is random. The termination criterion is $f(x) = 1$ or 10,000 evaluations.

The parameters of the RL system have to be tuned, which has been done through extensive tuning and testing resulting in the parameter settings shown in Table 2. We used the REPTree algorithm [16] as the regression model for the State-Action Evaluator.

As mentioned in the introduction, the Success Rate (SR), the Average number of Evaluations to a Solution (AES) and its standard deviation (SDAES), and the Mean Best Fitness (MBF) and its standard deviation (SDMBF) are calculated after 100 runs of each GA.

The results of the experiments are summarised in Figure 3. The experiments 1-10 on the x-axis correspond the different landscapes with 1, 2, 5, 10, 25, 50, 100, 250, 500 and 1000 binary peaks, respectively.

---

[2] The test suite can be obtained from the webpage of the authors of this paper.

Table 2. Parameter settings of the RL system

Parameter	Value
Reward discount factor (γ)	0.849643
Rate of on- or off-policy learning (δ)	0.414492
Memory limit	8778
Exploration probability (ε)	0.275283
ε-discount factor	0.85155
ε-minimal	0.956004
Probablility of uniform random exploration	0.384026
Optimization effort	0.353446

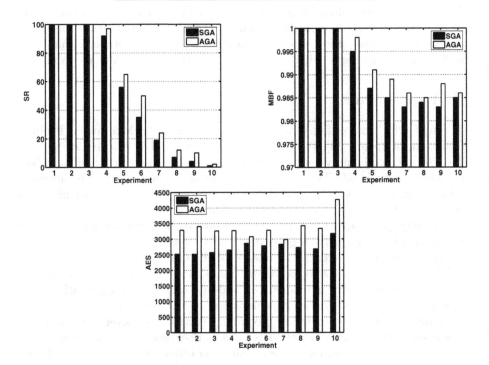

Fig. 3. SR, MBF and AES results for SGA and AGA

The results shown in Figure 3 contain sufficient data to answer our research questions from Section 2 – at least for the test suite used in this investigation. The first research question concerns the performance of the benchmark SGA vs. the RL-enhanced variant. Considering the MBF measure it holds that the AGA consistently outperforms the SGA. More precisely, on the easy problems SGA is equally good, but as the number of peaks (problem hardness) is growing, the adaptive GA becomes better. The success rate results are in-line with this picture: the more peaks the greater the advantage of the adaptive GA. Considering the third performance measure, speed defined by AES, we obtain another ranking. The SGA is faster than the AGA. This is not surprising, because of the RL learning overhead.

We are also interested in the overhead caused by reinforcement learning. From the systems perspective this is measurable by the lenghts of the GA runs. The AES results indicate the price of using RL in the on-line mode: approximately 20-30% increase of effort.[3] From the users perspective there is an overhead as well. The RL extension needs to be implemented (one-time investment) and the RL system needs to be calibrated. This latter one can take substantial time and/or innovativeness. For the present study we used a semi-automated approach through a meta-RL to optimize the parameters of our RL controlling the GA. We omit the details here, simply remarking that the RL parameter settings shown in Table 2 have been obtained by this approach.

5 Conclusions and Further Research

This paper described a study into the usefulness of reinforcement learning for online control of evolutionary algorithms. The study shows: firstly, concerning fitness and succes rate, the RL-enhanced GA outperforms the benchmark GA; concerning speed (number of evaluations), the RL-enhanced GA is outperformed by the benchmark GA. Secondly, also for the overhead of RL the user needs to tune the RL parameters causing overhead.

For future work, we consider a number of options. Firstly, our results indicate that on-the-fly control can be effective in design problems (given time interval, in search of optimal solution). To find best solutions to a problem, we hypothesize it is better to concentrate on solving the problem rather than finding the optimal control of the problem. This hypothesis requires further research. Secondly, the RL systems may be given more degrees of freedom: choice of probability of applying different operators, type of selection mechanism, include special operators to jump out of local optima. Finally, whereas RL in the presented work controls global parts of the EA, we consider the inclusion of local decisions like selection of individuals or choosing the right operator for each individual.

References

1. J. Clune, S. Goings, B. Punch, and E. Goodman. Investigations in meta-gas: panaceas or pipe dreams? In *GECCO '05: Proceedings of the 2005 workshops on Genetic and evolutionary computation*, pages 235–241, New York, NY, USA, 2005. ACM Press.
2. A. Eiben, R. Hinterding, and Z. Michalewicz. Parameter control in evolutionary algorithms. *IEEE Transactions on Evolutionary Computation*, 3(2):124–141, 1999.
3. A. Eiben, E. Marchiori, and V. Valko. Evolutionary algorithms with on-the-fly population size adjustment. In X. et al, editor, *Parallel Problem Solving from Nature, PPSN VIII*, volume 3242 of *LNCS*, pages 41–50. Springer, 2004.
4. A. Eiben and J. Smith. *Introduction to Evolutionary Computing*. Springer, 2003.

---

[3] We assume that fitness evaluations constitute the huge majority of computational efforts running a GA.

5. O. Francois and C. Lavergne. Design of evolutionary algorithms – a statistical perspective. *IEEE Trans. on Evolutionary Computation*, 5(2):129–148, 2001.
6. J. Grefenstette. Optimization of control parameters for genetic algorithms. *IEEE Trans. Syst. Man Cybern.*, 16(1):122–128, 1986.
7. L. P. Kaelbling, M. L. Littman, and A. P. Moore. Reinforcement learning: A survey. *Journal of Artificial Intelligence Research*, 4:237–285, 1996.
8. M. Littman, N. Ravi, E. Fenson, and R. Howard. Reinforcement learning for autonomic network repair. In *Proceedings of the International Conference on Autonomic Computing (ICAC 2004)*, pages 284–285. IEEE Computer Society, 2004.
9. S. D. Mueller, N. N. Schraudolph, and P. D. Koumoutsakos. Step size adaptation in evolution strategies using reinforcement learning. In D. B. Fogel, M. A. El-Sharkawi, X. Yao, G. Greenwood, H. Iba, P. Marrow, and M. Shackleton, editors, *Proceedings of the 2002 Congress on Evolutionary Computation CEC2002*, pages 151–156. IEEE Press, 2002.
10. V. Nannen and A. Eiben. Relevance estimation and value calibration of evolutionary algorithm parameters. In *Proceedings of IJCAI'07, the 2007 International Joint Conference on Artificial Intelligence*. Morgan Kaufmann Publishers, 2007. to appear.
11. M. E. Samples, J. M. Daida, M. Byom, and M. Pizzimenti. Parameter sweeps for exploring GP parameters. In H.-G. Beyer, U.-M. O'Reilly, D. V. Arnold, W. Banzhaf, C. Blum, E. W. Bonabeau, E. Cantu-Paz, D. Dasgupta, K. Deb, J. A. Foster, E. D. de Jong, H. Lipson, X. Llora, S. Mancoridis, M. Pelikan, G. R. Raidl, T. Soule, A. M. Tyrrell, J.-P. Watson, and E. Zitzler, editors, *GECCO 2005: Proceedings of the 2005 conference on Genetic and evolutionary computation*, volume 2, pages 1791–1792, Washington DC, USA, 25-29 June 2005. ACM Press.
12. B. D. Smart. Reinforcement learning: A user's guide. Tutorial at International Conference on Autonomic Computing (ICAC 2005), 2005.
13. W. Spears. *Evolutionary Algorithms: the role of mutation and recombination.* Springer, Berlin, Heidelberg, New York, 2000.
14. R. S. Sutton and A. G. Barto. *Reinforcement Learning: an Introduction.* MIT Press, 1998.
15. G. Wang, E. D. Goodman, and W. F. Punch. Toward the optimization of a class of black box optimization algorithms. In *Proc. of the Ninth IEEE Int. Conf. on Tools with Artificial Intelligence*, pages 348–356, New York, 1997. IEEE Press.
16. I. H. Witten and E. Frank. *Data Mining: Practical Machine Learning Tools and Techniques.* Morgan Kaufmann, San Francisco, 2 edition, 2005.

Greedy Cheating Liars and the Fools Who Believe Them*

Stefano Arteconi, David Hales, and Ozalp Babaoglu

University of Bologna
Dept. of Computer Science
{arteconi,hales,babaoglu}@cs.unibo.it

Abstract. Evolutionary algorithms based on "tags" can be adapted to induce cooperation in selfish environments such as peer-to-peer systems. In this approach, nodes periodically compare their utilities with random other peers and copy their behavior and links if they appear to have better utilities. Although such algorithms have been shown to posses many of the attractive emergent properties of previous tag models, they rely on the honest reporting of node utilities, behaviors and neighbors. But what if nodes do not follow the specified protocol and attempt to subvert it for their own selfish ends? We examine the robustness of a simple algorithm under two types of cheating behavior: a) when a node can lie and cheat in order to maximize its own utility and b) when a node acts nihilistically in an attempt to destroy cooperation in the network. For a test case representing an abstract cooperative application, we observe that in the first case, a certain percentage of such "greedy cheating liars" can actually improve certain performance measures, and in the second case, the network can maintain reasonable levels of cooperation even in the presence of a limited number of nihilist nodes.

1 Introduction

Recent evolutionary "tag" models developed within social simulation and computational sociology [7,16] have been proposed as possible candidates for robust distributed computing applications such as peer-to-peer file sharing [9]. These models exhibit a mechanism by which even greedy, local optimizers may come to act in an unselfish manner through a "group like" selection process.

Evolutionary models rely on the concept of a "fitness" or "utility" which can be derived by each individual within a population, usually based on how well it is performing some task. Variants of behavior within the population are assumed to be selected and reproduced in proportion to relative utilities, resulting in fitter variants growing in the population.

In order to apply these evolutionary models to distributed systems, we need to capture the notion of fitness or utility, as well as the process of differential

---

* Partially supported by the EU within the Sixth Framework Programme under contract 001907 "Dynamically Evolving, Large Scale Information Systems (DELIS)".

S. Brueckner et al. (Eds.): ESOA 2006, LNAI 4335, pp. 161–175, 2007.

spreading of behavioral variants. In previously proposed P2P applications, each node derived its utility from some measure of on-going performance. For example, in a file-sharing application, the number of successful downloads can be used [9]. Nodes then periodically compared their utility with another peer chosen randomly from the population. Of the pair, the node with the lower utility then copied the behavior and links of the "fitter" peer. This sort of "tournament selection" rule can be seen as "reproducing" fitter nodes and replacing the less fit ones. Alternatively it can be viewed as less fit nodes copying fitter nodes to improve their performance.

For this mechanism to work, however, nodes must behave correctly and report their local state to other nodes honestly. Yet, a node may deviate from its expected behavior or lie to other nodes about any one of the following: its utility, its behavior and its neighbor links (when the other node wishes to copy them). What happens if such "cheating liar" nodes are allowed to enter the network? What if they cheat for their own benefit or act maliciously to destroy cooperation that may exist among other nodes?

In this paper we make a distinction between different kinds of node behaviors. Nodes that follow a protocol specification but act selfishly to increase their own performance rather than cooperating to improve global system performance (e.g. leechers in a file-sharing system) are called *selfish* nodes. On the other hand nodes that do not follow the protocol specification we term *deviant*, while nodes which use their knowledge of the protocol to act against it and to achieve some local goal we call *cheaters*.

In an earlier work, we have shown that an evolutionary inspired protocol called SLACER can achieve and maintain small-world networks with chains of cooperating nodes linking all node pairs (so-called artificial social networks) in a robust manner [8]. In this paper, we study SLACER when it is subjected to four different types of deviant node behavior. In each case, deviant nodes use their knowledge of the SLACER protocol and the application task at hand (the canonical Prisoners' Dilemma game) in an attempt to exploit those that are faithfully following the protocol. The four variants of deviant behavior fall into two classes based on their goals: 1) Greedy Cheating Liars (GCL) try to maximize their own utility; 2) Nihilists (NIH) try to degrade the utility of the entire network, even at their own expense.

We find that the SLACER protocol is surprisingly robust, exhibiting graceful degradation of performance measures even when large proportions of nodes are Greedy Cheating Liars. Even more interestingly, we observe that under certain conditions, GCL nodes actually improve certain network performance parameters. In a way, we can view GCL nodes as performing a sort of "service" for which the honest nodes are "taxed". This observation suggests that P2P applications can perhaps be designed to accommodate certain deviant behaviors rather than trying to detect and isolate them.

Nihilist nodes, on the other hand, are more disruptive for the SLACER protocol and even relatively limited proportions of such nodes can degrade the performance of other nodes significantly.

The rest of the paper is organized as follows: in Section 2 we briefly discuss related work on deviant and selfish nodes. In Section 3 the SLACER protocol is described and its vulnerabilities are presented. In Section 4 experimental results for SLACER with honest nodes are analyzed. We introduce the four deviant behavior variants in Section 5 and in Section 6 present experimental results in their presence. Finally in Section 7 conclusions are drawn.

2   Related Work

Given the decentralized nature of P2P systems and the consequent lack of central control, cooperation between nodes is fundamental. To achieve this goal, different incentives and trust mechanisms have been developed [11,14].

Classical approaches to detect deviant nodes and avoid system inconsistencies include data replication, quorum techniques [12] and distributed state machines (DSM) [4]. Although originally designed for client-server systems to solve problems such as data consistency between replicated servers, such methods have recently been used to address cooperation as well as reliability in closed P2P systems requiring some kind of central authority to manage node identities and capabilities to join the system [1]. On the other hand, open P2P networks, where nodes can freely join the system without any cost, can be extremely large and dynamic due to continuous joining and leaving of nodes and rewiring of their neighbor links. In such environments, the proposed techniques appear not to be feasible. Alternative solutions are given by fully decentralized, probabilistic punishment schemes as in [5], but again dynamicity remains a problem in that a deviant node can subvert such a system by frequently rewiring to different nodes.

A more sophisticated approach, able to deal with free-riding nodes as well as cheating and deviant ones, is described in [6]. Here a distributed shared history mechanism is used to calculate trust values for all nodes including strangers (new nodes). This method can limit the incentives for selfish and cheating behavior as well as deterring colluders (cheating nodes jointly operating to exploit other nodes in the network). This approach is limited, however, because no distinction is made between new nodes joining the system (strangers) because a single entry in the shared history is used to take all of them into account as if they were a single node. This means whitewashers - nodes that constantly adopt new identities to escape detection of their deviant behavior - can potentially make the system expensive to join, in the sense that strangers (even non-deviant ones) may be initially punished as if they were deviant nodes, hence they might be discouraged from joining the network.

Our approach called SLACER (see next section) is based on simple, local node interactions with no need for notions and mechanisms such as trust, incentives and shared histories.

Algorithms based on reciprocity (e.g., the well-known tit-for-tat strategy [3]) require that each node store the last interaction it had with each other node it encounters. The strategy works by punishing non cooperative behaviour in future interactions. This can be a problem in a large and dynamic system where nodes often interact with strangers they have never met before. In this case, tit-for-tat dictates that strangers be treated with unconditional cooperation, and this allows selfish nodes to exploit tit-for-tat. Our solution draws on an evolutionary approach that does not require reciprocity [18,16]. The novel approach used in SLACER obviates the need for maintaining histories of past node behaviour or on-going interactions between the same nodes.

3   The SLACER Protocol

SLACER (Selfish Link Adaptation for Cooperation Excluding Rewiring) is a decentralized, local protocol that builds small-world like artificial social (overlay) networks with high levels of cooperation between nodes [8].

Each node in SLACER has a *strategy* which is an application-defined behavior (for example, how willing the node shares files with others), a *view* which is a bounded-size list of immediate neighbors in the network and a *utility* which is again defined by the application and measures how well the node is performing. SLACER assumes that nodes are able to modify their local views and strategies, as well as copy them from other peers, in an effort to increase their utility. It requires a random peer sampling service selectPeer() to be used in reproduction and view mutation steps[1]. The basic steps of the SLACER protocol consist of each node periodically selecting a random peer, comparing the local utility with that of the random peer, and copying the peer's strategy and view if it has a higher utility.

By copying another node's view, a node performs a *rewiring* of its links to a new neighborhood and effectively "moves" to a new location in the network[2]. A node's life is divided into *cycles*. In addition to performing application-specific tasks, at each cycle every node tries to increase its performance by copying nodes with higher utility with a given probability ρ. This action, also called *reproduction* after the evolutionary inspiration, is illustrated in Figure 1.

```
j ← peerSelect() //pick a random node
if i.utility ≤ j.utility then
  for each element e of i.view do
    remove e with probability ω
  i.strategy ← j.strategy
  i.view ← i.view ∪ j.view ∪ j //add j and j.view
  i.utility ← 0         //reset local utility
```

Fig. 1. Slacer reproduction phase pseudocode

After the reproduction phase nodes "mutate". Mutation can affect both node strategy and view. With some (low) probability μ, a node replaces its strategy with a different one. With some other (low) probability ν, a node changes

---

[1] In our implementation, we use the NEWSCAST protocol for peer sampling[10].

[2] If node view exceeds size-limit random elements are dropped.

its view by removing each link with probability ω (the same value used in the reproduction phase) and then linking to a node selected randomly over the population.

SLACER can be seen as a middleware layer (see Figure 2) for building dynamic artificial social (overlay) networks that are conducive to cooperation. To use SLACER, an application must define an appropriate *utility function* capturing the effective local benefit derived from the behavior adopted by a node (for example, number of packets received in a routing scenario, downloaded files in a file sharing application, detected spam messages in a collaborative spam filter, etc.).

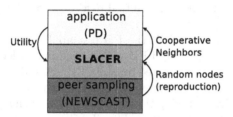

Fig. 2. SLACER middleware architecture

In this paper the Prisoners' Dilemma game is used as a benchmark application to test SLACER performance. This is an interesting and relevant application for our study since it captures the tension between "individual rationality" and "common good" that is typical of many P2P scenarios.

3.1   Prisoners' Dilemma Test Application

The single-round *Prisoners' Dilemma* (PD) game consists of two players selecting independently one out of two possible choices: to *cooperate* (C) or to *defect* (D), and receiving different payoffs according to the four possible outcomes as illustrated in Table 1.

	C	D
C	R, R	S, T
D	T, S	P, P

Table 1. Prisoners' Dilemma payoff matrix

The game captures scenarios where collective interest contradicts the individual one. This game has been selected as a test application because it captures a wide range of possible application tasks where nodes need to establish cooperation and trust with their neighbors without any central authority or coordination. Some practical examples include file or resource sharing, routing messages to facilitate communication between senders and receivers, or warning friends about a virus program and supplying them with a locally available fix.

The dilemma originates from the following constraints among the payoff values under the assumption that players wish to maximize their own payoff: $T > R > P > S$ and $2R > T + S$. Hence although both players would prefer the highest payoff T, only one can obtain it in a single round of the game. When both players select D this leads to the *Nash equilibrium* [13] as well as an *evolutionary stable strategy* (ESS) [17]. Hence, in a population of randomly paired players, a rational selfish player (one that is trying to maximize its own utility) would always play D. If both players select C, they would both perform better (earning R each) than if they both selected D (earning P each) but evolutionary pressure and individual rationality result in mutual defection, so players are pushed to play D and consequently earn P.

In the context of SLACER, the PD test application consists of nodes periodically playing a single-round PD with a randomly selected neighbor from the social network that is constructed by SLACER[3]. A node can only choose between the two pure strategies "always cooperate" or "always defect". The node utility value is obtained by averaging the payoffs received during past game interactions as defined by the PD application. The SLACER protocol then adapts the links and strategies of nodes in an evolutionary fashion as discussed previously.

4   Experimental Results Without Cheaters

In order to obtain a base-line performance, we simulated the SLACER protocol without deviant or cheating nodes — all the nodes follow the protocol faithfully. All of the simulations were performed using *PeerSim*, a P2P overlay network simulator developed at the University of Bologna [15]. We examine cooperation formation (how long it takes for cooperation to spread and the levels reached) and network topology (connectivity, clustering coefficient, etc).

The SLACER parameters used were: $\omega = 0.9, \rho = 0.2, \mu = 0.01$ and $\nu = 0.005$ with a view size limit of 20. Our results show averages over 10 different runs along with 90% confidence intervals when present.

4.1   Cooperation Formation

Figure 3 shows the evolution of cooperation level during a single, typical SLACER run, starting from a random network of all defector nodes. Cooperation reaches very high levels (about 95% of the nodes are cooperating) within a few hundred cycles.

When starting from complete defection, for cooperation to start increasing, it is necessary that two neighboring nodes mutate to cooperating strategies and play a PD round obtaining payoff R. From this point onwards, since cooperating node clusters perform better than defecting node clusters, cooperation rapidly spreads throughout the network by reproduction.

---

[3] Note that the reproduction phase utilizes a *different* random overlay network: that constructed by the NEWSCAST protocol for peer selection.

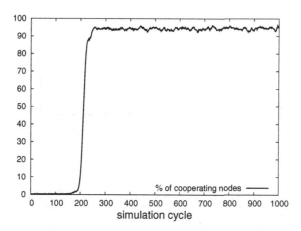

Fig. 3. Cooperation evolution for 4000 nodes

In Figure 4, the time needed to achieve a 95% cooperation level for different network sizes is shown. It is interesting to note that the larger the network, the less time it takes to achieve the same level of cooperation. Furthermore, for larger networks, the results have smaller variance. This is a consequence of fact that the mutation rate and the maximum view size are independent of the network size, and the probability for triggering cooperation as described above increases with network size.

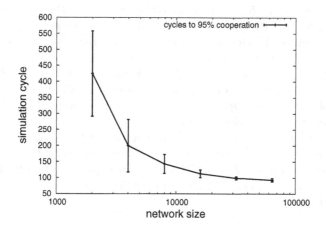

Fig. 4. Time to achieve cooperation for different network sizes

4.2 Network Topology

To analyze properties of the network resulting from SLACER, we adopt traditional topology metrics such as *clustering coefficient* (CC) and *average path length* (APL) in addition to specific metrics *largest cooperative component*

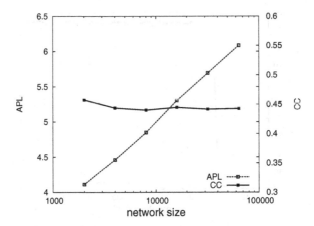

Fig. 5. Clustering Coefficient and Average Path Length for different network sizes

(LCC), *connected cooperative path* (CCP) and *connected cooperative path length* (CCPL).

LCC measures the size of the largest cluster in the subnetwork formed by cooperative nodes only, relative to the total network size. CCP is the proportion of node pairs that are connected through cooperative paths — paths of either length one or that contain cooperating nodes exclusively. CCPL measures the average length of such cooperative paths.

Observing the CC and APL for networks of different sizes produced by SLACER (see Figure 5), we note that they belong to the small world family — CC is high and APL small. Moreover, APL scales log-linearly with respect to network size while CC remains constant suggesting that the network is composed of a growing number of interconnected clusters.

The very large LCC values displayed in Figure 6 indicates a single connected component that accounts for almost the entire network. In other words, partitioning of the network appears not to occur even though SLACER is highly dynamic due to the rewiring of nodes.

Finally, because the CCP values are high and CCPL values are similar to APL (as discussed in [2]), we conclude that selfish nodes in the network (those that have opted to play D in the PD) do not occupy important positions blocking paths between cooperating nodes or resulting in cooperative clusters to be partitioned.

5   Four Kinds of Cheating Nodes

So far we have shown how SLACER can effectively handle selfish nodes — nodes that adopt the defect strategy. What happens if nodes not only act selfishly, but deviate deliberately from the protocol specification?

One way for a node to deviate is to lie about its state to other nodes. When asked during the reproduction phase, a node can report arbitrary values to a peer

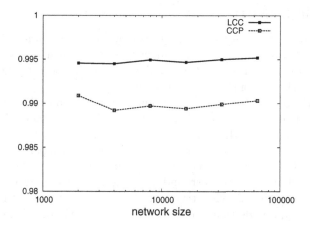

Fig. 6. Largest Connected Component and Cooperative Connected Path for different network sizes

for its strategy, its utility or its view. A deviant node may have the objective to *exploit* or to *destroy* the network. A node that wants to exploit the network wants to maximize its own utility without any regard for the rest of the system. A node aiming to destroy the network wants to lower the utility of all others. We term both such kinds of nodes as *cheating* nodes. In the next sections we outline four possible types of cheating behaviors.

5.1 Greedy Cheating Liars (GCL)

Let us first consider nodes that want to maximize their own utility at the expense of others. In the PD application, but the reasoning applies to any other similar scenario, the maximum possible payoff is obtained by a defecting node when it plays against a cooperating one.

To achieve a high utility then, a node will play the pure strategy "always defect" and never change it. To force its neighbors to behave altruistically, it will report a cooperating strategy when asked. So as not to be excluded from cooperative clusters (through rewiring), it has to rig the utility comparison to guarantee being the "winner" of any utility comparison by another node. This can be easily achieved by lying about utility, reporting always a very large value. Finally, when a node finds itself in a neighborhood that is unsatisfactory (i.e., playing against defectors resulting in an average payoff less than T) it rewires its view causing it to move to a new location in the network.

In summary, a node that wants to exploit the network behaves as follows:

- Always plays D.
- Always declares to be playing C.
- Always declares a high utility (e.g., $2T$).
- Rewires when surrounded by mostly defectors (average payoff less than T).

We call such nodes *Greedy Cheating Liars* (GCL).

5.2 Nihilists (NIH)

Nihilist nodes try to destroy the network by forcing it towards defection, irrespective of their own utilities. To achieve this, a nihilist node itself needs to play the pure strategy "always defect" and bring other nodes to defection as well through a technique similar to GCL nodes.

Since the goal is to spread defection, a nihilist node does not need to lie about it's strategy. On the contrary, it always defects and always reports a defecting strategy. On the other hand, to spread defection and build clusters of only defecting nodes, it needs to win all of the utility comparisons it participates it. This can be obtained by declaring very high utility.

When a nihilist node is surrounded by mostly defectors (i.e., average payoff close to P) it rewires its view trying to destroy other parts of the network.

In summary, a node that wants to destroy the network behaves as follows:

- Always plays D.
- Always declares to be playing D.
- Always declares a high utility (e.g., $2T$).
- Rewires when surrounded by mostly defectors (average payoff close to P).

We call such nodes *Nihilists* (NIH).

5.3 Lying About Views

We have also tested what we call "GCL+" and "NIH+" nodes that lie about views as well. When asked for their view, GCL+ nodes report only a link to themselves in an effort to become "hubs" for other nodes and exploit them. NIH+ nodes, on the other hand, report a set of random links from the population as their view in an attempt to spread defection to a wider population. These two cheating variants do not lead to significant differences in cooperation formation behavior with respect to the original GCL and NIH cases. They do, however, affect network topology which we discuss elsewhere [2].

6 Experimental Results with Cheaters

SLACER performance when cheating nodes are present will be now evaluated. We will analyze how cheating nodes influence previously studied cooperation formation and network topology. Moreover, the relative performances of cheating and non-cheating nodes will be compared and discussed.

6.1 Cooperation Formation with Cheaters

Cheating nodes force other nodes to adopt strategies by lying about their state, and as a consequence, cooperation formation follows a different pattern from the case where all nodes are truthful. In Figure 7 the cooperation levels that are achieved and time necessary to achieve them are shown as a function of percentage of cheating nodes in a network of 4000 nodes.

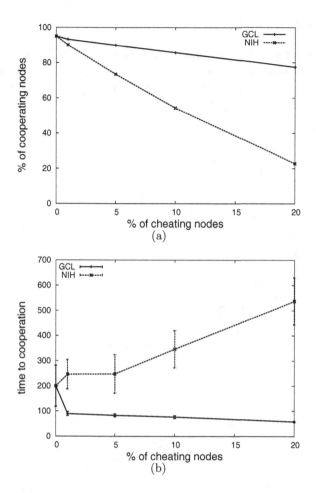

Fig. 7. Cooperation formation with cheating nodes. (a) Cooperation level achieved, (b) Time to achieve cooperation.

GCL nodes try to force other nodes to be cooperators so that they can exploit them (by defecting). As a result their presence in the network accelerates the spread of cooperation. Almost all the non-GCL nodes become cooperative with high cooperation reached in a shorter time than in a network with no cheaters (see Figure 7(b)).

Having more NIH nodes, on the other hand, increases the time to cooperation. Even though the presence of NIH nodes generally has a negative effect on the network, large numbers of them are needed to bring cooperation down to critical levels as can be seen in Figure 7(a). This indicates the network is resilient though not immune from this kind of attack.

The irregularity in Figure 7(b) for low quantities of NIH nodes results from the fact that NIH nodes make time to cooperation quite unstable (highly variable over different runs) as illustrated by the large confidence interval.

6.2   Network Topology with Cheaters

The presence of GCL and NIH nodes does not affect SLACER network topology formation. Even though cooperation performance could be significantly changed, GCL and NIH nodes use SLACER defined drop and rewiring rules, hence no significant topology modification is involved.

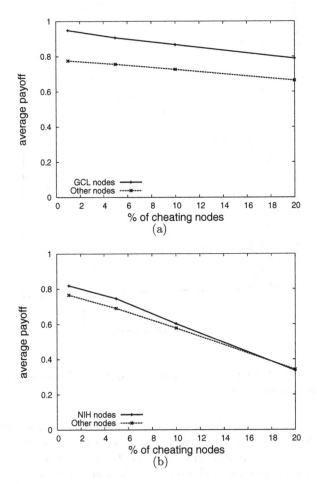

Fig. 8. Utility values in the presence of (a) Greedy Cheating Liars, and (b) Nihilists

6.3   Utilities

Here we consider how node utilities change when there are cheating nodes in the network.

PD payoffs used are $T = 1, R = 0.8, P = 0.1, S = 0$ so average payoff should be equal to 0.8 for a totally cooperating network and 0.1 for a totally defecting one, while the main goal is to have average payoff equal to 1 for GCL nodes, and 0.1 for NIH nodes[4].

Looking at Figure 8, with a small amount of GCL nodes, both cheating and non-cheating nodes have average payoff close to the maximum possible value (1 and 0.8 respectively), but increasing the number of cheating nodes results in both their payoffs decreasing. Normal nodes' payoff decreases because a larger quantity of them is being suckered by cheaters, while GCL nodes' payoff decreases because the more of them there are in the network the more likely two of them end up linking to each other and obtaining payoff $P = 0.1$.

Even for big quantities of GCL nodes there is no dramatic drop in achieved utilities, in fact increasing the number of GCL nodes seems to be more harmful to cheating nodes than to non-cheating ones.

With NIH nodes the average utility decreases linearly with increasing quantity of cheaters (as in GCL), but a large proportion of them is needed to seriously decrease utility (i.e. 20% cheating nodes needed to halve global average payoff value).

7   Conclusions

A protocol called SLACER has been presented to build cooperative artificial social networks in P2P systems. It is based on periodic state comparisons between random nodes and copying of the better-performing node's characteristics.

SLACER has been shown to lead to cooperation, even when initiated in a completely non-cooperative network, and has been tested against four types of malicious, deviant nodes that attempt to subvert the protocol. Such nodes lie about their state according to the goal they want to achieve. Two principle cheating categories have been described: Greedy Cheating Liar (GCL) nodes, whose aim was to optimize their own utility, and Nihilist (NIH) nodes, whose aim was to destroy cooperation in the network.

SLACER was shown to be robust against such behaviors in simulations. Although NIH nodes managed to decrease system performance, a large proportion of them were needed to bring performance under a critical level. Since P2P networks can be very large (thousands or millions of nodes), a relatively large fraction, such as 10%, of cheating nodes would seem improbable — although, of course, certain types of coordinated attacks are possible.

Interestingly, GCL nodes that exploit the network for their own benefit, offered a kind of "service" to SLACER. When GCL nodes were present in the network, cooperation spread faster at the expense of a small decrease in the non-cheating nodes' average payoff.

Robustness against misbehaving entities, as well as cooperation between nodes, are important features for P2P systems since they usually lack any central control and have an open structure. SLACER not only succeeded in reaching

---

[4] These values are chosen so the PD payoffs could be parameterized over the R value while keeping T, P and S fixed. Results similar to the one presented here were obtained with different R values as long as PD constraints hold ($0.5 < R < 1$).

both of these goals but, from a cooperation formation point of view, it even benefited (for the "time to cooperation" measure) from the presence of cheating nodes trying to exploit the system.

It is important, however, to emphasize that our results show that cheating nodes *do* obtain higher relative utilities than non-cheating nodes. But we assume that cheating nodes would not report honestly their cheating strategy to other nodes since they have a negative incentive to do this. Why would a liar be honest about its lying, and moreover, what would this mean? These are subtle yet crucial points which we expand on in another work [8].

Our results suggests a provocative idea: in open systems, perhaps the best strategy for dealing with malicious cheating nodes is not trying to detect and stop them, but to let them act freely yet turn their misbehaving into a social benefit for the whole system while trying to minimize their damage. Perhaps those who believe what greedy cheating liars tell them are not such fools after all!

Acknowledgements

We are grateful to Mark Jelasity, Simon Patarin, Geoffrey Canright, Alberto Montresor and Gian Paolo Jesi for stimulating discussions, advice and comments.

References

1. A. S. Aiyer, L. Alvisi, A. Clement, M. Dahlin, J.-P. Martin, and C. Porth. Bar fault tolerance for cooperative services. In *Proceedings of the 20th ACM Symposium on Operating System Principles (SOSP)*, October 2005.
2. S. Arteconi and D. Hales.   Greedy cheating liars and the fools who believe them.   Technical Report UBLCS-2005-21, University of Bologna, Dept. of Computer Science, Bologna, Italy, Dec. 2005.   Also available at: http://www.cs.unibo.it/pub/TR/UBLCS/2005/2005-21.pdf.
3. R. Axelrod. *The Evolution of Cooperation*. Basic Books, New York, 1984.
4. M. Castro and B. Liskov. Practical byzantine fault tolerance. In *Proc. Third Symp. on Operating Systems Design and Implementation*, New Orleans, Feb. 1999.
5. L. P. Cox and B. D. Noble. Samsara: honor among thieves in peer-to-peer storage. In *Proceedings of the ACM Symposium on Operating Systems Principles*, volume 37, 5 of *Operating Systems Review*, pages 120–132, New York, Oct. 2003. ACM Press.
6. M. Feldman, K. Lai, I. Stoica, and J. Chuang. Robust incentive techniques for peer-to-peer networks. In *EC '04: Proceedings of the 5th ACM conference on Electronic commerce*, pages 102–111, New York, NY, USA, 2004. ACM Press.
7. D. Hales. Cooperation without memory or space: Tags, groups and the prisoner's dilemma. In *MABS '00: Proceedings of the Second International Workshop on Multi-Agent-Based Simulation-Revised and Additional Papers*, pages 157–166, London, UK, 2001. Springer-Verlag.
8. D. Hales and S. Arteconi. Slacer: A self-organizing protocol for coordination in peer-to-peer networks. *IEEE Intelligent Systems*, 21(2):29–35, Mar/Apr 2006.

9. D. Hales and B. Edmonds. Applying a socially-inspired technique (tags) to improve cooperation in p2p networks. 35(3):385–395, 2005.
10. M. Jelasity, R. Guerraoui, A.-M. Kermarrec, and M. van Steen. The peer sampling service: Experimental evaluation of unstructured gossip-based implementations. In H.-A. Jacobsen, editor, *Middleware 2004*, volume 3231 of *Lecture Notes in Computer Science*, pages 79–98. Springer-Verlag, 2004.
11. S. D. Kamvar, M. T. Schlosser, and H. Garcia-Molina. The EigenTrust Algorithm for Reputation Management in P2P Networks. In *12th International World Wide Web Conference*, Budapest, Hungary, 20-24 May 2003.
12. D. Malkhi and M. Reiter. Byzantine Quorum Systems. *The Journal of Distributed Computing*, 11(4):203–213, October 1998.
13. J. Nash. Equilibrium points in n-person games. *Proceedings of the National Academy of Sciences of the United States of America*, 36:48–49, 1950.
14. T. Ngan, A. Nandi, A. Singh, D. Wallach, and P. Druschel. On designing incentives-compatible peer-to-peer systems. In *T.-W. J. Ngan, A. Nandi, A. Singh, D. S. Wallach, and P. Druschel. On designing incentives-compatible peer-to-peer systems. In Proc. FuDiCo'04*, 2004.
15. PeerSim. http://peersim.sourceforge.net/.
16. R. Riolo, M. D. Cohen, and R. Axelrod. Cooperation without reciprocity. *Nature*, 414:441–443, 2001.
17. J. M. Smith. *Evolution and the Theory of Games*. Cambridge University Press, 1982.
18. R. Trivers. The evolution of reciprocal altruism. *Q. Rev. Biol.*, 46:35–57, 1971.

Evolution and Hypercomputing in Global Distributed Evolvable Virtual Machines Environment

Mariusz Nowostawski and Martin Purvis

University of Otago
Information Science Department
Dunedin, New Zealand
{mnowostawski,mpurvis}@infoscience.otago.ac.nz

Abstract. Inspired by advances in evolutionary biology we extended existing evolutionary computation techniques and developed a self-organising, self-adaptable cellular system for multitask learning, called Evolvable Virtual Machine (EVM). The system comprises a specialised program architecture for referencing and addressing computational units (programs) and an infrastructure for executing those computational units within a global networked computing environment, such as Internet. Each program can be considered to be an agent and is capable of calling (co-operating with) other programs. In this system, complex relationships between agents may self-assemble in a symbiotic-like fashion. In this article we present an extension of previous work on the single threaded, single machine EVM architecture for use in global distributed environments. This paper presents a description of the extended Evolvable Virtual Machine (EVM) computational model, that can work in a global networked environment and provides the architecture for asynchronous massively parallel processing. The new computational environment is presented and followed with a discussion of experimental results.

1 Introduction

This paper extends previous work [1] and presents more extensive experimental investigations of the model. The extended EVM computational model provides a unified architecture that is asynchronous, can span computers over the network, and can utilise different existing computational components. With this architecture independent crawlers and search engines[1] can be used to search computers over the Internet for specified computational resources, and individual components can assemble into co-operating distributed computational units. The proposal also addresses a main challenge in multi-task learning (and one of the

---

[1] Crawlers and search engines for computational resources work based on analogous principles as the text-based equivalents, however, instead of matching textual patters, the computational crawlers try to match computational sequences (code snippets) that match a predefined behaviour).

S. Brueckner et al. (Eds.): ESOA 2006, LNAI 4335, pp. 176–191, 2007.
© Springer-Verlag Berlin Heidelberg 2007

problems of the original EVM architecture) which concerns the enormous computational resources required to tackle non-trivial program-generation problems. The extended EVMs architecture not only offers new possibilities for unifying the way evolutionary, self-organising and self-adaptable computing research is performed, but also offers a framework that can span millions of computers on the Internet, providing researchers with the required computational resources to tackle more challenging problems.

2   The World Wide Web Analogy

In 1945 Vannevar Bush published an article "As We May Think" in Atlantic Monthly [2]. In the article, Bush theorised that people do not think in linear structures[2], and he proposed a visionary, at the time, model of a computing machine: Memex. Memex was designed for information retrieval and cross-referencing based on high-resolution microfilms coupled to multiple screen viewers, cameras and electromechanical controls. On the design diagrams it looked like a big desk with a camera recording what users wrote and then linking it to other pieces of information indexed in the machine storage space. Bush described Memex as a "device in which an individual stores his books, records and communications and which is **mechanised so it may be consulted with exceeding speed and flexibility**. It is an enlarged intimate supplement to his memory." (Emphasis added.)

There are two important points about the Memex machine. First, it represents a belief that the way humans think goes beyond Turing computability models. The Memex description, which was written years before the first digital computers had been successfully built and utilised, is a clear reference to what these days would be called *hypercomputation*. Bush's beliefs are now shared by contemporary researchers from different fields working in the area of hypercomputing. Our asynchronous model of the EVM computing architecture in some way is similar to the principles of the Memex architecture.

The second important point about the Memex machine is the stress on the ability to mechanically crawl, index, re-index and generate new information from the vast amount of available textual documents. That directly inspired and led to a shift of how we store and process information today. This line of thinking has been continued by Theodor Nelson through the invention and development of hypertext and his efforts for the Xanadu project [3] and later by the work on World Wide Web by Tim Berners-Lee in 1989-91.

The extended EVM architecture, aims at addressing the two points mentioned above. On one hand, it provides a hypercomputing infrastructure for information processing by utilising multiple hosts with multiple asynchronously executed

---

[2] Interestingly enough, it contrasts profoundly with what his contemporary, Alan Turing, assumed for his models of computation. The collection of independently computing and asynchronously communicating agents is believed to be a more powerful model of computation, and some believe that it closely mimics the way human cognitive processes work.

threads of operation. On the other hand, we propose an analogy of hypertext and Word Wide Web to computation itself. We present a model of computation, that can be hyperlinked with other computational units, in a global framework where all computational units are exposed and shared in a way that is analogous to sharing textual information on WWW. The aim is to allow mechanised crawling, indexing, assembling and executing computational units in a similar fashion to text-oriented web pages on WWW.

We first present the extension of the single threaded, single machine based implementation of the Evolvable Virtual Machine (EVM) architecture [1] for the global distributed environment such as the Internets[3]. We then present the new extended EVM computational model which is asynchronous, is not limited to a single machine but can span computers on the Internet, and which can utilise existing computational components written in EVM assembly language[4]. Our expanded EVM model provides a unified architecture to share and inter-link any computational resources (programs). This generalises the way that the WWW is used (by human users) to share and link textual information. The power of the architecture resides in the possibility of independently developed crawlers and search engines that can utilise this global computing environment. One of the simple automated "computing search agents" or crawlers can be as simple as stochastic search discussed earlier in [4]. The biggest challenge in multi-task learning and one of the issues with the original EVM architecture is that it requires enormous computational resources to be able to tackle more difficult problems. The character of our EVM architecture not only presents possibilities for unifying the way evolutionary, self-organising and self-adaptable computing research is performed, but it also provides us with the architecture that can span millions of computers on the Internet, providing researchers with enough computational power. It opens up new possibilities and challenges, e.g. integrating and assembling distributed independently found solutions for sub-problems into a coherent solution for bigger tasks.

3   Existing Efforts

There are several existing technologies that try to address different aspects of global heterogeneous computing architectures. On the lowest level of operation, we have some very popular and powerful computing virtual machines, such as the Java Virtual Machine (JVM) by James Gosling et al., or the Common Language Infrastructure (CLI, also known as .NET) virtual machine (Microsoft et al.).

---

[3] Due to the flexible and hierarchical nature of the EVM architecture, the term EVM can be used in the context of a single machine, or in a context of multiple inter-linked machines alike. Usually, we refer to a single computing cell as *emlet*, and to the overall architecture with multiple cells as on extended EVM, or just EVM for short. The distinction should be easy to infer from a given context.

[4] We plan to extend the current implementation with the Java bytecode to EVM assembly compiler, and develop tools that allow arbitrary programming languages integration.

These technologies facilitate possible cooperation between multiple programming languages and between independently developed software components. With these technologies it is relatively easy to combine independently developed software programs together. However, locating appropriate components, and understanding their function is difficult. It strongly relies on humans programmers – automated search engines cannot do that. This situation will not improve much with the availability and uptake of UDDI and other semantic information for web-services – again, human programmers must do the appropriate decisions, linking and bindings. There is a need for automated indexing and referencing of computational resources. It should allow automated discovery, linking and re-linking of individual computing modules. This requirements have led to the burst of agent-oriented technologies and web services.

Objective 1. Virtual Machine. We believe that an important property of the virtual machine for the global computing architecture is the ability to introspect and reify itself. In other words, we believe that the base virtual machine cannot be rigidly designed. Instead, it should be flexible and allow ongoing customization and reification mechanisms, so in time, multiple, individually crafted and specifically targeted virtual machines can work and cooperate together. The virtual machine must allow itself to evolve and adapt to changing requirements and needs.

Objective 2. Indexing and semantic information. Similarly to the premise above, we believe that the way computational modules are semantically indexed, should be achieved through ongoing refinement and hierarchical descriptions, that are automatically generated. The semantic information should not be rigid and should not be specified in advance. Instead, it should be flexible, customizable and created on-the-fly for a given context. Descriptions and indexing mechanisms will vary, depending on the needs, applications, and uses, and the global computing architecture should provide mechanisms that make it possible. The architecture should facilitate multiple "search engines" and many "indexing and description" directories with specialized methods of combining and presenting information about computational modules.

The two objectives described above are interlinked. In order to facilitate the dynamic indexing and semantic description of the piece of code (Objective 2) the executable program itself must be exposed for inspection and introspection (on the virtual machine level). That puts us back to the demand of introspective and reflective virtual machine of the objective 1.

Objective 3. Learning. We believe that as more computational units become available, the more complex problems can be solved by re-use and cross-linking of existing solutions for simpler problems. The overall goal of the EVM architecture is to provide a global environment to facilitate the learning process by combining existing computational units – the process of learning that can be automated and mechanised.

4   Biological Inspirations

Current research in evolutionary computation (EC) emphasises information-centric methods that are inspired by Darwinian theory of random mutations and natural selection. This is visible in well-established computational optimisation methods, such as genetic algorithms (GA), genetic programming (GP), and their variations, such as assorted artificial life systems. Despite some successes, the typical simple single-layer evolutionary systems based on random mutation and selection have been shown to be insufficient (in principle) to produce an open-ended evolutionary process with potential multiple levels of genetic material translation [5,6].

The Evolvable Virtual Machine architecture (EVM) is a novel model for building complex hierarchically organised software systems [4,1]. From the biological perspective, the learning in our extended EVMs model is primarily based on Darwin's principle of natural selection, which is widely used in current computational models of evolutionary systems for optimisation or simulation purposes, and in evolutionary computation (EC) in general. Some authors regard natural selection as axiomatic, but this assumption is not necessary. Natural selection is simply a consequence of the properties of population dynamics subjected to specified external constraints [5].

Symbiosis is defined as the interaction between two organisms living together. At least one member benefits from the relationship. The other member (the host) may be positively or negatively affected. Proponents of symbiogenesis argue that symbiosis is a primary source of biological variation, and that acquisition and accumulation of random mutations alone are not sufficient to develop high levels of complexity [7,8] and also [5,6].

K. Mereschkowsky [9] and I. Wallin [10] were the first to propose that independent organisms merge (spontaneously) to form composites (new cell organelles, new organs, species, etc). For example, important organelles, such as plastid or mitochondria, are thought to have evolved from an endosymbiosis between a Gram-negative bacterium and a pre-eukaryotic cell. A similar hypothesis can also be made regarding the origin of the nucleus [11]. Based on global phylogenies of numerous protein sequences, it is suggested that the ancestral eukaryotic cell arose by a unique endosymbiotic event involving engulfment of an eocyte archaebacterium by a Gram-negative eubacterial host. According to Margulis [12], "Life did not take over the globe by combat, but by networking".

Another phenomenon widely spread in nature which occurs at all levels of biological organisation from molecules to populations, is *specialisation*. As an example, the cells of a vertebrate body exhibit more than 200 different modes of specialisation [13]. Specialisation is the process of setting apart a particular subsystem (reducing its complexity) for better efficiency of a particular function. Our working hypothesis is, that specialisation together with symbiosis facilitate reaching higher complexity levels.

Recent work in incremental reinforcement learning methods also advocate retention of learnt structures (or learnt information) [14]. The sub-structures developed or acquired during the history of the program self-improvement process are kept in the program data-structures. It is therefore surprising that this general procedure is not being exploited by any of the (standard) evolutionary programming models, such as GP or GAs [15]. Although these evolutionary programming models are inspired by biological evolution, they do not share some significant aspects that are recognised in current evolutionary biology, neither can they be used (directly) in an incremental self-improvement fashion. In our EVM model, on the other hand, the central architectural element is based on the notion of retaining previously developed structures. The structures are retained as long as possible, and replaced only when they are not useful in any of the current system configurations (tasks to be solved). This aspect of the system will be discussed later in more details.

5   Hypercomputing

Any computation that goes beyond that defined by the Turing machine is called *hypercomputation*. Such computation is also known as super-Turing, non-standard or non-recursive computation. Hypercomputing is a relatively new, multi-disciplinary research area, spanning a wide variety of fields: computer science, mathematics, philosophy, physics, biology and others.

Even though hypercomputing is a theoretically possible and mathematically sound concept, there are many controversies as to the physical realisation of a machine capable of hypercomputing. Some believe that human mind, even though embodied in a finite physical entity, is capable of hypercomputing. Others believe that hypercomputing can be achieved by so called trial-and-error machine [16]. Inspired by Kugel's seminal paper, we argue that evolutionary processes work in similar fashion to what can be called trial-and-error computing. The EVM architecture provides a sound model of computation that potentially goes beyond the Turing limit. Due to possible uncomputable asynchronous processing of independent hosts, the overall characteristics of the computing may exhibit hypercomputing. This somewhat speculative area of research will be pursued further when the EVM architecture is successfully deployed on large numbers of hosts.

6   EVM as a Virtual Machine

The EVM Virtual Machine[5] is designed with Objective 1 in mind. It is composed of a processing unit and the program together with data structures, all coded as 64-bit integers. Our current implementation of the EVM architecture is based on a stack-machine, such as Forth, or the Java Virtual Machine (JVM). In fact, with small differences, it is comparable to an integer-based subset of the JVM (the design was inspired by existing virtual machines, among others: Forth, JVM, CLI, Smalltalk, and Lisp).

---

[5] The implementation is written entirely in Java, and developers can obtain the source code from CVS http://www.sf.net/projects/cirrus

The basic data unit for processing in our current implementation is a 64-bit signed integer[6]. The basic input/output and argument-passing capabilities are provided by the operand stack, called here *the data stack*, or for short *the stack*. The data stack is a normal integer stack, just as in the JVM, for example. All the operands for all the instructions are passed via the stack. The only exception is the instruction push, which takes its operand from the *program* itself. Unlike the JVM, our virtual machine does not provide any operations for creating and manipulating arrays. Instead, EVM facilitates operations on lists. There is a special stack, called *the list stack* for storing integer-based lists. Execution frames are managed in a similar way to the JVM, via a special execution frames stack. There is a lower-level machine handle attached to each of the execution frames. This is a list of lists, where each individual list represents an implementation of a single instruction for the given machine. In other words, the machine is a list of lists of instructions, each of which implements a given machine instruction. Of course, if the given instruction is not one of the Base Machine units (primitive instructions for that machine), the sequence must be executed on another lower-level machine. The Base Machine implements all the primitive instructions that are not reified further into more primitive units.

In our work we deal with programs capable of universal computation (e.g. with loops, recursion, etc.). In other words, the virtual machine running our programs must be Universal Turing-machine equivalent. Potentially, EVM programs can run indefinitely and therefore each thread of execution has an instruction time limit to constrain the time of each program in a multi-EVM environment. Each execution thread (a single program) has a maximum number of primitive instructions that it can execute. Once the limit is reached, the program unconditionally halts.

The EVM offers reflection and reification mechanisms. The computing model is relatively fixed at the lowest-level, but it does provide the user with multiple computing architectures to choose from. The model allows the programs to reify the virtual machine on the lowest level. For example, programs are free to modify, add, and remove instructions from or to the lowest level virtual machine. Also, programs can construct higher-level machines and execute themselves on these newly created levels. In addition, a running program can switch the context of the machine, to execute some commands on the lower-level, or on the higher-level machine. All together it provides near limitless flexibility and capabilities for reifying EVM execution.

The programming language used for search in EC plays an important role. Some languages are particularly suited for some, but not for all, problems. An appealing aspect of a multi-level search process is that, in principle, it is possible to specify a new base level and a new programming language that is specialised for a given task at that level. We want the EVM language to exploit this property.

The base instruction set is called EVM Base Machine. This set is implemented by at least one machine on each of the EVM hosts. The extension to 64-bits of our original EVM architecture allows us to link to arbitrary instruction in the global

---

[6] Note, in [1] we used 32-bit integer architecture.

computing environment. The way it is currently achieved is through a so called *EVM Communication Protocol*. This protocol can be implemented over any other lower-level networking protocols, such as HTTP. The initial implementation uses raw TCP/IP sockets to transmit the data. Each EVM instruction is indexed by the second half of the 64-bits. This is the 32-bit long instruction index (as it was in the original EVM architecture). The first 32-bits now code the IP address of the remote EVM host.

The EVM protocol offers two modes of operation. In the *passive mode*, a desired program is requested, and the implementation of this instruction, for the EVM Based Machine, is transferred back to the requesting host. This is analogous of downloading the source of a program and executing it locally with respect to the existing data. The *active mode* allows the requested code to be executed remotely. This is analogous to web services and other remote procedure calls, and facilitates computing modules that are not implemented in EVM assembly language, but with an arbitrary implementation instead. The local data stack and the list stack are transfered to the remote host, and a program with an appropriate index will be remotely executed with the existing data.

The EVM Base Machine contains instructions capable of performing reflection on and modifications of the Base Machine itself. Because of this reflective nature of the EVM, remotely executed code may alter the instruction sets on the remote host. The architecture splits the space of each of the EVM hosts into two parts - the Read-Only instruction set, and the Read-Write instruction set. The Read-Only part of the host can be altered only by the owner of the host. The Read-Write part can be altered by any of the EVM programs – local and remote alike.

7   EVM as a Self-adapting Cellular System

The architecture consists of individual EVM machines (emlets), this includes a list of primitive or complex individual programs. and of the external environment that manages the individual machines, executes programs, schedules tasks, and collects statistics on the use of individual programs. The system described here is just one of the many possible implementations of the actual environmental mechanisms for EVM architecture. The strength of the EVM architecture is that the users are not locked into a rigid design, but instead, there are many possible implementations of the management layer, all working together on the same network of EVM hosts.

Cellular systems are characterised by many locally interacting components (cells), therefore performing a parallel, decentralised, highly redundant computation e.g. [17]. In biology, cellular systems, such as insect colonies, cellular tissues, or animal brain, have proven to be efficient, adaptive, and robust. Because of the non-reliance on a global, central control, they are not prone to major failure. Their emergent properties have been successfully applied in diverse fields of computer science, e.g. Cellular Automata [18], Membrane Computing [19], or Ants Algorithms [20].

A cell is the fundamental component of our system. All cells run asynchronously and in parallel on multiple EVM hosts. Each single host is potentially composed of up to 2^{32} cells indexed by a single 32-bit integer. All individual cells react to local interactions with their neighbours and with the environment. From a machine learning perspective, the goal of each of the cells is to solve one of the tasks available in the environment, whereas from an artificial life perspective, the cell aims at collecting enough food to survive. The cell without enough food is "recycled", which means the content is substituted with a new content (old program is replaced with a new program).

Every cell maintains a program[7] The cell's goal is to find a successful program: one that, by solving a task, yields enough food for the cell to survive. Programs can call other programs (Figure 1. Moreover, if a program gets a reward, it will share it with any programs used as "assistance" to compute the solution. All of them will benefit from their relationship. In other words, symbiotic relationships will appear between programs. This ability to access other programs has thus opened the door to complex hierarchical organisation (self-assembly). As a consequence, cells are now able to collaborate to solve complex problems (Figure 2).

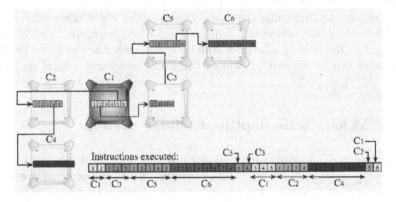

Fig. 1. The dark cell executes its program. Arrows show instructions that call neighbours' programs.

Cell specialisation. The cell self-adapts to a particular task in the environment, and must find a successful program. Several specialisation mechanisms have been studied by the authors: classic genetic algorithm, ad-hoc stochastic search maintaining a tree of probabilities of potential building blocks, or an adaptation of an environment-independent reinforcement learning method proposed by Schmidhuber [21]. However, since this paper focuses on the global behaviour of our system, we present without lose of generality only the results obtained with the simplest specialisation mechanism: random search (Figure 3).

---

[7] A program is a sequence of instructions in EVM assembly language.

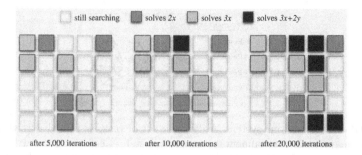

Fig. 2. Typical run exhibiting self assembly. 3 tasks: $2x$, $3x$, and $3x+2y$. After 5,000 iterations, several cells can solve the two simple tasks ($2x$ and $3x$). After 10,000 iterations, one cell ($C_{1,3}$) uses its left and down neighbours to solve the hard task ($3x+2y$), and all these 3 cells share the rewards (symbiosis). Shortly afterwards, some of its neighbours take advantage of it: they simply solve the task by calling $C_{1,3}$ (parasitism). Finally, after 20,000 iterations, we can observe another cluster of solutions at the bottom of the grid.

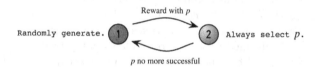

Fig. 3. The **random search mechanism** has two states. In the first, initial state, it randomly generates a new program for P. If a selected program p is rewarded, the mechanism transits to the second state. In the second state, p is always selected for P. It will stay ('survive') in that state as long as p remains successful. It is implemented by storing the cumulative rewards (called *provisions*) gained by p. At every time step, a fixed amount is subtracted from *provisions*. If the cumulative rewards drops below zero, p is considered unsuccessful and the mechanism transits back to state 1 (the cell 'dies').

8   Environment

The environment represents the external constraints on our system (Figure 4). Its role is to keep the system under pressure to force it to solve the tasks specified from the outside. The environment is modelled as a set of *resources*. There is a one-to-one mapping between the resources and the tasks to solve (every resource corresponds to a task). The purpose of these resources is to give rewards to the cells when they solve their task. How many rewards are given and how accessible are the resources is the topic of this section. Every resource has two attributes: *quantity* and *quality*. Values for these attributes specify how much food (reward) will be given to the cell that consumes the given resource.

Resource's quantity. This parameter ($QUANTITY$, capitalized to highlight its static nature) represents the abundance of resources in the environment. This value is set *ab initio* and is the same for each of the resources. It allows us to tune the amount of cells that will be able to survive.

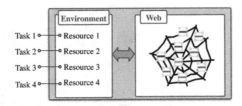

Fig. 4. Global view of our system. A dynamic set of tasks is provided to the system. Tasks are mapped to environmental resources. A web of cells interacts with the environment to try to solve the tasks. We use a schematic representation for the web to stress its flexible connectionism.

Resource's quality. The resource's quality must reflect how difficult a task is. It facilitates a mechanism to give more rewards for hard tasks (requirement 2), as more difficult tasks may involve several cells that will have to share the rewards. There are several ways of measuring the difficulty of a task. Some are *ab initio* (using expert knowledge), but it can be more interesting to adjust it dynamically based on the observed difficulty. For example, the resource's quality may be set based on the observed average time it takes to solve it, or on how many cells can solve it, etc. We decided to set the resource's quality to the current minimal number of cells required to solve the task. It will reflect dynamically the task's complexity without depending on randomness and without the use of an extra parameter that would need to be tuned for the search process.

Food. When a cell consumes a resource, it gets the following amount of food (rewards):

$$food = \frac{QUANTITY \cdot quality}{consumers} \ , \tag{1}$$

where *consumers* is the number of cells consuming the resource. Moreover, a cell is required to share its food with all the neighbours it used to solve the task. Every cell used will get the same share of food.[8]

At every iteration, a cell needs to eat one unit of food. If it eats more, it can makes provisions by storing the excess. If it eats less it will die from starvation once its provisions are empty.

$$provision_t = provision_{t-1} + food - 1 \tag{2}$$

This environmental model is the result of our previous investigations with different models and parameters. It ensures that all the tasks will eventually be solved (*requirement 1*)[9]. This may take a long time. However, if there is something in common between the tasks, our system will take advantage of it

---

[8] For these early experiments, we have chosen a very simple reward mechanism. More complicated models will be investigated in our future work.

[9] In some of the previous models, cells have been observed to tend to specialise in easy tasks only.

by reusing it, therefore speeding up the search process by exploiting correlations between tasks.

9   Multi-task Learning

Multitask learning is an area of machine learning which studies methods that can take advantage of previously learned knowledge by generalising and reusing it while solving a set of possibly related tasks [22]. Multitask learning has already shown promising results when applied to Artificial Neural Networks [23].

Some argue that multitask problems that share similar internal structure are much more common than one might imagine [24]. Most likely this may be a certain feature of all living systems. The human being, for instance, is continually confronted with new tasks. It must solve these tasks in parallel, using a single brain that has accumulated experience about all the previous tasks encountered since birth. On another level, populations work in a similar way. In computer science, traditionally multiple problems are translated into single task problems. The main advantage of multitask learning is the ability to reuse previously acquired knowledge. Solutions (or parts of them) of previous problems, can be reused to solve the current tasks. The system can shift its bias to search for a hypothesis space that contains good solutions to many of the problems in the environment.

Requirements. In order to be efficient in a multitask context, our model should fulfill the following requirements (these are the desiderata of all open multi-agent systems):

1. All tasks must be solved (eventually).
2. Solving difficult tasks should lead to greater rewards than solving easy ones.
3. Computational resources should focus on unsolved tasks.
4. Solutions must not be forgotten, as long as they are useful.
5. Knowledge diffusion should be facilitated (previous solutions must be accessible).
6. Dynamic environments should be supported: tasks can be added and/or removed at any time, dynamically.

10   Observations

For preliminary testing, we use a set of simple arithmetical tasks, such as $2x$, $|x|$, $3x + 2y$, $49 - x$, etc. These tasks enable the creation of related, incremental problems, that will highlight the main features of our model. What's more, it is straightforward to tune the desired difficulty level according to the computational resources at disposition.

Density. The two main environmental parameters: the resource's quantity and the food needed for a cell to survive can be represented as one parameter; *DENSITY*.

$$DENSITY = \frac{QUANTITY}{SIZE} \,, \tag{3}$$

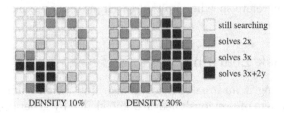

Fig. 5. Example with two different density settings: 10% and 30%. The parameter *DENSITY* enables to hand-tune the maximum percentage of cells that will be able to solve a task.

where $SIZE$ is the total number of cells. This simplifies the model, because only the respective ratio is really important. $DENSITY$ controls the utilisation of the cells in the web. Figure 5 depicts two different settings for that parameter.

This parameter may be extremely difficult to tune, since it involves a trade-off between requirements 5 and 3. Indeed, if it is too small, knowledge won't be accessible (few cells solving tasks). On the other hand, if the density is too large, there will be no room left to solve complex tasks.

Parasites and knowledge diffusion. There is another interesting behaviour of interacting cells that can be observed (see Figure 6). When a cell C_s solves a difficult task for the first time, the solution is almost immediately parasited by its neighbours (Figure 6b). That phenomenon enables the solution to be diffused around the successful cell C_s, thus rendering this solution accessible to an increasing number of cells. Since some cells may need this solution to compute a more difficult problem, knowledge diffusion is highly desirable. Competition between parasites is very intense. They usually appear, survive a couple of iterations, disappear, and after a while appear again, and so on. The dynamism exhibited looks like C_s is trying to reach something in its neighbourhood. For instance, if the diffusion manages to reach the neighbourhood of a cell C_1 that needs it, it will be used and thus the whole chain of parasites from C_s to C_1 will receive significant rewards and survive (Figure 6e).

Once some other cells in the web solve the same task as C_s on their own (without parasiting), it becomes more and more difficult for the parasites of C_s to survive (as they always have to share their food with the cells they use). As a consequence, knowledge diffusion will progressively decrease.

Equilibrum/stability. Another parameter, $PROVISION_{MAX}$, has been added. It sets a maximal bound for provisions stored by a cell. Its value drastically affects the dynamism of the web. If $PROVISION_{MAX}$ is high, most of the cells are stable and only a few appear and disappear (regime A). If $PROVISION_{MAX}$ is low, we observe much more dynamic structural patterns on the web, with cyclic episodes similar to a kind of *catastrophe* scenario [25]. Good solutions spontaneously appear in the web, and after awhile there are too many cells competing for the same resource. As a consequence, the quantity of the resource they are consuming decreases below 1. Since they don't have enough

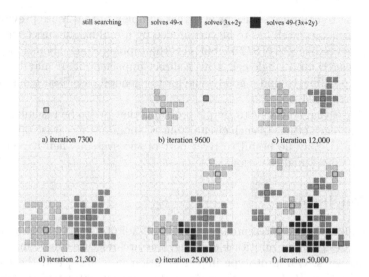

Fig. 6. Knowledge diffusion. Thanks to its parasites, the cell that manages to find the solution to $49 - x$ can diffuse it (a and b). A cell that computes $3x + 2y$ does the same (c). Eventually, in special spots surrounded by solutions to both problems, solutions to $49 - (3x + 2y)$ are likely to appear (d). In the long run, new solutions to $3x + 2y$ and $49 - x$ will appear (e and f). It thus becomes more difficult for parasites to survive. Parasites connected to the solution of $49 - (3x + 2y)$, however, receive more rewards from that solution and won't disappear. Cells with thick border are hosts.

provisions, they will soon almost all disappear. New cells can then start a new cycle (regime B).

There seems to be no smooth transition between these two dramatically different regimes. Regime A represents a stable and fixed solid state, similar to Wolfram's class 1 of cellular automata (CA) classification [18]. Regime B represents a cyclic state, and is similar to Wolfram's CA class 2.[10]

Robustness. Our system exhibits high levels of robustness. First, multiple solutions to the same task are available in the web. Due to this redundancy, losing one of them is not dramatic. Also, more food will be available for this resource (since *consumers* have decreased in Equation 1), creating a new solution to replace the lost one (a kind of self-repair). Second, if part of the solution is lost (e.g. one cell dies in a 5-cells solution), the *provision* variable enables the rest of the solution to survive for a short period, allowing the defective cell to have enough time to recover.

Locality. In living systems, locality has been shown to be an important factor for evolutionary processes (e.g. ecological niches). It also plays a prime role in

---

[10] Wolfram's Classes 3 and 4 can be achieved by tuning an extra parameter $PROVISION_{INITIAL}$, which specifies the initial amount of food a cell receives when it solves a task for the first time.

our system. To compute solutions of higher complexity that reuse previously acquired knowledge, a cell has to be surrounded by useful neighbours (requirement 5). Parameters like $DENSITY$, but also the topology (neighbourhood) or the program length for a single cell, have a direct impact on it. It may be difficult, or even impossible, to find a good value for the general case. Issues in scalability are to be expected, too.

The risk is that solutions to simple problems that are to be assembled remain too far from each other. In such circumstances, spontaneous catastrophic-events, like regime B, may be useful to reset part of the system when it seems to be stuck in a suboptimal situation.

11   Conclusion

In this paper, we have presented a general, self-adaptable, global computing architecture designed for multitask learning. The architecture can be implemented in various ways. Our prototype implementation uses Java, and the Evolvable Virtual Machines [1] framework as the underlying virtual machine. The implementation is composed of a network (a web) of interconnected computing programs (agents). Unlike existing cellular models, our cells are capable of universal computation on Turing-like virtual machines, and can modify and manipulate their own code via self-reflection. The cells can also autonomously self-specialise into simpler and more efficient instruction sets, allowing better exploration of the overall search space. Cells contain programs that can call each other; therefore the architecture facilitates collaboration in a symbiotic fashion. This system is self-adaptable in the sense that it can adapt to a dynamic environment without human input and/or predefined behaviour. It is also self-organising, as its internal structure emerges from the symbiotic interactions between cells. These symbiotic interactions enable reuse of previously acquired knowledge. Our architecture is designed to performs well in a multitask context. Up to now, interesting features have been observed at both the cellular and macroscopical levels. This includes, but is not limited to, parasitism, knowledge diffusion, self-assembly of inter-dependent symbiotic structures, and self-organising utilisation of resources. An interesting phenomenon regarding the cells connectivity has also been observed – the cells connectivity becomes an intrinsic (emergent) resource in its own right. Future research includes investigations of different search methods and dynamic indexing of the program spaces.

References

1. Nowostawski, M., Epiney, L., Purvis, M.: Self-Adaptation and Dynamic Environment Experiments with Evolvable Virtual Machines. In S.Brueckner, Serugendo, G.M., D.Hales, F.Zambonelli, eds.: Proceedings of the Third International Workshop on Engineering Self-Organizing Applications (ESOA 2005), Springer Verlag (2005) 46–60
2. Bush, V.: As we may think. The Atlantic Monthly (1945) http://www.theatlantic.com/doc/194507/bush.

3. Nelson, T.H.: A file structure for the complex, the changing and the indeterminate. In: Proceedings of the ACM 20th National Conference, Cleveland, OH. (1965) 84–100

4. Nowostawski, M., Purvis, M., Cranefield, S.: An architecture for self-organising Evolvable Virtual Machines. In S.Brueckner, A.Karageorgos, G.M.S., R.Nagpal, eds.: Engineering Self Organising Sytems: Methodologies and Applications. Number 3464 in LNAI. Springer Verlag (2004)

5. Eigen, M., Schuster, P.: The Hypercycle: A Principle of Natural Self-Organization. Springer-Verlag (1979)

6. Wright, S.: Evolution in mendelian populations. Genetics **16**(3) (1931) 97–159

7. Margulis, L.: Origin of Eukaryotic Cells. University Press, New Haven (1970)

8. Margulis, L.: Symbiosis in Cell Evolution. Freeman & Co., San Francisco (1981)

9. Mereschkowsky, K.S.: Über Natur und Ursprung der Chromatophoren im Pflanzenreiche. Biol. Zentralbl. **25** (1905) 593–604

10. Wallin, I.: Symbionticism and the Origin of Species. Williams&Wilkins, Baltimore (1927)

11. Gupta, R.S., Golding, G.B.: The origin of the eukaryotic cell. Trends in Biochemical Sciences **21**(10) (1996) 166–171

12. Margulis, L., Sagan, D.: Microcosmos: Four Billion Years of Evolution from Our Microbial Ancestors. Summit Books, New York (1986)

13. Alberts, Bray, D., Lewis, J., Raff, M., Roberts, K., Watson, J.D.: Molecular biology of the cell. 3rd edn. Garland Publishing (1994)

14. Schmidhuber, J.: A general method for incremental self-improvement and multi-agent learning. In Yao, X., ed.: Evolutionary Computation: Theory and Applications. Scientific Publishers Co., Singapore (1999) 81–123

15. Vose, M.D.: The Simple Genetic Algorithm: Foundations and Theory. A Bradford Book, MIT Press, Cambridge, Massachusetts/London, England (1999)

16. Kugel, P.: Thinking may be more than computing. Cognition **18** (1986) 128–149

17. Sipper, M.: The emergence of cellular computing. IEEE Computer **32**(7) (1999) 18–26

18. Wolfram, S.: Universality and complexity in cellular automata. Physica D **10** (1984) 1–35

19. Teuscher, C.: Information processing in cells and tissues. BioSystems **76** (2004) 3–5

20. Bonabeau, E., Dorigo, M., Theraulaz, G.: Swarm Intelligence: From Natural to Artificial Systems. Oxford University Press (2000)

21. Schmidhuber, J.: Environment-independent reinforcement acceleration. Technical Note IDSIA-59-95, IDSIA, Lugano (1995)

22. Baxter, J.: A model of inductive bias learning. Journal of Artificial Intelligence Research **12** (2000) 149–198

23. Caruana, R.: Multitask learning. In: Machine Learning. Volume 28. Kluwer Academic Publishers (1997) 41–75

24. Thrun, S.: Is learning the n-th thing any easier than learning the first? In Touretzky, D., Mozer, M., eds.: Advances in Neural Information Processing Systems (NIPS) 8, Cambridge, MA, MIT Press (1996) 640–646

25. Thom, R.: Structural stability and morphogenesis. Benjamin Addison Wesley, New York (1975)

A Decentralised Car Traffic Control System Simulation Using Local Message Propagation Optimised with a Genetic Algorithm

Martin Kelly and Giovanna Di Marzo Serugendo

School of Computer Science and Information Systems
Birkbeck College, London
jkell01@dcs.bbk.ac.uk, dimarzo@dcs.bbk.ac.uk

Abstract. This paper describes a car traffic control simulation realised in a decentralised way by message propagations: congested nodes (roads intersections) send speed-up or slow-down messages to neighbouring nodes. Different types of journeys have been modelled: regular car journeys, accidents and emergency cars journeys. These journeys have different lengths and speeds, and affect the system differently. Optimal values of parameters, used during the simulations for controlling the cars, have been determined through the use of a genetic algorithm (GA). This paper reports as well a preliminary experiment on different simulations realised with parameters values derived from the GA.

1 Introduction

Car traffic control and monitoring systems are receiving much attention since several years because of huge and increasing traffic volume and traffic flows (e.g. 27 million journeys, and 32.7 billion vehicle-kilometres in total in London in 2004 [1]). This raises obvious issues related to ecology, economy and safety.

Traffic managements are already in place, they assist traffic officers to monitor and control traffic on cities or motorways by allowing visualisation of traffic, or analysis of real-time traffic information. Decisions are usually taken from control centres and propagated to users by the means of road signs (traffic lights, motorway screens).

This paper reports on an initial experiment towards an adaptive decentralised control solution based on local propagation of messages among nodes (roads intersections). Optimisation of key parameters has been realised by running a Genetic Algorithm (GA).

Section 2 describes the elements of the model, while Section 3 provides details about the control system and the simulations. Section 4 describes the GA used to derive optimal parameters. Section 5 reports the initial experiments realised so far. The way how such a simulation can be useful in an actual scenario is highlighted in Section 6. Finally, Section 7 mentions some related works.

S. Brueckner et al. (Eds.): ESOA 2006, LNAI 4335, pp. 192–210, 2007.

2 Model

A simulation considers a set of 1000 car journeys travelling through a portion
of a city during a certain period (e.g. from 8am to 10am). Traffic is controlled
by locally propagating messages in the city. A graphical interface, representing
a town and depicting cars, allows visual animation of the simulations.

2.1 Town Model

The city is modelled merely as interlinked laneways representing individual
"sides" of the road. Figure 1 shows a GUI that represents a map modelling
the city as a series of dynamically adjusting throughways. The virtual city is
modelled on 3km * 3km with an on-screen view of 600m * 600m, with 1 pixel
equating to one meter. Vehicles are mapped as a point with a surrounding circle,
and a line indicating the direction with the line length as a function of speed.
Speeds are measured in metres per second and increase in discrete blocks rather
than from a continuous curve - a true production system would differ by following
a curve.

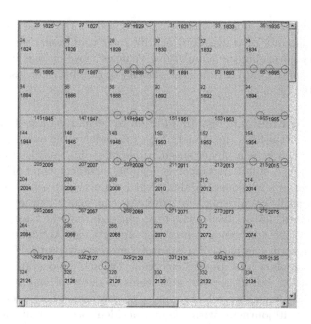

Fig. 1. Screen Shot showing a 600m * 600m portion of modelled town

Each cycle through the software model, calling each vehicle to move and consequent broadcast and evaluation of methods for up to 1,000 vehicles is regarded
as a *virtual second*, i.e. one complete iteration of all city artefacts.

Journeys. A set of 1000 pre-established journeys (or routes) has been established. A journey is a set of paths which are followed from start to finish. Table 1 shows the distribution of the 1000 routes according to their length. Journeys (or routes) are of varied length and speed and may occur in parallel. They typically represent the journeys taking place in a given portion of a city during a given time slot.

It should be noted that the set of 1000 routes is auto-generated, and therefore not necessarily the greatest distribution of journeys. In an attempt to better distribute the routes within the 3km * 3km block, the generation algorithm chooses equidistant points across and down the grid as starting points for journeys. Naturally this does not eliminate favouritism with some routes more heavily travelled than others, but neither does it blandly plan routes so that all traffic is distributed perfectly, this better represents actual traffic patterns without being completely random.

Table 1. Routes Distribution

Distance (km)	1.5km	1.8km	2.0km	2.2km	2.6km	2.7km	2.9km	3.1km	3.3km	3.4km
# Routes	119	122	144	131	90	88	80	74	79	73

Roads have various innate speeds, these speeds further vary according to the relative amounts of congestion, nearby road conditions, and the current parameters set governing the simulation. Vehicles move on one side of a road, known as a path, the path dictates the velocity of member vehicles. Speeds vary from 8km/h to 96km/h.

Accidents and Emergencies. In addition to regular vehicles that go at the speed dictated by the lane, the model supports accidents and emergency vehicles: emergency vehicles have a higher speed, while offending vehicles (accident) are blocking vehicles. A simulation involves regular, emergency and offending cars.

Accident journeys are journeys along which an accident will occur randomly on one of the paths comprising the route. An emergency journey is one taken at a higher speed. 25 accidents will take place during the execution of each simulation, with 25 emergency routes also undertaken. Accidents temporarily block traffic flow on one path of a roadway; emergency routes block traffic on both paths, but allow the routing emergency vehicle to operate at the roads optimal speed. On exiting a path, both sides of the road may resume normal operations. The emergency vehicles, and also journeys where accidents occur, take place every 40 journeys, with the first accident occurring at journey 35 for accidents, at journey 40 for emergencies, and at 40 journey intervals for both thereafter (35 & 40, 75 & 80, etc.).

Accidents and emergencies are not governed directly by the control system; they are a condition of the environment. However they do impact on throughput and efficiency, for example when an accident occurs all vehicles behind the accident vehicle are stalled, this can block the path, and have a knock-on or accumulative effect in inbound paths. Likewise for emergencies, for any path an emergency vehicle is on, the other vehicles on both sides of the road are stopped completely. This is to model the effect of pulling cars into the side of the road to make way for the emergency vehicle.

An accident merely blocks a path for a given number of cycles, stifling progress on one or more paths. An emergency is effectively a high priority journey, which halts all vehicles on a road (both sides) while it traverses at an emergency speed.

2.2   Parameters

The main idea behind the parameters selections has been the willingness to enforce a *decentralised* control over the cars using message propagation: congested paths send messages to neighbouring paths (Rearward and/or Forward).

The four following parameters have been chosen:

- *Threshold*: the level at which a path reacts to congestion;
- *Range*: the distance and direction a path is willing to broadcast messages to its neighbours relative to its level of congestion;
- *Sensitivity*: the elasticity of the reaction to inbound messages pertaining to neighbouring paths;
- *Persistence*: the durability and significance of messages.

The parameters model a throttling process. Our goal is to maximise throughput in the system and therefore to correlate speed with volumes as terms dictate. The parameters selected above, Threshold, Sensitivity, Persistence, Range, control local velocity and its residual short-term affects. The Threshold indicates when the path will start issuing control messages, while the Range indicates how far to broadcast. The Sensitivity and Persistence parameters control how much a path reacts to a message and for how long the path remains influenced by the message respectively. Each parameter has six possible levels of expression.

Threshold. The Threshold parameter is the controlling factor related to throughput. It is determined by the ratio of the current Population on the considered path to total Capacity of the path. Threshold represents the sensitivity of the path to the rate of increase and represents: Population/Capacity. It will trigger velocity changes on the current path, and depending on the Range parameter, may trigger broadcast messages to all neighbours. Table 2 shows the different values for Threshold. For instance, if the Threshold is set at 1, broadcast messages to all neighbours will start being sent as soon as the number of vehicles on the related path will reach 10% of the whole capacity of the path. On the contrary, if the Threshold is at 6, the messages will be sent only when the capacity of that particular path reaches 60%.

Range. The Range parameter represents the range and direction of communications or broadcast targets for the messages sent among the paths. As soon as a path reaches the threshold rate specified by Threshold, it will start sending

Table 2. Threshold Parameters Values

1	2	3	4	5	6
10%	20%	30%	40%	50%	60%

messages to its neighbouring paths. There are two types of messages used during the simulations: R (for Rearward messages) and F (for Forward messages). Rearward messages are almost always of the slow-down variety, forward messages are always indications to speed-up. It is left to each path to decay their messages and return to optimal state, the messages reflect a response to short-term prevailing conditions which tend to propagate traffic (rearward or forward) toward areas of less density as an emergent property.

The use of offset antagonistic pairs of messages was considered for this solution, i.e. send a speed-up message, and then when conditions alleviate, send a slow-down message. However the path controls its own destiny, may disregard messages entirely due to prevailing conditions (such as all-stop, or maximum speed reached), or may ignore messages.

Messages are actually propagated by *nodes* - the intersection points of the 3km * 3km grid modelling the city (see Figure 1). A node is simply a congruence of paths, nodes have inbound and outbound paths, they transmit and receive messages originating from paths, the node is also responsible for decrementing message range.

Table 3 shows the 6 possible cases of message range propagation. If Range is set at 1 (R1F0), this means that Rearward messages are sent to the immediate (connected) neighbours rearward the path (R1 stands for one hop - one node - Rearward), while no Forward messages are sent (F0). Similarly, if Range is set at 4, this means that Rearward messages are propagated for two hops rearward the path (R2 stands for two hops - two nodes - Rearward); and the same for Forward messages (F2 stands for two hops forward the path).

Table 3. Range Parameter Values

1	2	3	4	5	6
R1F0	R1F1	R0F1	R2F2	R2F1	R1F2

Sensitivity. Sensitivity represents the reaction of a node to inbound peer messages. It is not simply a one to one relationship: an arriving message from a neighbour does not immediately activate a reaction from the paths connected to the receiving node. Indeed, the reaction is also affected by the rate of inbound messages: faster the messages coming in, greater the reaction as determined by Sensitivity. An arriving message partially fills a "capacitor", when the number of messages has arrived which completely fills the capacitor the message effect is then triggered. This equates roughly to the activation function in neural networks. It is complemented by the Persistence parameter which works to diminish any elevated state.

Table 4 below shows the different values for Sensitivity. For instance, if Sensitivity is set at 3, as soon as the rate of incoming messages reaches 30%, the node receiving the messages will actually modify the speed of the corresponding path according to the messages received (slow-down or speed-up). A high Sensitivity will cause the path to react strongly to messages, while low Sensitivity will need many more messages to accrue an influence.

Table 4. Sensitivity Parameter Values

1	2	3	4	5	6
10%	20%	30%	40%	50%	60%

Persistence. This is the decay rate for known state, i.e. a road may be unused but has altered state due to inbound peer messages. The Persistence rate is the rate of reduction in the excited state, i.e. how long it perseveres in the altered state before returning to the normal state. This will also affect the message capacitor (see Sensitivity parameter), since it will serve to reduce its charge. This rate may be seen as similar to the evaporation rate used for modelling ant trails.

The table below shows the different levels for the Persistence parameter. For instance, if the Persistence parameter is set at 4, the simulation will keep memory of received (slowing-down or speed-up) messages for 20s (virtual seconds) before going back to the normal state.

When messages are received and evaluated, the Sensitivity and Persistence become important. How much of a reaction a path has to a message is governed by Sensitivity, i.e. how much will it speed-up or slow-down. Persistence dictates how long a period of time that message will be remembered, similar to the pheromone trail. Persistence does not dictate the period for which messages are sent. The age of a message has significance. Older messages exert less influence than new messages in proportion to what percentage of maximum persistence the message has reached.

Table 5. Persistence Parameter Values

1	2	3	4	5	6
5s	10s	15s	20s	25s	30s

3 Control Model and Simulation

This section describes how the different simulations are done. A single simulation involves 1000 (pre-established) journeys. The parameters values will be the same for all paths in the city for a given simulation, i.e. all paths will have the same propensity to communicate, will communicate over the same distances, will persist messages for the same time, etc.

Each operational cycle represents the passage of one virtual second. Each virtual second, each vehicle moves the number of metres per second equating to the speed dictated by the path they are on.

A simulation uses the following elements:

- *Packet*: represents a vehicle;
- *Path*: represents a side of a road;
- *Route*: represents a journey (it is a collection of serially connected paths);
- *Node*: represents an intersection between paths. Nodes connect paths in a single route, and join multiple routes together. Nodes are used in the propagation of messages within the system.

Congestion Detection: from paths to nodes. Paths are sensitive to congestion according to their Threshold value. When they detect congestion accruing they raise messages according to their Range parameter. These messages are sent to the paths inbound and outbound nodes (Rearward/Forward in accordance with Range), the nodes then transmit the message to the correct paths as appropriate.

Propagation: from nodes to paths. If a node must propagate a message to the next node, this is flagged to the connecting path and the notified path contacts its outbound node (or inbound node depending on the direction of propagation of the message) with the message as necessary.

When a node receives a message (speed-up or slow-down) it decrements the messages distance attribute. It then iterates through its set of outbound paths (for a forward messages) or its set of inbound paths (for rearward messages). Messages cannot "echo" back to a node as they propagate away from the originating path in the given direction. Even if the message range was sufficiently large to allow a message to travel back to the point of origin it would not continue indefinitely as the message's distance is decremented as it passes through each node.

Reaction: change of path's speed. When the path receives the message, it adds it either to its increasing messages collection or to its decreasing messages collection based on the message type, i.e. whether it is a speed-up or a slow-down message. The path will evaluate its messages when cars enter or leave - messages are evaluated no more than once per real second to avoid thrashing unnecessarily.

When a path receives a message (to speed up or slow down) its reaction is based upon its Sensitivity parameter, this acts as a type of suppressor or multiplier (depending on the activation level) which tends either to retard message influence or to promote it.

The Sensitivity is effectively a multiplier on the stock increase or decrease in speed undertaken during message evaluation, the values range from a 10% increase to a 60% increase. It is not based on message direction, it augments the paths reaction when evaluating messages (speed-up versus slow-down, the age of the messages, etc.) to determine the current velocity for a path.

The Sensitivity rate is never "reached" per se. It is a multiplier, an augment on how the path reacts to messages. The cars themselves don't receive messages. When they move they proceed at the prevailing velocity for the current path, in a real world scenario there would be some transmission to vehicles. In the model vehicles know the set of path's which comprise their route, when they move they use the current path's velocity to determine how far to travel in metres per second.

The Persistence parameter works either to prolong or curtail the duration of message influence. Path velocity is a combination of self-determined and peer-group influenced factors. Its own velocity is a function of congestion, its peer group may influence that velocity through messaging, i.e. a road is uncongested with a velocity of 14 metres per second, however due to congestion ahead, the messages received by its peer cause the path to reduce speed by 50%, the level of persistence is similar to the rate of evaporation of ant-trails. It determines the rate at which messages' influence is reduced. If a path maintains a peer-influenced rate for a very long time it may falsely report max speed, as above, 50% lower than its true maximum. If Sensitivity is also low, an inbound path may have to raise many messages for it to alter its state. Persistence helps to ameliorate this factor over time, meaning that state will change on request (according to Sensitivity) but will decay over time and the influence of contrary messages.

Throttling Messages. Forward (speed-up) messages are transmitted forward, triggered by the Threshold parameter value to attempt to clear the route forward to alleviate congestion on a given path.

Rearward (slow-down) messages are transmitted rearward to anticipate congestion, i.e. when a path fills up, the feeding path cannot enter. Therefore throttling by congestion is an emergent state, slowing down inbound paths when Threshold is hit may help to avoid a stalled path condition.

Messages serve to alter the optimal state of a pathway. The pathway has an innate tendency to maintain its optimal state, reflected in the Persistence parameter which tends to maintain or direct a path towards this state. Messages may also serve to excite or inhibit path velocity, how a path responds is controlled by the Sensitivity parameter, high values for this parameter exhibit greater response to inbound messages.

As said before, the Threshold and Range (distance) parameters are primarily responsible for the message propagation.

When a path hits a level of congestion that breaches the setting defined by threshold it initiates a message to intersecting paths, basically telling inbound paths to slow down, i.e. to feed fewer vehicles, and outbound paths to speed up, so it may feed vehicles to them faster.

The range of the message, or how far this message propagates is governed by the Range parameter.

An individual with a value of R1F2 in this parameter will propagate slow-down messages rearward to one node (and therefore to all inbound paths

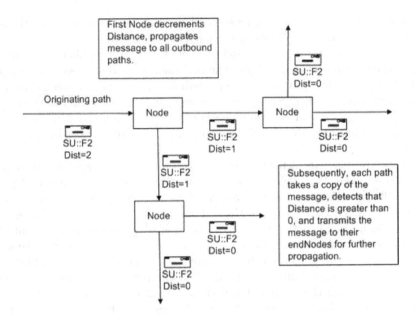

Fig. 2. Messages Propagation

registered with that node), it will also send speed-up messages to its outbound node (and consequently to all outbound paths), when these paths receive the speedup message, they notice that a range counter is not zero and therefore further propagate the message to their outbound nodes. When a node receives a message for propagation it first decrements this counter to register the consumption of the message before passing it to each neighbouring path (see Figure 2).

The Persistence parameter controls the period of influence of the message, once the time is past the message is removed entirely. Also older messages exert lesser influence than newer messages (a 28 second old message is inferior to a brand new arrival as the new arrival more correctly reflects prevailing conditions). Paths use the decay rate/persistence level for two purposes: to modify path velocity appropriate to congestion levels both of itself and of the conditions of the local group; and also to control the return to optimum speed for the path. This optimum speed is the speed it attempts to maintain. When a path returns to its optimum speed through message decay, it informs any paths that it sent slowdown messages to disregard the message; thereby influencing neighbouring paths which may reflect and artificially slow velocity to snap back to equilibrium faster.

Cascading Message Propagation. When an accident blocks the path that it is on, this may have a knock-on effect on paths that connect to this path as vehicles may not be able to join as the path becomes blocked. A first node raises a series of slow-down messages, those messages are propagated as R1 (for instance), now the receiving nodes start actually slowing down the vehicles.

The nodes further up the path, or these receiving nodes themselves, will start observing congestion, and start sending messages for slowing-down, so a new series of R1 is propagated - but not from the original node.

In case of an emergency the behaviour is slightly different, both sides of a road are stopped to allow an emergency vehicle to traverse. When the emergency vehicle moves off the path to its next path, that road is freed up for travel once again, and the subsequent road is stopped, these actions continue until the emergency route is complete.

Collisions. Collision avoidance is undertaken by projecting a bounding rectangle forward from the vehicle's position; its width is set to the bounding circle indicating the vehicle's location, its length projects forward from the vehicle in proportion to the current speed. As a vehicle moves from one path to another, it ensures there is room for the vehicle at the point of entry (by calling a specific method on the target path). Otherwise as the vehicle travels it checks that it is not about to collide with a neighbour prior to executing the move. This allows vehicles to queue up behind one another. Vehicles will not take oncoming traffic into consideration when detecting potential collisions. Vehicles will overtake a blocking vehicle on the same path after a small random number of initial "waits" this prevents vehicles who are stuck waiting to turn onto an adjoining path from blocking all vehicles behind it from carrying on forward. This represents a simple model of typical behaviour, the turning vehicle normally assumes a position on one extreme side of their lane, rearward vehicles must ameliorate their behaviour to accommodate, hence the waiting for a random number of cycles (currently set to a maximum of 5).

4   Optimisation of Parameters with a Genetic Algorithm

The purpose of genetic algorithms is to derive *solutions* to optimisation problems. A genetic algorithm starts with a *population* made of randomly chosen *individuals* each represented by its own set of *genes*. Each individual represents a possible solution to the optimisation problem.

GA Overview. Our goal is to find the set of parameters values which result in the most efficient resolution of the congestion problem. Therefore, the *optimisation problem* consists in determining parameters values (i.e. genes) that, when used to control the runs of 1000 journeys in a city, the (total) time to complete (to simulate) these 1000 journeys is the shortest possible time.

An *individual* is then a 4 tuple (i.e. 4 genes) and represents the run (one simulation) of 1000 journeys in the 3km * 3km city (see below for a description of the genes). When the 1000 journeys are being simulated the values of the 4 genes are used for running these journeys; consequently the time implied to complete these 1000 journeys is then an indicator of how "good" (fit) the corresponding individual is. The 4 gene values stand for the values of the 4 parameters of Section 2.

The *initial population* is made of 1024 (4^5) individuals. The simulations are run on those 1024 individuals. Each simulation starts with 1000 vehicles in the city (each driving one of the pre-established routes). As vehicles complete their journeys they are removed from the city. When fewer than 200 vehicles remain, the simulation stops. The fitness function is then evaluated on this simulation. The fitness function is given by the total amount of time the simulation has implied to complete the 800 first journeys.

After the initial population of 1024 simulations is evaluated, we pick the top 100 individuals, the rest is discarded. The GA crossover and mutation (2%) aspects are enabled in order to evolve the population from that point. A new generation of individuals will be produced, which will then undergo another simulation-selection-crossover/mutation process for another 1000 generations.

Each organism represents a gene sequence equating to individual genotype. The organism is tested against the same criteria, and with the same input data: the same set of 1000 journeys is used throughout the whole experiments (among which only the 800 first completed are considered for the fitness function evaluation). The testing environment only differs according to the influence of the individual organism's genotype.

The *goal* of the whole system is then to find optimal parameters values that when applied in the car control simulation allow minimising the total length (in time) of all undertaken journeys.

GA Genes. As said above, the GA genes are exactly the parameters: Threshold, Sensitivity, Range and Persistence. The possible values are those given by tables 2 to 5. Each gene has then 6 levels of expressions: this ensures a population large enough with enough variety so that evolution would demonstrate successful candidates but not so large or finely tuned as to represent a great many wasted cycles comparing with almost-like candidates. Of equal importance is not selecting a population of such small size and coarsely-grained attributes that would render evolution unnecessary for purposes of evaluation.

GA Initialisation. The GA starts with 1024 randomly chosen individuals (4-uples of genes) but with a central tendency. Indeed, i.e. the first population contains few if any 1 or 6 strength genes. This was chosen to avoid evaluation of sets of genotype with all minimum or all maximum attributes in the initial population.

GA Selection and Termination. Once the simulations (a set of 1000 journeys each) are run on the initial population of 1024 individuals (1024 different genes), the fitness function is applied on each of these simulations. It is given by the total amount of time in virtual seconds needed to complete the first 800 (out of 1000) journeys. This measurement is based on the distance travelled, and the virtual time taken.

This initial population provides a gene-pool for further searching through crossover and mutation. Indeed, a set of 100 fittest candidates is maintained for a further 1000 generations. At the end of each simulation if the current candidate is fitter than the minimum it is added to that set, the minimum candidate is dropped off the end of the list.

The process is the following:

```
select the two fittest candidates from the set of 100 individuals
loop:1000
  create two offspring and evaluate them
  take the fittest of these
  if they are fitter than the minimum, then
          add them to the set of 100
end loop
```

This requires 2000 evaluations to proceed through 1000 evolutions (1 per off-spring). This also means that if the fittest candidate were in the initial population it will not be replaced.

GA Crossover/Mutation. When two candidates are identified for breeding, a random number is chosen between zero and 3, representing the point of crossover. Two new individuals are then generated from the complementary pairs due to the parent genotype split at the point chosen at random. Mutation applies to the new chromosome at a rate of 2%.

About the 800 first completed journeys. The fact that we choose the 800 first completed routes for computing the fitness function could be seen as introducing a bias factor in the evaluation of the results. Indeed, it could be argued that the worst journeys would not complete correctly, or some may be blocked somewhere in a deadlock or in a similar situation. According to the experiments done, the remaining 200 are not blocked in a deadlock as all the simulations complete for all journeys. They are cut off deliberately at this point because of the fact that on a 3km * 3km city the last couple of hundred vehicles have the streets to themselves. At this low congestion level there is no contention for resources and no comparison to be found between differing individuals. Thresholds would not be hit at such low congestion levels, and it is not a good representation of an urban traffic environment. We believe that all performance related aspects of the system will have demonstrated their fitness through the evaluation of 800 journeys, in contention for resources with up to 1000 other vehicles, and one or two journeys in the latter stages of evaluation should have no bearing on the calculation. If a set of genes is not fit, its weaknesses will have been demonstrated by mismanagement of the traffic scenario for the preceding journeys.

5   Experiments

This section describes two sets of results obtained when running the GA described in the previous section as well as a modified version of it. These results

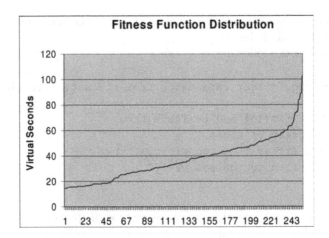

Fig. 3. Fitness Function Distribution Over Last 256 Generations

need to be complemented by additional experiments in order to further confirm and better analyse these results. However, they already show that the determination of the parameters, by running a GA, help finding optimal solutions, and thus enhancing the city performance.

Experiment 1: Fitness Function Distribution. Figure 3 shows an ordered distribution of the fitness function value over the last 256 generations (out of the 1000 initial, and 2000 (1000 * 2) generations).The fitness functions values range from 102s to 15s of virtual time. This measurement is based on the actual distance travelled, and the virtual time taken. As said above, a virtual second elapses when an entire cycle of all city artefacts has been realised (calling each vehicle to move the number of meters corresponding to one second of the speed specified by the road they are currently in, broadcast of all the necessary messages, and evaluation of corresponding methods).

The resulting data show that there are many viable (optimal) solutions, i.e. 95 of these solutions are below 30s, of which 50 are below 20s. The above figure shows an ordered distribution of the solutions, however the solutions produced by the consecutive generations do not demonstrate any convergence of the fitness values.

Experiment 2: Modified GA. A modified version of the original GA of Section 4 has been realised in order to try to observe more quickly any convergence of the solutions.

The genes types and values are the same except for the Persistence gene that now takes the values given by Table 6 below. By running the simulations, it appeared that with efficient 4-uples of genes, the fitness value function is below 20s, thus the Persistence does not need to exceed this value.

In the modified GA, the first generation has been created from 100 randomly selected individuals (instead of 1024 in the original GA). A global set of the fittest individuals is maintained throughout each generation.

Table 6. New Persistence Parameter Values

1	2	3	4	5	6
3s	6s	9s	12s	15s	18s

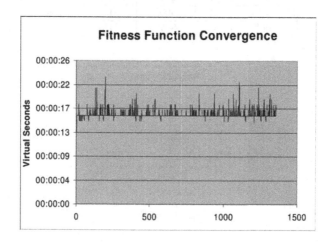

Fig. 4. Fitness Function Distribution Over Last 12 Generations

Next generations are produced in the following way: individuals are selected at random from the set of fittest individuals. A random number is selected to indicate the point of crossover. Each individual is then subject to a 5% potential for mutation on each gene, however only one gene may be mutated per individual. Once the set of candidates is complete, the evaluations begin again. Thirty generations were executed with values remaining stable and consistent in the later 12 generations.

The simulations of the first generation (made of 100 individuals with pure random selected gene values) show fitness functions ranging from 53s to 13s. The 12 last generations have fitness functions for the set of individuals comprised between 13s and 22s, and the last ones clearly around 17s (see Figure 4).

Examples taken from the best solutions obtained during this experiment, among the 12 last generations, are given by Table 7 below. High Sensitivity and Persistence are frequently observed for good solutions.

An interesting point to report is the apparently direct correlation between the Range value and the Fitness Function on *random* individuals (first generation). Indeed, Figure 5 shows on the lower part an ascending arrangement of the fitness function, and on the upper part the corresponding Range values: when the Range values are 3 or 5, the fitness function stays between 13s and 20s, when the Range value is 2, 4 or 6, then the fitness function raises above 25s.

However, in the last 12 generations, such a correlation does not appear (Range values are indifferently distributed among the 6 possible values). A possible explanation would be that the set of 4 parameters, modified through the GA procedure, have a combined influence on the fitness function.

Table 7. Examples of Efficient Genes Values

	Threshold	Range	Sensitivity	Persistence	Fitness
1	30%	5	50%	18s	13s
2	30%	5	20%	9s	14s
3	40%	2	50%	15s	15s
4	60%	6	50%	15s	16s

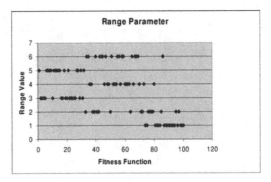

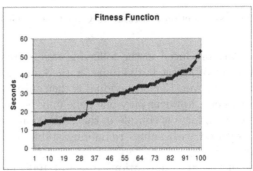

Fig. 5. Range vs Fitness Function in Random Population

A similar phenomenon has been observed on the last 256 generations of Experiment 1 as well. This lets presuppose that in Experiment 1, more cycles would be necessary before any convergence could be visible, and that the results are similar to randomly chosen individuals.

Results. Results reported here are very preliminary, and simply show (confirm) that the use of a GA is actually useful in determining specific optimal parameters further used to control the city car traffic.

Additional experiments are necessary to investigate the actual influence of the parameters, their correlation, as well as the behaviour of the city under different conditions (other sets of journeys), and under different control schema (e.g. different sets of parameters).

The current model is simple and consequently has some limitations, for instance it uses the same parameters values for the whole city portion considered. However, since the size of the considered city is rather small, this may be acceptable here. Further extensions should consider a bigger city, or a combination of smaller portions having each their own sets of genes values.

6   Towards an Actual Traffic Simulation System

By communicating traffic levels in real-time, we could apply the decentralised message propagation system today by controlling throughput using traffic signals. In the future vehicles will be given a maximum upper or optimal speed limit, thus allowing an actual implementation closer to the proposed model. Modification to vehicles would be unnecessary: some vehicle recognition system to measure inbound and outbound vehicles would be sufficient. Such recognition systems are already available in major cities. Of course, the GA should first be run on actual (recorded) traffic values related to a well identified city zone, so that optimal parameters could be derived.

Currently, most traffic control systems are not tuned to prevailing dynamics. The system described in this paper demonstrates the improvements in efficiency capable by cooperation and coordination at local level. For example, in the system above the widest broadcast signal is two nodes forward and two nodes rearward; this avoids the complexity of centralised command and isolates the grid from massive message propagation which could flood the network. Applying the principal of decay to the message allows it to have influence on a curve rather than a simple digital switch. This is taken directly from ant-colony optimisation; it reduces the complexity of message management (i.e. having to fire messages as transactions in antagonistic pairs). It is particularly important in allowing the local conditions to adapt and recover to dynamic conditions. However it should be pointed out, that any path which sends slow-down messages to inbound nodes will always send a speed-up message to it closest inbound node once its own velocity resets to optimum.

In addition to communication among nodes, direct communication among cars can be envisaged in the future thanks to current works on wireless inter-vehicle communication. In this case, the system described here could be extended in different ways: to act according to the school of fish metaphor, where each car maintains a sufficient but minimal distance from neighbour cars favouring fluidity of traffic; or to propagate information along a series of cars (several hops) to support re-routing in case of congestion, etc.

7   Related Works

Car Traffic Control Systems Projects. Actual implemented systems use one or several control centres receiving real-time traffic data, and from which both manual and automated decisions can be taken and propagated to the vehicles through different means.

The technology aiming at *acquiring* real-time data related to traffic conditions is already available: traffic detectors able to detect the volume of traffic, the average speed of vehicles, time between vehicles, blocked traffic; visual control of traffic is available through video surveillance cameras. Similarly, the technology, aiming at *informing* the drivers are also quite advanced: either through specific devices on the vehicle, or through signs on the motorways.

Complete traffic managements, combining acquisition, decisions, and information to drivers are of different nature: detection of accidents, fluidity of traffic, delivery of traffic information to drivers via broadcasting media such as radio; enforcement of traffic policies (e.g. London congestion charge).

The city of Athens has a particularly interesting complete system, built for the Olympics, which uses cameras, an airship, and distributed command to control traffic light phases and durations[1]. From one hand, it incorporates data traffic acquisition using diverse techniques such as TV cameras or ground detectors; official vehicles used as mobile sensors to continuously monitor traffic recording of traffic volume via sensors. On the other hand, a decision making system designs solutions to solve traffic problems, and sends automatically corresponding information to vehicles on the road (traffic signals), or alerting police. Several similar projects are currently under way in large cities such as Beijing or Hong Kong.

Adaptive Control Strategies. Several works can be mentioned that make use of different techniques in order to provide car traffic control strategies that adapt to real-time situations.

Swarm-based traffic control usually employs ant metaphor for inducing a decentralised traffic control. We can cite [3] who apply the pheromone metaphor to provide a decentralised traffic congestion prediction system: cars deposit pheromone along their route which is later retrieved by forthcoming cars. The amount of pheromone deposited depends on the speed of the car, and represents the density of traffic: low speed produces high concentrations of pheromone, while high speed produces low concentrations of pheromone. The amount of pheromone later retrieved by other cars provides an indication about traffic congestion and thus serves for short-time traffic predictions.

Similarly [4] uses the ant metaphor to communicate among cars and to provide a simulation of traffic dynamics in different scenarios. In this case, an additional evolutionary algorithm, including a swarm voting system for preferred traffic light timing, is introduced in order to minimise the average waiting time of vehicles.

As an alternative to swarm-based techniques, we can mention the works on intelligent transportation systems focusing on self-managing and self-organising solutions based on service-oriented architectures and the corresponding middleware[2].

As far as the use of genetic algorithm is concerned, we can mention works at the Utah Traffic Lab on the use of GA for optimising traffic signal timings[3]. This

---

[1] http://www.roadtraffic-technology.com/projects/athens/

[2] http://www.dsg.cs.tcd.ie/transport

[3] http://www.trafficlab.utah.edu/

work makes use as well of a simulation used for evaluating the different identified timing plans; or the works of [2] reporting as well the use of GA for optimising light traffic timing. GA have also been used for finding optimal solutions to air traffic control, for instance [5] uses GA to derive flight plans and optimise time-route problems.

8   Conclusion

This work will be continued and the model, the GA and the simulations will be revised. A series of future directions for enhancing this work have already been identified.

Evaluations will have to extend past a mere 800 journeys, and instead may focus on time-slices with fitness evaluated on the throughput achieved during each period. We would want to measure system performance under different conditions and states, and evaluate each of these with different sets of parameters. This is achievable by adding some conditions governing routes available and vehicles available to undertake those journeys, in different geographical areas, for each testing phase.

The initial population of 4^5 individual has been chosen randomly among the total possible population of 4^6 (4 genes with 6 level of expressions). Future versions will likely introduce performance improvement allowing an enhanced search among the whole population by increasing the size of the initial population.

Accident and emergency rates should be made somewhat relative to prevailing traffic conditions, for example more accidents will occur on congested streets, or streets pushed close to their maximum velocity, that is, there should be a cost function associated with allowing streets to build up congestion, or to permit too great an upper speed-limit. There should be an element of independent accident and emergency propensity per traffic period given that accidents and emergencies occur that are unrelated to traffic volumes.

In order to moderate a larger city and identify different areas or similar areas, different path categories could be included. In addition, by modelling each pathway as individual entities, the local clustering of pathways may better represent the dynamic and volatile requirements of urban traffic.

Further to the concept of nodes, it may be desirable to investigate cells in particular cells of varying area/population. This may be based on the concept of activation thresholds in ant/termite colony, e.g. removing workers will demonstrate worker behaviour in soldiers, albeit after a greater exposure to stimulus.

In the current version of the system re-routing does not occur (cars are slowing down, or blocked but do not change route). In the next version of the system, we would want to add a querying capability to the network, i.e. a vehicle can request alternative routes from nodes when progress is stifled.

References

1. London travel report 2005. Technical report, Transport for London, 2005.
2. H. Ceylan and M. G. H. Bell. Traffic signal timing optimisation based on genetic algorithm approach, including driver's routing. *Transportation Research Part B*, 38:329–342, 2004.

3. Y. Ando et al. Pheromone Model: Application to Traffic Congestion Prediction. In *Engineering Self-Organising Systems*, volume 3910 of *LNAI*, pages 182–196. Springer-Verlag, 2005.
4. R. Hoar, J. Penner, and C. Jacob. Evolutionary Swarm Traffic: If Ant Roads Had Traffic Lights. In *Congress on Evolutionary Computation (CEC'02)*, pages 1910–1915. IEEE, 2002.
5. S. Oussedik, D. Delahaye, and M. Schoenauer. Dynamic Air Traffic Planning by Genetic Algorithms. In *Congress on Evolutionary Computation*, pages 1110–1116. IEEE Press, 1999.

Author Index

Lecture Notes in Artificial Intelligence (LNAI)

Printing: Mercedes-Druck, Berlin
Binding: Stein+Lehmann, Berlin